Kerouac in Ecstasy

Kerouac in Ecstasy

Shamanic Expression in the Writings

THOMAS R. BIEROWSKI

McFarland & Company, Inc., Publishers
Jefferson, North Carolina, and London

LIBRARY OF CONGRESS CATALOGUING-IN-PUBLICATION DATA

Bierowski, Thomas R., 1962–
    Kerouac in ecstasy : shamanic expression in the writings /
Thomas R. Bierowski.
    p.   cm.
    Includes bibliographical references and index.

    ISBN 978-0-7864-5967-4
    softcover : 50# alkaline paper ∞

    1. Kerouac, Jack, 1922–1969 — Criticism and interpretation.
2. Shamanism in literature.   I. Title.
PS3521.E735Z5773   2011
813'.54 — dc22
                                                      2010052512

BRITISH LIBRARY CATALOGUING DATA ARE AVAILABLE

© 2011 Thomas R. Bierowski. All rights reserved

*No part of this book may be reproduced or transmitted in any form
or by any means, electronic or mechanical, including photocopying
or recording, or by any information storage and retrieval system,
without permission in writing from the publisher.*

On the cover: Jack Kerouac (Photofest); background image
© 2011 Elena Ray

Manufactured in the United States of America

*McFarland & Company, Inc., Publishers
  Box 611, Jefferson, North Carolina 28640
    www.mcfarlandpub.com*

To Robert and Elizabeth Bierowski

Table of Contents

List of Abbreviations — viii
Preface — 1
Introduction: Kerouac in Ecstasy — 3

1. *Visions of Gerard*: Modern Hagiography — 29
2. The Shrouds of Eternity: *Doctor Sax* as Shamanic Journey — 42
3. *Visions of Cody*: "Kidnapped, Shanghaied, and Orphaned" — 73
4. *The Subterraneans* as Nadiral Ecstasy — 99
5. "In-stasy" and the *Book of Dreams* — 122
6. *Old Angel Midnight*: "Space Prose for the Future" — 144
7. *Big Sur* and the Memoir of Disintegration — 153
8. Conclusion: "Be Lamps Unto Thyselves" — 179

Chapter Notes — 187
Bibliography — 197
Index — 201

List of Abbreviations

The following abbreviations are used for works
that are cited frequently in the text.

BOD	*Book of Dreams* (Kerouac)
BS	*Big Sur* (Kerouac)
DS	*Doctor Sax* (Kerouac)
GBO	*Good Blonde & Others* (Kerouac)
JKSL 1940–1956	*Jack Kerouac: Selected Letters, 1940–1956* (edited by Ann Charters)
JKSL 1957–1969	*Jack Kerouac: Selected Letters, 1957–1969* (edited by Ann Charters)
OAM	*Old Angel Midnight* (Kerouac)
OTR	*On the Road* (Kerouac)
SOGE	*Scripture of the Golden Eternity* (Kerouac)
TEOR	*The Encyclopedia of Religion* (edited by Mircea Eliade)
TS	*The Subterraneans* (Kerouac)
VOC	*Visions of Cody* (Kerouac)
VOG	*Visions of Gerard* (Kerouac)
WHTK?	*What Happened to Kerouac?* (documentary, directed by Richard Lerner and Lewis MacAdams)

Preface

The present work considers Jack Kerouac's writing as a modern shamanic expression. I became interested in this while reading Mircea Eliade's *Shamanism: Archaic Techniques of Ecstasy* and noting the parallels between archaic shamanism and Kerouac's modern prose. The spiritual import of Kerouac's work, especially in terms of his Catholicism and Buddhism, has been well documented by Beat biographers and scholars. I take that spirituality as a given and proceed (and regress) from there. The shamanic view of his writing is worth a closer look, first, because it places Kerouac (and all artists through time) on a continuum with his archaic predecessors who originated the techniques of ecstasy; and, second, because Kerouac's rise and fall describe the precarious position of the shamanic figure in modern America, and in so doing, reveal as much about that society as it does about the writer. To this end, I explore the shamanic substrata of Kerouac's content and investigate his writing style as ecstatic technique in five novels and two experimental volumes that represent the critical phases of his development as writer-shaman.

Regarding religious practice, mysticism, and myth, I have found the classic works of William James and Joseph Campbell to be extremely helpful. In terms of shamanic performance in the arts, then and now, I also have benefitted greatly from the work of Kelly Bulkeley, Robert Ellwood, Gloria Flaherty, Lewis Hyde, I.M. Lewis, Gerhard Mayer, Ted Spivey and Michael Tucker. Other important published works that discuss the relationship between Kerouac (or the Beats in general) and shamanism cited in this book are Ben Giamo's *Kerouac, The Word and the Way*, Tim Hunt's *Kerouac's Crooked Road: The Development of a Fiction*, and John Lardas's *The Bop Apocalypse*.

Introduction
Kerouac in Ecstasy

Ecstatic Tradition: Archaic Shaman to Modern Artist

> There is a blessedness surely to be believed,
> and that is that everything abides in
> eternal ecstasy, now and forever.
> — Kerouac, *The Scripture of the Golden Eternity* 30

From the Greek *ekstasis*, ecstasy means "to be placed outside" the "static" (hence limited) self, and brought into a union with the ultimate reality. Ecstasy is the technique of the shaman. The process, style, and content of Kerouac's fiction demonstrate a modern ecstatic impulse. Years before Mircea Eliade's *Shamanism: Archaic Techniques of Ecstasy* brought a neo-shamanic awareness to Western consciousness, Kerouac had been on a journey ("his life on the road"), and developed the technique of performing the ecstatic experience in his fiction. Shamanism comments significantly on his work throughout the arc of his career.

Shamans were (and still are) the men and women called apart from their society to gather power by "dying." The shaman suffers a death-like initiation out of the static old self. He then flies or dives in ecstasy to experience the soul as a sacred fact of his being. Consequently, the new self transcends the old by the ritual performance that is ecstasy. This performance, this show, is identified with the ecstatic union itself. As Eliade puts it, "shamanism = *technique of ecstasy*" (4). In so doing, the shaman can look after the "soul-troubles" of the tribe by pursuing his own trip. The influence of the shaman on the human experience has been profound and positive. As Gloria Flaherty notes, "The shamans were the originators of magic, music, medicine, mathematics, laws or codes of behavior, writing, all the things that contribute to beneficial social frameworks" (139). The first artists were shamans, and in this context, the project of writers, dancers, musicians, painters, performers — the goal of any artist to this day — continues to be the revelation of visions in the ecstasy of art. In this view, Kerouac's writing is a modern expression of an archaic shamanic tradition. He is a post-shamanic figure on the page where he introduces alternative states of consciousness, other realities, through words.

Many critics have aptly commented on the mystical import of Kerouac's writing. Mysticism is an iteration of a foundational shamanic impulse.[1] The "most important expression of ecstasy, and the prototype of mysticism, is found in the life of the shaman" (Ellwood 55). John Lardas observes that "Beat poetics began to develop along the lines of mysticism in that the act of writing became the means of submission and an avenue of transcendence.... [W]riting became an encounter with the most inscrutable truths of existence; the source of the world's being and the limits of human understanding" (153). Kerouac's writing echoes the shamanic experience and technique, an active encounter with the mystical IT from which he composes the vast myth of a life that he beholds and creates again as the god of his art. I.M. Lewis writes, "What is proclaimed is not merely that God is *with* us, but that he is *in* us. Shamanism is thus the religion *par excellence* of the spirit made flesh" (183). Similarly, Kerouac's spontaneous prose was the perfect technique of the "spirit made word" that belies the "belief that a direct knowledge or immediate perception of the ultimate reality, or God, is possible in a way different from the normal sense experience and rationalization" (*TEOR*, vol. 15, 14).

Translating the mystical experience is problematic. Though such encounters reveal knowledge and insight ("noesis"), they are highly ineffable (James 380). Tim Hunt, in his insightful study, *Kerouac's Crooked Road: The Development of a Fiction*, elaborates on the roots of this problem:

> Our literacy builds on and transforms our orality; and in subsuming the oral to writing and print ... we align ourselves with the logic and norms of a society that relies on classification and analysis more than participation and narrative, on knowledge more than wisdom, and on product more than the experience of performance [xix–xx].

Introduction

To overcome the ineffable one needs to transcend the idiom, a challenge that is heightened as modernity rolls on. Therefore, as Lardas notes, Kerouac "located his art within the basic philosophical conundrum of the twentieth century — how to move beyond language in and through language" (Lardas 170). Through dedicated adaptation and innovation, Kerouac found the language and style to authentically communicate his ecstasy. Occasionally teetering on the threshold of passing out of language altogether, Kerouac's work shows authentic mastery and reveals a deep perception of a spiritual essence that is thoroughly human, and fading. The words become a post-shamanic drum on which he works out, practices, and plays at the ecstatic potential of language so that his readers might participate and be transported (that is, ecstatic). A shamanic reading of Kerouac's fiction, therefore, yields insight into the "visionary tics shivering in the chest" that wound up illuminating the visions of an entire generation of modern Americans (*GBO* 72). Understanding the nature of ecstasy, its process and dynamic, has helped me appreciate Kerouac's writing in a fresh and more generous way.

The Writer-Shaman

As noted, literature, like all art, carries some degree of shamanic import. The relationship between the shamanic and the literary impulse is intrinsic. Eliade expands on this:

> The shaman's adventures in the other world, the ordeals that he undergoes in his ecstatic descents below and ascents to the sky, suggest the adventures of the figures in popular literature. Probably a large number of epic "subjects" or motifs, as well as many characters, images and cliches of epic literature are, finally, of ecstatic origin [510].[2]

The affinity of creation myths across a broad cultural spectrum, for instance, argues for the shared characteristics of ecstatic experience in different places and times. The actual performances of the shaman (and our reception of them) are so interwoven into the fabric of human experience that it is still possible for an audience to enter into the alternative realities of virtual performances offered in books (or films, recordings, etc.). The writer-shaman must experiment in words to communicate the precise ecstatic moment. Percussion, movement and sound have always been more effective than writing in this regard as they are more immediate. Though words resist, the writer-shaman is compelled to tell because of the value of ecstasy to himself and, potentially, to his readers. In this way he builds up, explores, and chronicles the myth of himself and his time. Each performance, each book, authenticates the myth in real time. The writer-shaman is able to do this through a fantastic sequence of experiences that takes the shape of a journey.

"Lonesome for Home" (The Shaman Then and Now)

Both the would-be shaman and the tribe suffer an illness that can be understood in various ways. This soul condition manifests itself as a pathology of *deus otiosus*, a sense of "God withdrawn" from the very soul — a state of death. (It's a divine distance that we have, for the most part, grown comfortable with in our modernity.) Ejected from an Eden of mystical harmony, if not union, the split between God and man expresses itself in the hunger to once more savor that ultimate reality, to *be* there again. Eliade calls this yearning the "nostalgia for paradise" (508). He regards the shaman's ecstasy as "a recovery of the human condition before the fall," one that "reproduces a primordial condition accessible to the rest of mankind only through death" (493). This is a notion Kerouac could savvy. In a letter to Allen Ginsberg, dated July 21, 1969, he says it plainly: "Death is holy ecstasy" (*JKSL 1957–1969* 262).

Kerouac's (and all our?) preoccupation with death cannot be minimized here. Death is a hallmark of shamanic metaphysics and *the* context that defines the potential of ecstatic technique. Ecstasy is the means of leaving behind the profane human condition (Eliade 95). William James, in his classic work, *The Varieties of Religious Experience*, calls this profane condition "the sick soul" (127). In this lack, we find the germ of the shamanic cure. This "soul disease" is the condition the would-be shaman must recognize and suffer before he journeys to the ultimate identity of godly essence. It is, in Lewis's words, "the high level of adversity to which shamanism appears to respond" (183).

Introduction

Called by his own intuition to a mystical identity, the neophyte departs from the tribe and is dismembered to the very core of his limited being through an illness (actual or dreamed). This initiation empowers him with the means of voluntarily accessing the spirit world. Simply put, the shaman cures the terror of death by "dying." Ecstasy shows him that *deus otiosus* is a limiting illusion, self-imposed. He is now "the great specialist in the human soul; he alone 'sees' it" (Eliade 8).

The final, and in some ways, *key* aspect of this journey is the shaman's reincorporation into the tribe through his performance. The career of the shaman cannot be fulfilled without his recognition and acceptance. Reenacting the journey to the ultimate reality for the audience, the shaman-artist performs through time on the cave wall, the canvas, the drum, the stage, the horn, or the page. If the tribe identifies with the performance, it will be transformed and transported to the soul essence. The shaman achieves this metamorphosis in terms of Levy-Bruhl's principle of participation, wherein the primitive mentality completely identifies with a person or object in a pre-logical and mystical way (Levy-Bruhl 78). Carl Jung expands upon and modifies this dynamic as he sees it played out in the modern "civilized man" in his notion of "participation mystique":

> [A] peculiar kind of psychological connection with the object wherein the subject is unable to differentiate himself clearly from the object to which he is bound by an immediate relation that can only be described as partial identity. This identity is based upon an *a priori* oneness of subject and object. "Participation mystique," therefore is a vestigial remainder of the primordial condition ... in which the object (as a general rule) obtains a sort of magical, i.e., unconditional, influence over the subject [*Staub de Laszlo* 266–67].

Kerouac's experiential novels (of which I'll discuss *Visions of Gerard, Doctor Sax, Visions of Cody, The Subterraneans,* and *Big Sur*), and his even stranger experimental works (*Book of Dreams* and *Old Angel Midnight*) are the "magical objects" that best mediate his writing as ecstasy. Matt Theado astutely comments both on the goal and dynamic of this project: "Kerouac sought an immediate relation between the object and the writer. The prose that results from this relation is an unmediated representation in language that Kerouac suggests will be recognized by readers via a 'telepathic shock'" (33). The quality of the tribe's participation in this "telepathic shock" is proportional to the level of transformation it will experience. The tribe's reception also dictates the role of the shaman in it. In the modern hegemony of (supposed) reason and logic, the shaman is mostly viewed with considerable skepticism.

> Just as the French psychiatrist, Levy-Valensi, has claimed that in western society the spiritualist seance is often the ante-chamber of the asylum, so shamanism is regularly seen as an institutionalized madhouse for primitives.... [The] spirit-possessed shaman is presented as a conflict-torn personality who should be classified as seriously neurotic or even psychotic [Lewis 161].

Because the modern shaman's "madness constitutes a test case in the cross-cultural definition of normality and abnormality," his visionary performance, though baffling to the status quo, cannot be ignored through rationalization (Lewis 162). If shamanism isn't culturally defined (which was the case in Kerouac's modern America as it is today), if it has no place in the communal landscape, it is simply seen as eccentricity and relegated to the furthest margins of collective experience until we figure out what, if anything, to do with it (Lewis 170).

This isn't really "news." Our human penchant for, if not destroying, then ignoring our visionaries is epic. This unfortunate proclivity cuts us off from a great resource that is "a grand confluence of ageless human activities the world over" (Flaherty 13). The transcendence of the profane, soul-sick condition actualized in shamanic ecstasy represents what Joseph Campbell calls "the release potential within us all, and which you can attain, through herohood" (151). If, as A.T. Hatto asserts, "shamanism is but an extreme expression of a universal human capacity," then it is a phenomenon that is very far, yet very near (Tucker 19). We are very far from the archaic shaman who shape-shifts and flies through space and time, and very close to the artists of our time. They coexist at opposite ends of a continuous shamanic arc in decay. Eliade expounds on this notion: "For what the shaman can do today in *ecstasy* could, at the dawn of time, be done by all human beings *in concreto*, they went up to heaven and came down again without recourse to trance" (486). Jack Kerouac's trance was an evolving prose technique in modern America, and the fictional Legend he created using it strongly indicates his participation in the shamanic tradition.[3]

Introduction

Kerouac's Word Quest in Post-War America

Jack Kerouac's tribe, broadly understood, extends from the America of the 1940s and 1950s, the Beat Era, through the 1960s, the Counterculture Era, and beyond that to a worldwide readership today. At the outset, though, his tribe was the literary community and readership of a mid-twentieth century America that swung wildly from a dazed adherence to the status quo to an unparalleled freedom of expression from its margins. Kerouac and his written visions are both products of their place and time. All shamans, Eliade notes, internalize the zeitgeist of their culture (266).

The atmosphere of post–World War II America was complex, ambivalent, and highly distasteful to Kerouac and the rest of the Beats for a number of reasons that time and their legacy have made clear. Underlying America's euphoric prosperity, and behind the Allied victory in the war, loomed the destruction of Hiroshima and Nagasaki. This specter of atomic annihilation instilled a serious unease in the generation then coming of age. The onset of the Cold War and nuclear arms race darkened the optimism of Americans who, though victorious, money-capable, and ostensibly at peace, still lived with the fear of manmade apocalypse. The predominant impulse was to "hunker down in Levittown," so to speak. The instructions for happiness were simple: work and consume, enjoy conformity, and don't worry. And even though most Americans suffered nightmares of Communist threat and mushroom clouds, the military-industrial complex would prevent all that as long as everybody stayed calm; such was the shaky hope of status-quo America in the Fifties. As Walter Cronkite observed, "Eisenhower's intention was that we should try to settle down to some nice quiet American pursuits and not rock the boat (and that) it was time for us to ease off a bit. And he accomplished that. The country was pretty quiet" (Workman, *The Source*). John Tytell, in his analysis of the Beats, *Naked Angels*, summarizes the dominant ideology of the time in this way: "In the late forties and early fifties, the axioms of the upright in America were belief in God, family, and the manifestly benevolent international ambitions of the nation" (6). Trust in the ideologies of capitalism and consumerism as safeguarded by the government and the military under the ongoing guise of "the American Dream" was the ticket to a safe and comfortable life in post-war America. But the cost, the loss of the very individualism on which the nation purported to be founded, was appalling.

> [The] emergence of the new postwar values ... accepted man as the victim of circumstances, and no longer granted him the agency of his own destiny: the illusion of free will, the buoyantly igniting spark in the American character, had suddenly been extinguished [Tytell 9].

Although many Americans didn't seem to mind or even notice this, many artists, Kerouac among them, did.

In the documentary film *The Source*, Beat poet Allen Ginsberg notes that, in the Fifties, "there were all these marginalized cultures which were never represented in public," such as the African-American and gay communities, and the drug and criminal subcultures. In response to the severity of life beyond the threshold of the status quo, these groups often generate ecstatic experiences. Lewis writes that peripheral cults (where spirits take possession without any reference to "the moral character or conduct of their victims") "frequently embrace downtrodden categories of men who are subject to strong discrimination in rigidly stratified societies" (27). Because these "categories of men" remain vital in their marginalization and provide an authentic and critical perspective on the postwar status quo in America, like a peripheral cult, Kerouac and the other early Beats become, in a sense, possessed by these outsiders. The early Beats are restless, as only the suffocating can be, and running to the edges for some air. They want more of something they can barely define and will perhaps never attain, but they are moving away from the central sweet pocket of the status quo.

> [These came] of age into a Cold War without spiritual values they could honor. Instead of obeying authority and conforming to middle class materialistic aspirations, these young people dealt as best they could with what [John Clellon] Holmes called "their will to believe, even in the face of an inability to do so in conventional terms" [Charters, *The Portable Beat Reader* xx].

The stifling lifeless atmosphere of the times was ripe for an illuminating breakthrough to an alternative vision. Such it has always been, notes I.M. Lewis.

> [The] circumstances which encourage the ecstatic response are precisely those where men feel themselves constantly threatened by exacting pressures which they do not know how to combat or control, except through those heroic flights

of ecstasy by which they seek to demonstrate that they are the equals of the gods [30].

Kerouac's discomfort with the sad state of the American soul as he discerned it in the post-war status quo predisposed him to the ecstatic response of writing down his own heroic legend. In this way, he would authenticate his own mythos and break the hold of any conventional ideology that impinged on his freedom. In a time of conformity, Kerouac would bring the individual to center stage in bold light and real time. In a literary tradition iced over by the New Critic's claims of objectivity, the books he wrote in the Fifties and Sixties resurrected the subjective point of view with a hot vengeance. Kerouac's subjective ecstatic vision, his Beat apotheosis of the individual, draws a rhetorical line in the sand. Omar Swartz notes that Kerouac "does the one thing that cannot be tolerated by any repressive society: he suggests alternatives to traditional values and questions the ruling society's right to authority" (34).

Ginsberg, whose poetics always display a keen ability to cut through the hypocritical haze of "the ruling society," describes the Beat epiphany as "suddenly the realization: Why are we being intimidated by a bunch of jerks who don't know anything about life? Who are they to tell us what we feel and how we're supposed to behave? And why take all that?" (Workman, *The Source*). The nascent Beat impulse was secret and treasonous, a modern yearning that echoed the archaic shamanic ache for "new standards of conduct, a distinctive lifestyle, a sense of self-definition" (Charters xvii). So Kerouac deserted the status quo and in his life and art insisted on a paradise that, in Whitman's words, "was cheaper, easier, nearer" than middle-class America ever thought (194). Once he found his voice and started writing all about it, "Beat" didn't remain a secret for long.

What Ailed Jack and What He Did About It

Like many of us, Kerouac looked fondly upon his childhood. His was a shamanic nostalgia for the paradise of a pre-war America epitomized by his hometown of Lowell, Massachusetts, in the Twenties and Thirties. In that place and time, his experience was unself-conscious and immediate, though mysterious and often terrifying as well. His boyhood in Lowell, and his separation from it, proved to be the initiatory sickness in Kerouac's shamanic journey as an artist. His deeply felt and often morbid sense of Catholicism was marked by dark wonder. The boy's cringing fear of loss and death provided an abiding state of creative tension that Kerouac sought to work out in his prolific travels and writings.

As Kerouac saw it, shame was the contagion that had crept into the American psyche (and into its literature) in the years since he was a boy. "Shame," he writes, "seems to be the key to repression in writing as well as in psychological malady" (*GBO* 189). In biblical terms, this shame is the same essential "dis-ease" Adam and Eve felt in the Garden of Eden when God took affront at their transgression (i.e., their wanting to be like Him) and expelled them from paradise, initiating the phenomenon of *deus otiosus*. Only the shaman, by securing a sense of soul, can restore the human condition from its shame to its godly essence. This is the validation that Kerouac, flawed and troubled as he was, sought for himself and his readers.

"[G]enius and disease," Edmund Wilson writes, "like strength and mutilation, may be inextricably bound up together" (289). The shamanic-artistic enterprise has always embodied this paradox. Our modern capacity for tolerating paradox, however, has long grown weak. For this reason, most modern critics, depending on their point of view, are liable to demonize the visionary artist as psychopathic, blasphemous, even unpatriotic. Since the Beat vision that emerges in Kerouac's writing reflects the general insanity of his America, it was seen by many as a conscious threat to the status quo as opposed to a spontaneous alternative. Kerouac found himself in the precarious position of visionary artist in modern times because, as Tytell notes, "the acting out of repressed inhibitions and taboos relieves binding public pressures to conform, and the artist as scapegoat/shaman creates an alternative with his very being" (11). Because the soul-centered bent of his fiction was often overlooked in favor of, and separated from, his dissipate lifestyle (which was a significant aspect of his shamanism, as I will discuss in Chapter 7) in his time, Kerouac was mostly reviled by the critics and "scapegoated" by the literati who cared little for the shameless portrait he painted of himself and even less for the shame-free alternative his fiction heralded.[4]

The initiatory sickness Kerouac underwent can be understood in a

Introduction

few ways. Clearly, he suffered and worked through a crisis of literary paternity. Early on, he was most influenced by Thomas Wolfe, whom he revered as "a torrent of American heaven and hell that opened my eyes to America as a subject in itself" (Plimpton 117). After the publication of his first novel (*The Town and the City*) in 1950, several critics noted the affinity between the two writers. *The Town and the City* closely emulates Wolfe's *Look Homeward, Angel* with its sprawling Whitmanic prose and archetypal American theme of family. It falls short of a completely authentic voice. And in the process of literary emulation, Kerouac became, by turns, a *picaro* like Balzac, a confessionalist like Rousseau, a memoirist like Proust, and, closer to home, an American Transcendentalist like Emerson, a cosmic loner like Thoreau. As Ann Charters, his first biographer, has noted, "He could write any style you like" (*WHTK?*).

Kerouac exorcised his literary predecessors (died to them, in a way) through multiple artistic strategies. First, he heeded his intuition to resist literary convention and, if necessary, categorization. In a 1950 letter to Neal Cassady, he writes, "I aim to employ all styles and nevertheless I yearn to be non-literary. Dribbledrags. This is the odd beginning" (*JKSL 1940–1956* 248). As Charters comments:

> What Jack Kerouac was doing as a writer, as a stylist — spontaneous prose — was another reason that he came under fire. Jack Kerouac believed and put his whole career on the line justifying and performing it ... and that was an extraordinarily adventurous thing to do. He could write any style you like. He chose to do the hardest, most difficult thing which is fly in the face of convention and write the way he pleased to write knowing full well that people might call it "typing" rather than writing ... which they did [*WHTK?*].

Truman Capote famously called it "typing" on David Susskind's TV show, *Open End*. In the *Herald Tribune Book Review*, Gene Baro growled that Kerouac's work was "infantile [and] perversely negative." And in the *Hudson Review*, Benjamin DeMott referred to Kerouac as "a slob running a temperature."

What else *could* the literary establishment say about a writer whose project, in the final analysis, was so different from its own? "They all think writing is a profession that's their trouble," Kerouac griped. "To me it's the day" (*JKSL 1957–1969* 117). Fellow Beat author, John Clellon Holmes, however, recognized the breadth and scope of Kerouac's vision, suggesting that his writing "seemed to be describing a new sort of stance toward reality, behind which a new consciousness lay" (Charters xix). Tytell seconds this view, noting in Kerouac and the other Beats "a major shift in perspective from the conception of literature as entertainment to writing as a necessary mode of expressing a personal vision in hostile circumstances" (70). Kerouac rejected the pillars of literary expression that, in 1955, according to Kerouac biographer Dennis McNally, read "as if American high culture were a repertory theater that had only a handful of shows, and those by playwrights of remarkably similar values and background. The shows were all too often exercises in incestuous trivia" (201). Tytell interprets the break made by Kerouac and the Beats in this way:

> In the fifties, when the voice of personality seemed so endangered by an anonymity of sameness, the Beats discovered a natural counter for the silence of the day in a new sense of self, a renaissance of the romantic impulse to combat unbelievably superior forces [16].

This neo-romantic journey to self is of great shamanic import. Kerouac made that trip through performing the ecstatic technique of raw, exhaustive and spontaneous composition. While the literary critics of his day equated craft with art, Kerouac equated craft with deceit. "If you don't stick to what you first thought," he writes, "and to the words the thought brought, what's the sense of foisting your little lies on others, or, that is, hiding your little truths from others?" (*GBO* 189). The New Critic looks for craft in the face of its art, and nods in approval upon finding it. But through his spontaneous prose, Kerouac traded in that face for his very own. What he saw there ran the extreme gamut of his American experience, and the product insulted jaded critical sensibilities.[5] His "best novels are personal documents written out of his own torment and humor, with no mediation. They throw a scary light on just how essentially decorous and genteel most fiction is" (*East Bay Express*, May 92). Kerouac's genteel "well-written novel," *The Town and the City*, and his indecorous departure from it in his subsequent work, mark his progress to an authentic perspective and artistic statement. Kerouac's performance of his visions in letters, articles, poems, essays, and novels shows his commitment to the ecstasy of writing.[6]

Introduction

The "Half-Healed" Shaman

Literary style and lifestyle both played a role in Kerouac's persona, as the criticism has shown. Ellis Amburn, Kerouac's editor in the Sixties and one of his biographers, analyzes the inconsistencies (many of a sexual nature) between Kerouac-the-man and Kerouac-the-fictional-narrator. For my purposes, it will serve to understand the continuity between Kerouac-as-shamanic-performer and Kerouac-as-alcoholic. According to Amburn, Kerouac's "lifetime of alcoholism began over Thanksgiving dinner in 1938" when his father forced the sixteen-year-old to have a drink (38). His mother, Amburn claims, was also an alcoholic, and Kerouac often drank with her for the rest of his life. Amburn places Kerouac in the tradition of American writers who turn to alcohol for relief of a variety of internal conflicts:

> Temperamentally and psychologically, he was already firmly entrenched in the mainstream of mid-century American writers, such as Nobel laureates Ernest Hemingway and William Faulkner, who felt that writing was not a red-blooded masculine pursuit and who were both alcoholics. They typified an American era that was uncertain about sexuality, obsessed with ambition, morbid about religion, and incurably alcoholic [51].

Shamanic practice also has a long tradition of substance-induced ecstasy. William James explains the taking of spirits in this way: "The sway of alcohol over mankind is unquestionably due to its power to stimulate the mystical faculties of human nature, usually crushed to earth by the cold facts and dry criticisms of the sober hour" (387). To say Kerouac sought and found God in a bottle is to oversimplify. This was just one of many techniques he employed. He also "sought God" in Catholicism, Buddhism, travel, narcotics, jazz and classical music, his heroes, and mostly in his writing (which embraced all of them). Alcohol and drugs were primary mechanisms for reaching the ecstasy he reenacted in his fiction. "A variety of means such as dancing, drugs, and self-mortification have been used across cultures, climes, and at various times to induce ecstasy" (*TEOR* vol. 5, 12). Eliade elaborates upon the historical significance of the substance-induced ecstasy in shamanism and its place in the arc of shamanic decadence:

Introduction

> We must also take into consideration the symbolic value of narcotic intoxication. It was equivalent to a "death"; the intoxicated person left his body, acquired the condition of ghosts and spirits. Mystical ecstasy being assimilated to a temporary death or to leaving the body, all intoxications that produced the same result were given a place among the techniques of ecstasy. But closer study of the problem gives the impression that the use of narcotics is, rather, indicative of the decadence of a technique of ecstasy or of its extension to "lower" peoples or social groups [477].

The substance-induced ecstasy, then, is that of the common man, one Kerouac witnessed, favored, and participated in. In the self-medication of the Beat or fellahin personalities, he saw the "magical promises to heal the split between the reality of the dream and the reality of Western culture" (Hunt 63).

Kerouac's use of alcohol and drugs, his "low road" to ecstasy, is evidence of a decaying shamanic tradition that affirms the possibility of attaining ecstatic vision through self-destructive means. The practice of this aberrant ecstatic technique finally (and of course) killed him. The means of his vision wore him down. He remained, to borrow I.M. Lewis's term, a "half-healed" shaman, largely, but not only, because of his alcoholism (Lewis 180). Kerouac writes, "My manners, abominable at times, can be sweet. As I grew older I became a drunk. Why? Because I like ecstasy of the mind" (*Satori in Paris* 28).

As Kerouac's fiction is inextricably linked with his life, I must seriously consider his alcoholism as a technical aspect of his shamanic impulse, one that brings on the "physiological changes that must be produced before the visions can occur. In some mysterious way, then, the body becomes a perceiving organ for the sacred dimension of reality" (*TEOR* vol. 15, 282). (As Whitman notes in "Song of Myself," "If the body were not the soul, what is the soul?") Taking into account the agitated Catholicism that colored Kerouac's perception of this sacred reality, his alcoholism might be understood as a willful mortification of the body, a death ritual engaged. Allen Ginsberg elaborates on this notion in an interview with Lewis MacAdams at the Naropa Institute:

> So Kerouac weeping over Bach's *St. Matthew's Passion* which was the, probably, the last face I saw on him. Tears would come to his eyes very often in his later years in conversation when he [talked] about something he felt sentimental about: his mother, his cats, his writing, his novels, state of America, but par-

Introduction

ticularly music or Christ, particularly the Crucifixion, because he was going through a crucifixion, that is, the mortification of his body. That's what he was painting, incidentally, in his last ten years. He was painting cardinals, popes, crosses, and Christs on the cross [*WHTK?*].

His fascination with death and the creative possibilities of that fascination are significant themes throughout Kerouac's fiction. They account for the simultaneous (or oscillating) tones of sadness and joy, of self-affirmation and self-destruction in his body of work. Kerouac in ecstasy dissolves such dichotomies, intermingling pain and pleasure in the flow of a fiction that is often fueled by his self-annihilation. In the same interview quoted above, after Ginsberg describes Kerouac's dolorous condition in his last years, MacAdams suggests that, nevertheless, the primary legacy of his work is one of joy "more than the suffering." Ginsberg breaks this notion down to its ecstatic roots:

> Well it's about joy, but the kind of tears is tears of ... I mean ... it's one taste. Joy and suffering at a certain point become one taste, because it's existence itself, the crying over existence, not non-existence ... because the tears are an appreciation of existence and the beauty and mortality and sadness of leaving existence, and the suffering of existence which is so deep it's joyful. To exist is joyful just by its very nature of existing even if it's suffering existence. Grief is not unadulterated pain. Grief is also mixed with a sense of majesty and finality and realization of ultimate reality. That's why people weep, because they realize that the ultimately real is ultimately real ... and irrevocably so. There's only one life and this is it [*WHTK?*].[7]

By melding exhilaration and dejection and spontaneously confessing this seemingly impossible alloy, Kerouac at length achieved his authentic voice. Personally in crisis, artistically ecstatic, he performs the visions of a paradise that came off to many in post-war America as irresponsible, if not altogether barbarous. These visions allowed him to breathe in suffocating times, and his writing offered that same possibility to the American tribe.

Kerouac as Post-Shamanic Figure

Does Kerouac's fiction really describe the career of a soul seeker in ecstatic performance? Or put a different way, is the premise of my study here real or imagined? I suspect it's a little of both. I imagine it is my experience of reading Kerouac (whose style often requires an exacting level of reader participation) and finding the spiritual highlights and lowlights of his content that leads me to choose shamanism as the most effective paradigm for interpreting his work. But in reality, less than a year after the publication of *On the Road*, having achieved a significant amount of literary notoriety (though not acclaim), Kerouac explained his *raison d'être* as follows: "What are you searching for? they asked me. I answered that I was waiting for God to show his face" (*GBO* 51).

Although quite aware that he was on a journey toward the soul and the sacred, Kerouac never actually used the word "shaman" to refer to himself or any of his characters, nor would he have to for purposes of validating the shamanic significance of his art and vision. He *is* a writer of extensive, shaman-like skills, participating in a tradition that precedes and transcends literary convention. I agree with Omar Swartz, who asserts, "The power of Kerouac's writing is rooted in and amplified by that 'ancient and unconscious source,' the timeless essence of ultimate reality, that finds it expression in art; i.e., dance, music, painting, writing" (ix).

The shamanic vision (like the artistic impulse it subsumes) dances between and connects what is real and imagined. As John Clellon Holmes notes, "The interaction between imagination and reality is the source of all literature" (*WHTK?*). Since mystical reality has always been primarily intuitive (i.e., unfathomable, impossible to the rational mind), the shaman depends on imagination to express it. Shamans save imagination from being overwhelmed by the consensus reality. The modern creative imagination offers an alternative experience that merges the fragmented status quo into an ecstatic singularity. According to William James, this monism is characteristic of all mystical experiences.

> They all converge towards a kind of insight to which I cannot help ascribing some metaphysical significance. The keynote of it is invariably a reconciliation. It is as if the opposites of the world, whose contradictoriness and conflict make all our difficulties and troubles, were melted into unity [388].

The same might be said of Kerouac's "IT."

His writing became the performance of a personal ecstatic vision that, in part, incited a cultural phenomenon in America. As Lardas accurately notes, "The emphasis on shared moments of ecstasy and honest dialogue

Introduction

in Beat literature revealed an alternative social reality" (148). That social alternative was played out, for good and bad, in the Sixties. Though he loathed his role as "King of the Beats" (and mostly disparaged both the hipster and the hippie phenomena that came in his wake), Kerouac's field of cultural (if not literary) influence cannnot be doubted. In a 1986 interview, William Burroughs makes his case for Kerouac's legacy as follows:

BURROUGHS: Well, the whole Beat movement has become a worldwide cultural revolution of absolutely unprecedented proportions; there's never been anything like it before.... Although the Beats were originally non-political, others who were political were really following the Beat movement to its logical conclusion.
INTERVIEWER: But Kerouac didn't seem to have any sense of that or desire for it or acceptance of it.
BURROUGHS: Well, no, he didn't. He was completely apolitical. I don't think he ever took part in a demonstration or signed a petition — but *he started it*. As Jesus Christ said, "By their fruits ye shall know them," not by their disclaimers [*WHTK?*]

COSMOLOGY OF THE ROAD

If nothing else, Kerouac, like Whitman before him, offered the great American Road to his readers. This motif evokes a modern shamanic journey, a trip from the limited reality to an ultimate reality of unlimited freedom and kicks where Kerouac believes we all belong. "The theme of travelling or wandering refers to a flexibility which counteracts the imminent (mental) torpor of daily life" (Mayer 89). The road, in shamanic terms, is an all-encompassing end unto itself, a technique of ecstasy. "The road," Kerouac famously proclaims in *On the Road*, "is life" (199). Movement for the sake of movement, epitomized by his many portrayals of Neal Cassady, shows this shamanic marriage of ecstatic technique with ecstasy itself. Cassady became the primary Beat avatar and muse for Kerouac in ecstasy. Of Cassady, Ken Kesey said his "page was this highway, and his writing tool was one of these cars" (Workman, *The Source*). Kerouac embodied the road ecstasy in his characterization of Neal Cassady (as Dean Moriarty in *On the Road*, and Cody Pomeray in numerous other novels). In Cassady, Kerouac beheld the glory and desolation of the modern American journey. Where does the ecstatic road lead? How? Why?

The archaic cosmology comprises three cosmic regions, which are connected by an axis and can be accessed by the shaman (Eliade 8). Ellwood also cites three possible destinations for a shaman whose "psychological experiences during the ecstasy are generally pictured as a journey into the land of souls, the beyond, the underworld or the sky or over wide geographic areas; real, known regions" (73). The three regions, then, are the heavens, this world, and the underworld. The central axis is a hole or a locus where the ecstatic flight can occur — up, down or around — from one region to another. The mystical locus for Kerouac was the road and/or his childhood Lowell, the axis was the page, and the ecstatic technique was spontaneous prose.

A flight to the sky yields God in his heaven. A descent to the underworld reveals the lost souls of the sick and dead. And a road trip in this world reveals to the reader everyone from the great-souled heroes to the lost and derelict, often at the same time.[8] The journey to the ultimate essence of each of these three worlds (which are iterations of the same ultimate reality) is the ecstasy of the road.

The flight to the heavens can beget sublime theophany and, perhaps, an uplifting sense of participation in its audience. This is ecstasy as it is commonly understood — a wild, ultimate joyride. Kerouac performed many such flights that bear this hallmark: the encounters with "IT" in *On the Road* and *The Subterraneans*, the lessons of dharma found in the wilderness solitude of Mt. Hozomeen in *Desolation Angels*, and the visions of a fellahin Madonna in *Tristessa* (to cite just a few). Shamanic flight to the sky, connections to heavenly beings, and an indwelling paradisal reality are frequently seen in his work.

Journeys in the second cosmic region ("this world") might be the type of trip Kerouac performed on the page more than any other. His tombstone reads, "He honored life," which I take to mean "He honored *this* life." His visions were of what he saw first-hand on his "horizontal ecstasies" on the road. The incessant movement (in cars and buses, on trains, hitchhiking) in his life and on the page proves to be as much an ecstatic technique as the spinning of a whirling dervish. Kerouac explains the hope behind such movement in *On the Road*: "I was a young writer and I wanted to take off. Somewhere along the line I knew there'd be girls, visions, everything; somewhere along the line the pearl would be handed to me" (14). The "pearl," the lesson (or the "noesis," to use William James's term), is the mystical reward of the road.

Introduction

THE SOUL(S) OF JACK

One of the duties of the archaic shaman was to retrieve lost souls and bring them back for the psychic good of the tribe. At the height of his artistic powers, Kerouac renders all of his Beat heroes in order to provide his readers with the possibility of communing, as he has, with these great souls. Besides Dean Moriarty/Cody Pomeray, the Beat avatar and patriarch, other characters who fall under his heroic vision are Mardou Fox, his lover in *The Subterraneans*; Japhy Ryder, his young mentor in *The Dharma Bums*; Tristessa, his junky-goddess in the novella of the same name; and his dear dead brother in *Visions of Gerard*. To some extent these are all devotional soul portraits conjured in his ecstasies of relationship. They are characters who illuminate the holiness of his own experience. He performs his own illumination for the reader as he heads out on the road, hangs out in the tenements of Lowell and Mexico City, climbs the mountaintops and wanders the back alleys of America. He always beholds the wonderment of his flesh-and-blood saints right here, in the great cosmic region of this world, like a shaman seeking out souls to reveal their secrets as a matter of ecstatic record.

VIEW FROM THE BOTTOM

The third type of shamanic journey is the flight to the netherworld, what I call the "nadiral ecstasy." Harrowing, but no less valuable, these trips (like all ecstatic experiences) offer a paradoxical perspective. As noted, ecstasy melts any sense of contradiction, so that the flashpoint of all such experience, as Ginsberg recalls in the quote above, shares the single taste of our common human nature. Like Whitman before him, Kerouac, for much of his career, espoused an expanding, unifying consciousness, despite our modern sense of isolation. In "Song of Myself," Whitman writes, "I am of old and young, of the foolish as much as the wise,/ Maternal as well as paternal, a child as well as a man" (61). Similarly, in "Song of the Open Road," he bids the reader to contemplate the darker aspects of our common nature: "Behold through you as bad as the rest,/ Through the laughter, dancing, dining, supping, of people,/ Inside of dresses and ornaments, inside of those wash'd and / trimm'd faces,/ Behold a secret, silent loathing and despair" (143). The cosmic self, then, draws deeply on and reflects unsparingly the panoply of human life, the "good and the bad." Shamanic ecstasy explores the darkness and the light, the heights and depth of the human mystery.

Introduction

Therefore, a flight to the netherworld is as significant in its noetic import to the shaman and the tribe as a rapturous flight to the heavens. Kerouac's *The Subterraneans* is a work of nadiral ecstasy (as I discuss at length in Chapter 4), as are the closing sequences of *On the Road*, the lovesick bathos of *Tristessa*, the "Passing through the World" sections of *Desolation Angels*, and numerous entries in *Book of Dreams* and *Old Angel Midnight*. All of these show Kerouac in repeated journeys to the very depths of his existence. Time and again he dives to the bottom of his emotional, physical, and metaphysical being and reveals the lesson of those journeys on the page. While most of his novels plainly show this technique at one time or another, his most indicative nadiral works are the last three published in his lifetime: *Big Sur* (1962), *Satori in Paris* (1966), and *Vanity of Duoluz* (1968). These novels present a shamanic decay in its final throes, indicating one crash-landing after another. (I elaborate on the culmination of Kerouac's nadiral vision by examining *Big Sur* in Chapter 7.)

The publication of *On the Road* in 1957 was followed by ten years of predominantly critical vitriol and rejection by the literary community he wanted so badly to win over for years. By the late Sixties Kerouac's vision of "Beat" as an essentially religious term (i.e., a beatific, joyful, and "yea-saying" impulse) had first been transformed into the morose solipsism of the beatnik and then into the heartless and gutless solipsism of the hippie. Kerouac discussed his sadness at the twisting of his vision with William Buckley in a 1968 televised interview less than a year before he died.

> BUCKLEY: To what extent do you believe that the Beat Generation is related to the hippies? What do they have in common? Was this an evolution from one to the other?
>
> KEROUAC: We're just the older ones. See? I'm 46 years old, these kids are 18. But it's the same movement, apparently a Dionysian movement in late civilization and which I did not intend any more than, I suppose, Dionysus did, or whatever his name was.... We're all in our forties. We started this and the kids took it up. But a lot of hoods, hoodlums, and Communists jumped on our backs ... Ferlinghetti jumped on my back ... and turned the idea that I had that the Beat Generation was one of "beatitude," and a pleasure in life, and tenderness; but they called it in the papers "Beat Mutiny," "Beat Insurrection ..." words I never used. Being a Catholic, I believe in order, tenderness, and piety.

Introduction

BUCKLEY: Well then your point was, a movement which you conceived as relatively pure has become ideologized and misanthropic and generally objectionable?
KEROUAC: A movement that was considered what?
BUCKLEY: Pure.
KEROUAC: Yes. It was pure in my heart [Lerner, *WHTK?*].

It seems clear enough that Kerouac's vision, which he apprehended with an inward purity, was never fully understood by his contemporaries as he had hoped. This, along with his alcoholism, might be considered the other contributing factor to the "half-healed" status of his modern post-shamanic practice. The critical rejection, but also, even more, the popularization of what he valued most, wore him down. He felt that his writing had something to offer that was never accepted in the spirit it was given. He was either shuffled off to the mad margins or made an icon for purposes he never intended. In the first case, the sickness of conformity and shame Kerouac sought to cure remained, and he was labeled a lunatic. In the second case, his essentially religious vision was taken over and corrupted by political and social ideologies with agendas of their own.

By the Sixties, besides his critical rejection as a writer, Kerouac had abandoned (or been left behind by) the gang of heroes who were his primary muses at the height of his powers. Many of them had adjusted to the changing times more than he ever could. Cassady had gone on to be the driver of the Merry Prankster bus and a hippie emblem. Ginsberg was already a solid figure on the American literary landscape and was accepted by many of the critics who had rejected Kerouac. The losses had been piling up for Kerouac. His childhood soulmate, Sebastian Sampas, had been killed in the war. His saintly brother Gerard was dead much longer than that. His father and sister were both dead. His marriages had failed. All this, as well as his demonization by the literati, had taken its toll. Kerouac cited the dictum "accept loss forever" as an essential part of his modern prose technique, yet he never could accept, nor survive, the loss of his pure and immediate essence, which was his childhood in Lowell. Nor could he, in the end, ever fully escape the disillusionment with modern America, though he still wrote, in fits, as if his life depended on it.

The final three novels published in his lifetime show a heartbreaking attempt to retrieve what had been lost but not forgotten, what had been dreamed but never attained during his journey. And his prose technique in these works, somewhat frayed and drained, tells of a frightened, lonely man on a nadiral binge. It shows his ecstatic technique in decline: the shallow breath, the torn-down myths, the broken beat, and the horrific vision of loss. Burned out, Kerouac only reported the darkest of ecstasies at the end of his Legend. In his final years, despite the critical rejection and "even worse the nausea of false enthusiasms based on the wrong reasons" (as he lamented in a 1960 letter), and though addled with personal loss and addiction, Kerouac still wrote, as Robert Creeley put it, "long after anyone seemed to be listening" (*GBO* xii).

He remained fiercely protective of his individual Beat vision, went all to pieces, and was dead twelve years after *On the Road* promised so much. And those who read him until the end witness the whole spectacle on the page. "We are a nation of voyeurs," Swartz writes, "we like to watch (often from a safe distance) our idols, heroes, and our Messiahs live on the verge of insanity and chaos that we ourselves are afraid to court" (xi). The safe distance kept by critics and public alike, no matter how positive or negative their opinion of him, doomed Kerouac's shamanic career in his time and shrouded his final performances in black. His writing was always a stab at self-realization, though, in the end, he suffered doubt as to its value. On the last page of his final novel (*Vanity of Duluoz*), referring to his first novel (*The Town and the City*), Kerouac bitterly summarizes his career:

> And I settled down to write, in solitude, in pain, writing hymns and prayers even at dawn, thinking "When this book is finished, which is going to be the sum and substance and crap of everything I've been thru throughout this whole goddam life, I shall be redeemed."
>
> But, wifey, I did it all, I wrote the book, I stalked the streets of life, of Manhattan, of Long Island, stalked thru 1,183 pages of my first novel, sold the book, got an advance, whooped, hallelujah'd, went on, did everything you're supposed to do in life.
>
> But nothing ever came of it [268].

Language and Departure

Kerouac searched for and, at length, accessed the "secret language" that best translated his ecstatic visions. Spontaneous prose fed his need for new language forms. In a 1967 *Escapade* article, he wrote,

Introduction

> My position in the current American literary scene is simply that I got sick and tired of the conventional English sentence which seemed to me so ironbound in its rules, so inadmissible with reference to the actual format of my mind as I had learned to probe it in the modern spirit of Freud and Jung, that I couldn't express myself through that form any more [*GBO* 159].

This introspective impulse, so characteristic of twentieth-century art, was Kerouac's *entrée* to a deeper approach and form in his fiction, one that would approximate every wave, ridge, and trough of his consciousness in language. (*Visions of Cody*, *Book of Dreams* and *Old Angel Midnight*, as I will discuss in later chapters, prove to be his most experimental and successful works in this regard.) The entire Legend of Duluoz exhibits what Ellwood sees as "the modern responsibility for one's interior self [that] has led to rebirths of mysticism and paramystical processes" in our day (70).

Over his career, Kerouac produced a body of work he hoped would enfold and cure his own modern sense of fragmentation. On his television show, Steve Allen asked the writer, "How would you define the word 'beat?'" and Kerouac answered, "Well, sympathetic" (*WHTK?*). Kerouac's motivation for, and the goal of, his writing was much broader in scope than literary craft. It archives a sense of soul and communion that he saw vanishing before his own eyes in America. This task required a "modern prose" that, for Kerouac, meant

> following free deviation (association) of mind into limitless blow-on-subject seas of thought, swimming in sea of English with no discipline other than the rhythms of rhetorical exhalation and expostulated statement.... Blow as deep as you want — write as deeply, fish as far down as you want, satisfy yourself first, then reader cannot fail to receive telepathic shock and meaning-excitement by same laws operating in his own human mind [*GBO* 69].

This modern prose embodies significant shamanic motifs throughout his work. Besides direct references to ecstasy, trances and dreams, skeletal visions, sky visions, and depictions of mentors (or helping spirits), there is much evidence of a shaman-like "secret language" that takes the form of neologisms, poetic compounds, glossolalia, linguistic conversions, and unconventional punctuation. He conjures his nostalgia for the paradise of pre-war America by repeatedly invoking contemporary pop icons throughout his work. As James Fisher observes in *The Catholic Counterculture in America, 1933–1962*,

Introduction

> Like no Catholic before him, Kerouac was able to blend mystical imagery with materials from the American popular culture he adored with equal fervor.... Kerouac's early love for the Three Stooges and the Shadow, Krazy Kat and Harpo Marx reflected an early desire for experience beyond the limits of immigrant Catholicism [208].

Kerouac builds a personal mythos by melding his individual (French Canadian Catholic) experience with that of such American popular archetypes. He often emphasizes the reader's participation in that mythos by frequent use of direct address, thereby arguing for the universal significance of his subjective ecstatic forays on the page. His work consistently shows the shamanic preoccupation with death and the mystical perception of the writer's experience: simultaneous, chaotic, yet indicative and reflective of his times. Kerouac devised an authentic language and style that best convey the ineffability of his mystical encounters with an alternative and ultimate reality. In *Desolation Angels*, he expands on the nature of that language and style:

> Strangely enough, these scribblings were the first of their kind in the world, I was originating (without knowing it, you say?) a new way of writing about life, no fiction, no craft, no revising afterthoughts, the heartbreaking discipline of the veritable fire ordeal where you can't go back but have made the vow of "speak now or forever hold your tongue" and all of it innocent go-ahead confession, the discipline of making the mind the slave of the tongue with no chance to lie or re-elaborate [229].

Kerouac's spontaneous prose proceeded, then, from a pre-lingual impulse, and is more akin, as he explains it, to the oral tradition than the written. His was a new way of writing that bravely answered an archaic call to confess what he saw as the ecstasy of being. A shamanic reading of his work shows that *all* of his writing — from the wonder of his youth (as mythologized in *Visions of Gerard* and *Doctor Sax*), through the dark confused wonder of his maturity (as confessed in *Visions of Cody* and *The Subterraneans*), to his disastrous notoriety and demise (as recorded in *Big Sur*) — is ecstatic in origin and style. "It's hard to explain," he writes in *Big Sur*, "and the best thing to do is not be false" (29).

Kerouac dedicated himself to the truthful expression of his experience, equally sacred and profane, through the ecstatic language and technique of his prose. His career traces a distinctly shamanic arc. Throughout the gathering of his literary powers and even in their decay, his body of work,

Introduction

at once fictional and autobiographical, stood fast to his Beat vision of sympathy, and held to a radical notion of cosmic ecumenism whereby anyone might actualize his own mystical nature through the subjective experience. Anytime. Any place. Right now.

> He is called a Yogi, he is called a Priest,
> a minister, a Brahmin, a Parson, a Chaplain,
> a Roshi, a Laoshih, a Master, a Patriarch, a Pope,
> a Spiritual Commissar, a Counselor, an Adviser,
> a Bodhisattva-Mahasattva, an Old Man, a Saint,
> a Shaman, a Leader, who thinks nothing of
> himself as separate from another self, not
> higher nor lower, no stages and no definite
> attainments, no mysterious stigmata or secret
> holyhood, no wild dark knowledge and no
> venerable authoritativeness, nay a giggling sage
> sweeping out the kitchen with a broom. After
> supper, a silent smoke. Because there is no
> definite teaching: the world is undisciplined
> Nature endlessly in every direction inward
> to your body and outward into space [*SOGE* 42–3].

1

Visions of Gerard
Modern Hagiography

> An early taste of death is not necessarily a bad thing.
> —"How to Be a Great Writer," Bukowski 93

In July 1926, when Kerouac was four, his sickly brother, Gerard, died at the age of nine. The formative influence this event had on the writer has been well documented in the Duluoz Legend and in the biographical and critical body of work that came in its wake, and rightly so. The impact of a loved one's death (or the impression of the first funeral we attend in childhood) cannot be minimized in any of our experiences. It marks, most likely, the first time we come face to face with the ultimate mystery and witness the ways in which we deal with its imminence. Death is the common proof of our worldview. Kerouac was no different. As I consider Kerouac vis-à-vis the shamanic technique that his body of work evinces, I'm compelled to take another look at the meaning of this singular event as he recreated it in his novel, *Visions of Gerard*. Even as the death ecstasy is fundamental to the shamanic perspective, it is also the linchpin on which all of Kerouac's writing hinges. "Death," he writes, "is the only decent subject, since it marks the end of illusion and delusion—Death is the other side of the same coin, we call now, Life" (*VOG* 103). Gerard's suffering and death set the stage for Kerouac's life-long search for, and interrogation of, the divine essence.

Although the extraordinary power of Kerouac's memory has been widely and appropriately recognized (as in Gerald Nicosia's excellent biography titled *Memory Babe*), *Visions of Gerard* is not a photographic report of that summer's events. How can it be? Written in January 1956, it is a reconstruction, a creative bridge between the thirty-three-year-old Kerouac and his toddler experience between 1922 and 1926. Therefore, in it we see the Catholicism of his upbringing mingled with the Buddhist key of his adult interest. It is a work of childhood hagiography recreated by a man who is actively struggling with his faith and striving to redeem mortal loss.

The Saint as Tutelary Spirit

The goal of the hagiographer is to retell the lives of the saints in order to edify the living faithful and convert the skeptic (i.e., "you can do this too"). The life of Gerard as seen by his family (and much of Lowell, it seems) demonstrates the characteristics of a child saint. Deeply compassionate, pious, gentle, stoic, generous, desirous of sanctity, hungry for theophany, wise beyond his years, and somehow "otherworldly" for all of these qualities, *Visions of Gerard* attributes a "definite and immortal idealism" to his little brother who grows up to reveal the same to the reader of this novel (*VOG* 6). Gerard embodies a remedy for the hardhearted and hateful world in which Kerouac finds himself in 1956. At various times in the novel, Gerard is described in terms of (or likened to) the wounded Sacred Heart of Jesus (7), Jesus clearing the temple (11), and St. Francis (19). He is personified along the lines of the suffering servant portrayed in the Old Testament as one whom "the Lord was pleased to crush ... in infirmity" (Isaiah 53:10). The signature color of the always pale Gerard is, of course, white, as he is a soul made pure through suffering in a profane world.[1] Gerard is an innocent lamb led to the slaughter through the mortification of his body, and a child who is privy to "astonishing revelations of heaven" on account of it (*VOG* 1).

The role and function of the saint in general, and Gerard in particular, closely resemble those of the tutelary spirit in the shamanic paradigm. The presence of, and communication with, the tutelary spirit validates the shamanic career (which is all about accessing the spiritual realm) (Eliade 95). He is one who has crossed over, experienced the ecstasy of death, and, therefore, actualizes the mystical identification with the divine. From this angle, in his brief suffering life, Gerard is like a wounded shaman, and his death provides Kerouac all the proof he needs to seek "religion."[2] In the life and death of Gerard, Kerouac receives the lessons by which he might access the mystical essence.

1. Visions of Gerard

Kerouac describes his earliest childhood as a complete identification with Gerard, a kind of "possession." "For the first four years of my life, while he lived, I was not Ti Jean Duluoz, I was Gerard, the world was his face ... bending over me and being me and blessing me" (*VOG* 2). As an adult writing this and other chapters of his Duluoz Legend, Kerouac possesses Gerard's spirit to recreate his ecstasies for the reader. This "spirit possession," then, is both active and passive in *Visions of Gerard*.[3] The title itself has a double meaning. The first might be translated as "The Acts of Gerard" (referring to what the child Kerouac saw Gerard doing), while the second is best understood as "What Gerard Saw" (with his own eyes as mediated by Kerouac in his writing).

"The Acts of Gerard"

The young Kerouac witnesses Gerard's unending acts of compassion. Gerard brings a poor boy named "Plourdes" home to be fed (*VOG* 4). He frees a mouse from a trap and nurses it back to health only to have the family cat eat it (*VOG* 10).[4] He feeds the neighborhood birds from his sickbed (*VOG* 21). When little Ti Jean pokes out the eye of a murderess pictured in the newspaper, Gerard advocates non-judgment and understanding (and together they fix the picture!) (*VOG* 23). Sickly as he is, Gerard ventures out on a bitter cold night to get his mother some aspirin to alleviate *her* suffering (*VOG* 41). All of these acts impart the idea that kindness and disregard for self are the hallmarks of right living.

On his final Christmas Eve, the failing Gerard is brimming with the ineffable mysteries of death (*VOG* 59). Of all his acts recounted in this novel, most importantly, Gerard suffers and dies heroically before Ti Jean's eyes. This sequence bears many of the qualities of the Passion of Jesus as recounted in the Gospels, and all the characteristics of the shamanic initiation. There is a value inherent in suffering from these perspectives that is absent in the secular worldview, namely, the belief that suffering reveals the sacred and leads to the common ecstasy of all our deaths. (This outlook is not lost on the nuns who are present at Gerard's deathbed to witness his agony and record his words, nor is it lost on the adult Kerouac casting about for a spiritual foundation to supplant his profane experience.) This significance stands in opposition to the predominant view of suffering as an evil to be avoided at all costs. That is not to say the dying child, as portrayed, is joyful (i.e., unnatural or somehow spared) in his suffering. Like Jesus on the cross, who exclaims, "My God, my God, why have you forsaken me?" (Mark 16:34), Gerard on his deathbed cries out, "Oh my Jesus you've left me alone and you're hurting me" (*VOG* 68). Nevertheless, all this suffering yields an "ecstasy [that] unfolds inside his mind like a flower and says, Yes" (*VOG* 69). And for all this, Kerouac writes, "unceasing compassion flows from Gerard to the world" (*VOG* 70). This is the greatest lesson of Gerard's supreme act of suffering. He accomplishes the seemingly impossible: he loves the world, fallen and ignorant as it is of all his intuitions about our spiritual essence.

"What Gerard Saw"

Many important episodes in *Visions of Gerard* take place when the narrator (Ti Jean) is absent from the scene. In them, the narrator's point of view becomes omniscient and wholly dedicated to Gerard. In these sequences, what Gerard sees, thinks, says, does, and otherwise experiences are pure fiction. They are a product of Kerouac filtering the imagined past through his present consciousness in the ecstasy of writing. (In other words, in Kerouac's poetics, the omniscient point of view equals the ecstatic point of view.)

For example, when Gerard leaves Ti Jean at home and turns the corner en route to the parish school, his (Gerard's) thoughts clearly betray the Buddhist bent of the adult Kerouac (*VOG* 25). This section also introduces the motif of "the sky" in the novel. Kerouac dedicates much descriptive and allusive detail to the sky as the heavenly context of the Passion play that is *Visions of Gerard*. (See, for example, 25, 27–28, 30, 58–59, 98, 129.) Equally shamanic and Christian in its import, Gerard is fascinated with the sky, which he sees as both his mentor and his destiny. "Gerard has his eyes up to the sky and knows he'll never learn in school what he'd like to learn this morning from that sky of silent mystery, that heartbreaking sayless blank that won't tell men and boys what's up — 'It's the eye of God, there's no bottom'" (*VOG* 27–28).

1. Visions of Gerard

Especially telling as regards this omniscient point of view and the "imagined experience" it yields is the extended section that shows Gerard going to confession. It begins with a long diatribe on sin and the fallen condition of mankind: Catholic guilt accented with Buddhist notions of void and samsara. "Even Gerard was a sinner" and went to confession on Fridays (*VOG* 31).[5] The acute detail of this vision shows Gerard moving through the church, engaged in the ritual, saying prayers, the "mystic priestly secret" words that he cannot fathom (*VOG* 32). He contemplates the sad injustice of the crucifix with great empathy and prepares his confession. Kerouac imagines the dialogue in the confessional where Gerard owns up to pushing a younger schoolmate who accidentally knocked down his house of cards, looking at another boy's penis in the lavatory, and lying to a nun about having studied his catechism (which he knew and understood anyway). The priest absolves Gerard and assigns him the penance of reciting a rosary and fifteen additional "Hail Mary's." As he fulfills his penance at the altar rail, the narrative point of view waxes divine and shifts to God looking down at little Gerard, "the mortal angel" (*VOG* 38). Gerard experiences an ecstasy of forgiveness and silence alone in the church and soon returns home. This sequence describes a vision both true and mystical. Gerard in the confessional becomes the hub of the universe. The scene resolves in an all-embracing awareness as Kerouac writes, "None of the elements of this dream can be separated from any other part, it is all one pure suchness" (*VOG* 39).

The very next episode in the novel further displays Kerouac's omniscient point of view in imagining Gerard's experience as he heads out into the winter night alone to get aspirin for his mother. This becomes a kind of essay that interrogates our suffering humanity, which Gerard seeks to understand and, at least as far as his mother is concerned that night, to heal. He (Gerard through Kerouac) perceives a dark cold world, inhospitable and completely indifferent to the misery of its inhabitants. On this trip Gerard concludes (in a rather Gnostic tone) that ours is a mistaken creation, one that is incongruous with the feeling nature of mankind. God, it seems to him, created a "world not made for men ... something dead to sympathy" (*VOG* 42). He asks God why this is so and, more importantly, on returning home, he asks his mother the same thing. The exchange reveals Gerard's mystical awareness of our divine origin and his yearning to return to it. When he inquires, "Why didn't God leave us in heaven?" and his mother responds, "You're sure we were there?" Gerard says, "Yes, I'm sure" (*VOG* 44). That we're not "in heaven" (and the "why" of that) is a difficult question for any afflicted person of any faith in any era, especially when some of us (like "millionaires in yachts") apparently suffer very little in this life (*VOG* 45). It is a problem that any believing (or thinking) person — even a "saint" like Gerard — has to struggle with. (Thus, as discussed earlier, in *Visions of Gerard* we have the sacred value of suffering unseen by the secular world.)[6]

In a subsequent sequence (perhaps based on a story told to him by his mother), Kerouac re-imagines a day when Gerard is exhausted and falls asleep at his desk in school. What follows defines a shamanic experience (i.e., initiatory illness, celestial flight, and helping spirits in animal form) and "looks" like a Catholic holy card. In Gerard's dream, the earth dematerializes and he finds himself in the presence of "a Great White Virgin Mary ... held aloft by countless swarms of grave bluebirds" (*VOG* 52). Gerard is beckoned by the Blessed Mother. He follows her to heaven in a wagon being hauled by two white lambs as two white pigeons perch on each of his shoulders. When the nun wakes him up, Gerard says, "Well I was in heaven" (*VOG* 53). The revelation of his vision, as Gerard explains it, is that we're all in heaven already, although we don't know it. This good news is greeted with stunned amazement by the nun and his classmates in the scene. The critics, you might say, were also "stunned."

It is because of this scene and others like it in *Visions of Gerard* that many critics of his day dismissed the novel as sentimental, bathetic, and self-indulgent. The job of the hagiographer (and one's ability to "keep the faith" in general) has never been easy. *Visions of Gerard* as Kerouac saw it (namely, a sincere portrait of the compassionate life and death of his brother) was mostly greeted with a "you've GOT to be kidding me" reaction from the critical corps of the day. That was the first target of the disparaging attacks: the book's "prideful sincerity" (*JKSL 1957–1969* 370).[7] It is easy (too easy) to scorn the experiences of Gerard (and Kerouac's re-creation of them) simply because we have not shared them. Celestial visions? By the early Sixties, they ranked right up there with alien abduction in our skeptical collective consciousness. Our receptors for sincerity and compassion in art (like our capacity to have and apprehend the shamanic expe-

1. Visions of Gerard

rience overall) had already been dulled in the slick modern milieu. Kerouac recognizes this and comments on it often in his correspondence, sometimes with a rueful humor (*JKSL 1957–1969* 371). The negative criticism (frequently in the form of pointed personal attacks) that dogged Kerouac almost from the beginning reveals more about the state of our modern culture than it does of the writing itself. *Visions of Gerard*, I think, gets down with some very profound problems and questions of our existence. But suffice it to say that, by the time of its publication, the age of miracles was long gone. And who needs visions of heaven when you've got a TV in your living room and other profane alternatives?

Profane Interlude: The Aberrant Ecstasy of Emil's Night Out

It is interesting that prior to the final "agony and death" of Gerard in the summer of 1926, the novel abandons Gerard altogether. Instead, Kerouac's omniscient narrator is dedicated to the maundering spring evening his father (Emil) spends cavorting with his cronies, the "bar standers and beer eaters" of Lowell (*VOG* 61). This long sequence of 25 pages only mentions Gerard twice. This makes sense because Emil is trying to escape his bleak situation for an evening. It is a "style" of escape that we see played out again and again throughout the Duluoz Legend: leave the wives behind to take care of things, go hang out with the boys, work a little, and drink a lot. In the overall structure of the novel, this is a reprieve from the sacred suffering of Gerard, and Emil's foray into the profane night.

As soon as Emil leaves the house, the narrative situates him in the Duluoz genealogy. This close attention to heritage is a pet motif throughout Kerouac's work, whether it is his own roots or the roots of his characters. (He further explores this theme in works such as *Visions of Cody, Doctor Sax, The Subterraneans*, and *Satori in Paris*.) Now in *Visions of Gerard*, we flash back to Emil's Canadian birth, baptism, and childhood. We witness the family's move to New Hampshire, then another to Lowell. We see Emil graduate from insurance salesman to independent businessman. Eager, intuitive, and gregarious, Emil is painted by Kerouac as a real mensch with a distinctly fatalist streak before the narrative snaps into the particular action of this spring night (*VOG* 80).

In an otherwise largely reverent work of hagiography, once the story leaves the deathbed behind and walks out the door with Emil, the scenes take on a decidedly lighter and irreverent tone. Emil's interplay with his print shop partner Manuel in this episode can be downright comic and reminiscent of the exchanges of Abbot & Costello. They complete their work in short order and head out into the night to drive around on Manuel's motorcycle-with-sidecar, to chew the fat and drink with other denizens of Lowell. It's a "boys' night out" and the idea is to leave behind (transcend?) the troubles of the day. There's a lot of talk about vaudeville, much wife-bashing, and card playing. Throughout the Duluoz Legend, the "game," real or imagined, is often a hedge against the pressures of life, and always an alternative to the real-world experience. "Emil leans over to rub his thigh in the night of the world forgetting his family, lost in the eye to eye the game of men in America" (*VOG* 94). But as dawn breaks and Emil rakes in his winnings, the thought of his dying son overwhelms him with shame (*VOG* 96). All that's left now for Emil (as for his son, Jack, so many times later on) is to drink more.

As discussed in the introduction, from a shamanic perspective, the use of alcohol (or any substance) is a legitimate, though aberrant, ecstatic technique. It is aberrant because chronic exercise of this technique will kill the practitioner (as the shortened alcoholic life of Kerouac attests). Yet it is a legitimate kind of religious experience because, as William James notes, "Sobriety diminishes, discriminates, and says no; drunkenness expands, unites, and says yes ... it makes [the drinker] for the moment one with truth" (387). This long "boys' night" sequence in *Visions of Gerard* establishes the heritage and appeal of alcohol in the Duluoz Legend. Emil, Manuel, Old Bull Balloon and others drink to excess and drive on through the Lowell dawn. They blather at one another. They keep their troubles and angst at bay, and, yes, they attain an ecstatic perspective that's "only stored in bottles" (*VOG* 101).

However, when Kerouac intervenes in this bacchanal with an enigmatic authorial aside, he seems to question the real worth of any of it.

> Experience has made a man of Emil, and you may take man and weigh him on the scales with his weight in goldshit on the other pan, the measurement

1. Visions of Gerard

may come out, legible—If so, write me a letter—I see no reason for man—But his value, I buy—Dawns white with drunkness I've had myself with my boys—And there'll be more [*VOG* 98].

This passage typifies an ambivalence that many critics and readers of Kerouac find exasperating. It seems that he is often on both sides of the fence from book to book, even page to page. Here Kerouac sings the glory of drink; there he bemoans its ravages. Elsewhere in this novel, he writes about the holiness of life, but here he comments on its pointlessness. Why? This is the paradox, the contradiction inherent to Kerouac writing in ecstasy. As Whitman says, "Do I contradict myself? / Very well then I contradict myself / (I am large, I contain millions)" (96). Besides, it seems that such contradiction is a realistic expression of human nature and the paradox of the individual experience. No problem. I find it entirely believable and natural. It's important to note that the tone and meaning of the passage from *Visions of Gerard* quoted above comments upon the profane experience of the drunken Emil as contrasted with the sacred experience of the compassionate Gerard. Emil's night out sums up the aberrant alcoholic technique and its fleeting ecstasy while the saintly Gerard is home dying, about to access ecstasy for real and for good.

At 10 the next morning, Emil returns home stinking drunk with Bull Balloon in tow. Nothing is changed. Mother makes them breakfast. This profane interlude is over.

Kerouac's next line appears in quotes: "'And time bids be gone'" (*VOG* 102). Time is up for Gerard, and soon for this book (which is Gerard).

The Death of Gerard

Bedridden, Gerard spends his last days teaching his little brother kindness and compassion for all things: cats, birds, even flies. He explains that God includes such fragile beings in his creation to see whether or not we will break them. Those who protect the weak and vulnerable out of a sense of compassion are bound for heaven (*VOG* 104). Gerard dispenses deathbed blessings and lessons "concerning the kinds of fearlessness, or the proof of faith, or the ethereality of pain, or the unreality of death (and life too), or the calm hand of God everywhere slowly benedicting" (*VOG*

109). Gerard is now well established as Ti Jean's spiritual hero. He is a shaman and saint bound for "the other side." He has what the hagiographers call "the odor of sanctity." Gerard's "breath smells like crushed flowers" and his "room takes on the quality of a lily, white, wan, fragrant" (*VOG* 107). The priest is called to confer the last rites to the dying boy. Then the nuns ask him questions and record his last words on paper. It is a scripture that remains undisclosed. Kerouac can only conjecture on the questions asked and the answers given. This is notable because up to this point in the novel he hasn't shied away from using the omniscient point of view to project thoughts, words and actions onto Gerard (and other characters, such as Emil, as we've seen). However, here, Kerouac simply writes, "I'm afraid to say what I really want to say" (*VOG* 109). I'll not conjecture as to why.

The actual moment of Gerard's death happens "off stage." We get no details of it at all. The passing of a loved one is a crisis for the living left behind, not the deceased who has moved on. Kerouac notes that it was "as if a curtain had opened, and innumerably revealed the scene behind the scene" (*VOG* 111). For the living, *that* is the vital question precipitated by death: How do you deal with your peek at the ultimate mystery?

As Kerouac describes Gerard's home wake, we see a variety of reactions to the boy's untimely passing. Ti Jean greets his brother's death with an innocent joy that's augmented by the adult writer's mystical sensibilities: "It was some great event that would make a change that would make everything better" (*VOG* 109). Later, Kerouac summarizes the extended family's response with the characteristic fatalism of the Duluoz clan: "Gerard is dead and the soul is dead and the world is dead and dead is dead" (*VOG* 111). His mother rails at the injustice of it and, when reminded that we all will die, she shocks the group by saying, "Good, damn it, good!" (*VOG* 115). Each of these responses, in its own way, flies in the face of the typical somber and tragic pose of the mourner. But Kerouac has been "schooled" in the mysteries by Gerard. In their "head-to-head confabs [listening] to the holy lazy silence of Time," Gerard has imparted a secret knowledge to his little brother (*VOG* 116).

As Gerard's classmates file past his coffin, Kerouac addresses the reader directly with an analogy of ecstatic/shamanic import. The realization of death that one perceives looking at a corpse, he writes, is the same thing

1. Visions of Gerard

"you learn the first time you get drunk at sixteen.... 'Don't you realize you are God?'" (*VOG* 117). This observation elaborates upon the meaning of what I have referred to earlier as "Emil's night out." To put it simply, the consequence of alcohol use in the Duluoz Legend is the same as that in the shamanic tradition; namely, what you experience temporarily by drinking, you experience eternally by dying: ecstasy. Kerouac will revisit this theme in fact and fiction for the rest of his life.

The Funeral Procession

In *Visions of Gerard*, the procession to the funeral Mass shows a style of shifting, simultaneous, and omniscient perspective analogous to the "Wandering Rocks" chapter of Joyce's *Ulysses*. The scene opens with the narrative "camera" aimed at the sky (the heavenly context of the novel, and Gerard's destination). The point of view then shifts to look down on the whole earth before it focuses incrementally ("Coming down, far, sad, wide, the world, the earth, this pot, this parturience organizer") on Massachusetts, then Lowell, then a store in Lowell, then a butcher standing in the doorway of the store, then the blood on the butcher's hands, then to the man about to buy the pork chop the butcher has prepared (*VOG* 120–121). The function of this sequence is multiple. As a "vision of being," it is a rhapsody on our samsara earth, and an argument that reality is solely a matter of perspective. Most importantly, it introduces us to "Mr. Groscorp."

As his name implies, "Mr. Groscorp" is the voice of our physical reality. So it is fitting that as he sits down to lunch in his apartment across the street from St. Louis Church, he spies Gerard's funeral procession pull up in front. This reminder of mortality annoys Mr. Groscorp, spoiling his lunch. His viewpoint is entirely secular in that he sees no reason for the ritual and ceremony of the Catholic funeral, and no reason for him to be reminded of his own mortality by it. "I'm eating — We'll think about it later" (*VOG* 122).

The perspective shifts again as a crew of house painters observes the funeral procession. They serve as a profane chorus to the sacred scene (*VOG* 121). Their commentary is insensitive and wise-cracking. They let fly one cheap joke after another in the longest run of dialogue in the novel. But when they see the child-sized coffin, they fall into silence and self-recrimination.

The funeral procession sequence in *Visions of Gerard* is another example of how Kerouac uses the omniscient point of view to swing the narrative focus from the primary plot to a variety of viewpoints, and, thereby, perform the story in its fullest context. It is a technique by which he can juxtapose the profane and the sacred and show them, as much as possible in words, in a simultaneous manner. As Mr. Groscorp feeds himself in the apartment, and the joking house painters get back to work across the street, the scene resolves inside the church as the organ intones the beginning of the funeral Mass.

Funeral and Burial of Gerard: "Here and Now I see the ecstasy" (VOG 127)

From a shamanic point of view, the last five pages of *Visions of Gerard* are some of the most exciting in the entire Duluoz Legend. They are plainly indicative of the function and primacy of ecstasy in Kerouac's style and content. If in many places, the rest of this novel has proven to be a dialogue between the sacred and the profane, the funeral and burial of Gerard establish the view that, at the end of the day, each of Kerouac's books is about realizing the divine essence.

A long prayer from the "old" Latin Mass kicks off this final episode. Appearing on the page *in toto* and untranslated, it gives the impression of a writer reveling in the musicality of the words themselves separated from their meaning for the average reader. It sets a symphonic tone that slowly crescendos. Then Kerouac re-creates what he claims is one of his earliest memories. Whether it is the child Ti Jean having this memory in the church pew during his brother's funeral or another authorial intervention in the novel is unclear. The substance of this memory is significant in *Visions of Gerard* (a story about Kerouac's first tutelary spirit). It also presages the following novel in the Duluoz Legend, *Doctor Sax* (a tale about the writer's next tutelary spirit). In a curious blend of active and passive voice Kerouac recollects what seems to be a prototype of Doctor

1. Visions of Gerard

Sax himself—an old man in a slouching hat—who is walking toward "some inexpressibly beautiful opening in the rain where it will be all open-sky and radiant, but I will never go there.... He, on foot, heads for the pure land" (*VOG* 126). This memory melds with the rain outside the church as well as the priest's chanting and organ music within. Heading for "the pure land," the man in this memory is on the same journey as Gerard, and, as we will see in *Doctor Sax*, he will "serve" Kerouac in the same manner as Gerard, that is, as teacher and mentor in the mysteries.

The memory, the music, the incense, the tearful mourners, the tolling church bell, the prayerful incantations, and his dear Gerard dead in the coffin all combine to yield a deeply joyful vision that shows Ti Jean "the divine and perfect ecstasy, reward without end, it has come, has always been with us" (*VOG* 127). Gerard's idea in life that "we're all in heaven already" has been made apparent as he lay in the casket and crossed into the pure land. Gerard's mentorship of Kerouac helped him come to terms with the essential paradox and puzzle of the human experience: Why must we die? The answer: To live. Die to your bodily life, and be born to your spiritual life, that's the shaman's way. This novel shows the suffering and death of Gerard to be sacred and ecstatic (even as it shows Emil's drunken foray into the Lowell night to be profane and ecstatic). This tension between the sacred and the profane, and Kerouac's ecstasies in both these realms, are the twin foundations for Kerouac's career. While Doctor Sax will catalyze the idea of himself as a writer, his memories of Gerard sparked them in the first place. He tells himself, "Write in honor of his death" (*VOG* 112).

"[The] gravedigger picks up his shovel and closes the book" (*VOG* 129).

2

The Shrouds of Eternity
Doctor Sax *as Shamanic Journey*

> Genius is nothing more or less than childhood recaptured at will.
> — Baudelaire
>
> In slumber the eye of the soul waxes bright,
> but in the daytime man's doom goes unforeseen.
> — Aeschylus, *Euminides*

Dream, Myth, and Apocalypse

In 1948, Jack Kerouac is 26 years old, living in Ozone Park with his mother. Unable to interest publishers in his first novel, he despairs of ever making a living as a writer. That fall, he has a dream about his childhood Lowell. Four years later, in the summer of 1952, in a stoned fit of imagination, he writes this dream out (in pencil and pocket notebooks) in the squalor of William Burroughs's bathroom in Mexico City. Burroughs, at this point a full-blown junky, still shaky after shooting his wife in the head, is trying to lay low. He prefers that Jack smoke his marijuana in the bathroom. Granted, by this time Kerouac has published *The Town and the City*, but five years will pass before publication of *On the Road*, and he is hardly assured of a career as an author. In fact, he is nearly destitute, and Burroughs will soon ask him to move on.

Faced with this dubious future, Kerouac enters upon the most creative period of his life (thirteen books in six years) and produces his own multi-genre apocalyptic vision, *Doctor Sax*. For the shaman, personal turmoil begets the dream that calls for the ecstatic performance. The performance then establishes the myth. Apocalypse marks a common human passage, the "reduction" and return to the soul. Apocalypse gets us all home.

2. The Shrouds of Eternity

Apocalyptic dreams, like apocalyptic literature in general, reflect withdrawal from the present social and political world and from the realm of sense impression to an imaginary, internal universe where, as in Blake, we can see truly only with the eyes of the soul [*TEOR* vol. 4, 482].

Kerouac's situation in Mexico City 1952 is clearly critical, therefore ripe for an ecstatic response. Far from home and in financial straits, he suffers his initiation into the writer's life. Such an "indomitable urge to flee into the wilderness" and undergo hardships there is characteristic of the shaman's "illness," which is "preceded, accompanied by, or followed by visions" (*TEOR* vol. 15, 283–84). Kerouac's answer to this personal crisis is radical and written. "Perhaps only by writing," notes James T. Jones, "could he explore all the ramifications of the primal scene in his life and thereby come to know it fully" (47). The nostalgia he evinces for the lost paradise of his childhood Lowell in *Doctor Sax* is not sentimental, but terrifying and comedic in turns. Finding the prospect of maturity and responsibility inhibiting and, perhaps, frightening in Burroughs's bathroom, Kerouac ritualizes the death of his boyhood innocence to re-create a time when his fear was tinged with wonder and humor.

So in 1952, Jack Kerouac, the thirty-year-old author having a tough time in Mexico City, uses "Jackie Dulouz," the teenage neophyte from Lowell, to express the meaning of the dream he had four years previous. Like all of his best writing, *Sax* is driven by a notion of revelation and myth that will spontaneously find its own form, literary convention be damned. Attentive to the ecstatic nature of the project in *Sax*, Kerouac finds himself delving into "the secret of what God has done with my Time" (*DS* 6). In this way, through a shamanic lens, one life might comment on our common human experience.

Playing with Language, Leitmotif, and the Bildungsroman Gone Wild

> I am beginning to discover something beyond the novel and beyond the arbitrary confines of the story ... into the realms of revealed Picture ... revealed whatever ... revelated prose ... *wild form*, man, *wild form*. Wild form's the only form holds what I have to say.
> — Kerouac, letter to John Clellon Holmes, June 5, 1952[1]

Kerouac in Ecstasy

> I can hardly bring myself to call it a novel.
> — Barnaby Conrad reviews *Doctor Sax*,
> *Saturday Review*, April 1952

The story begins, "The other night I had a dream..." (*DS* 3). The opening paragraph of *Doctor Sax* primes the reader for an unconventional foray into the writer's past. In one sentence (85 words, eight lines long), Kerouac explains that what follows will not be a traditional narrative, but an actual dream he will enact and re-present. "In *Doctor Sax* dreaming is equated with art, and the artist is identified with the perpetual child or, even more pertinently, with the child's fantasy" (Nicosia 394). In a 1951 letter to Neal Cassady, Kerouac asserts the significance of dreaming (and, by inference, *Doctor Sax*) in no uncertain terms: "Dream and vision are intertwinable with reality and prophecy" (*JKSL 1940–1956* 269).

In "The Neal Book" (later called *Visions of Cody*) and *On the Road* (both works-in-progress during the composition of *Sax*), Kerouac describes his writer's vocation as a divine mandate. (That is, he sees a vision of God in the clouds pointing to him and saying, "Write!") In *Doctor Sax*, however, even as the shaman re-creates his own initiation (illness and cure) at will in the ecstatic technique, the directive to write comes from Kerouac himself. "Describe the wrinkly tar of this sidewalk ... and let your mind off yourself in this work" (*DS* 3). As in other works of this most fertile period (1951–1957), here Kerouac shows a paradoxical coupling of self-consciousness and abandonment. He used various names for his modern prose technique as it rapidly evolved. In *Visions of Cody*, it was "sketching"; in *The Subterraneans*, "spontaneous prose." He calls the technique of *Doctor Sax* "wild form," and using it recounts his initiation as an adolescent into the mysteries of the cosmic struggle between good and evil, reality and fantasy, present and past, life and art. Though this story is on one level a personal meditation on the narrator's coming of age as a writer, it is also turned inside-out to conceivably belong to us all.

In *Sax*, "wild form" looks like six books of shifting genres, tones, and voices. The oscillation of form in the novel is experimental and requires a high level of reader participation. Throughout the narrative Kerouac employs a wide range of stylistic strategies to perform the vision of *Sax*, including stage directions (11), a script (29–30), a map (42), a screenplay

2. The Shrouds of Eternity

(81–97), a racing program (89), a newspaper clipping (90), incantations (117, 149), poetry (157–62), and embedded text (135–43). Perhaps the form of the novel shifts unconsciously with his visions, or, perhaps, Burroughs just needed to use the bathroom. As Kerouac explained to Ginsberg in November 1952, "*Doctor Sax* was written high on tea without pausing to think, sometimes Bill would come in the room and so the chapter ended there, one time he yelled at me with his long gray face because he could smell the smoke in the yard" (*JKSL 1940–1956* 383). Kerouac's "wild form" in *Doctor Sax* has no rational motive or explanation; rather, it is felt. "I'm sure," he wrote Cassady in 1951, "that someday science will prove what I intuitively claim now" (*JKSL 1940–1956* 268). As he perfected his technique, Kerouac became convinced "that the urgency of explaining something has its own words and rhythm, and time is of the essence — Modern Prose" (*JKSL 1940–1956* 450).

The prose in *Doctor Sax* often evokes an authentic, shamanic use of language. Eliade notes,

> The purest poetic act seems to re-create language from an inner experience that like the ecstasy ... of the "primitives," reveals the essence of things. It is from such linguistic creations ... that the "secret language" of the mystics and the traditional allegorical languages later crystallize [54].

The writer's greatest potential for magical performance is proportional to his ability to play with language. Kerouac's use of onomatopoeia, for example, as a radical move toward the pre-lingual, shows his close attention to the primacy of sound and intuition over the rational narrative, and marks what he sees as the presence of the oral tradition within the act of writing. Critic Matt Theado points out that

> Kerouac relates the written word tightly with the spoken word, and both are yoked by the world of his mind as he sifts through dreams, memories, and various other thought associations to build up the sentences [33].

In a typical episode, a sound-vision yields the spiritual presence of Sax as the metaphysical playground of all the children of Lowell. Elsewhere, Sax is revealed in the fantasy "horse races" little Jackie holds on his bedroom floor on rainy days using marbles, races that begin with his mock playing of a bugle (*DS* 86).

As a means of distancing his writing from the arbitrary confines of the conventional narrative, the language throughout *Sax* is playful and entirely subject to Kerouac's whim. In the spirit of his belief that "something that you feel will find its own form," he often adapts or fabricates words, intuitively depending on their "sound" to carry the meaning or, more accurately, their felt sense (*GBO* 72). Thus, we find the narrator "goopy" with amazement as he perceives his interior and exterior worlds. Later he sees a "Bloop Moon shining by a jackpine in Pawtucketville" (*DS* 205). Devoid of any rational descriptive meaning, in the often-cartoonish *Sax* world, "bloop" works as an adjective to render the simple image of moon and tree, not because it makes sense, but because it is the word yielded by the spontaneous technique of the writer afoot with his vision. It's part of the show. An active, sympathetic reader gets the drift.

His "wild form" in *Doctor Sax* generates a neologistic abandon worthy of *Finnegans Wake*, as when the character Eugene Pasternak exclaims, "Geeyaw! The grooleman make my flingle dole ring soul make out — containt my comp! save my bomp!" (*DS* 178). That's a head-scratcher, and part of Kerouac's playful show of character. As a final point of language in *Sax*, it is significant that Kerouac renders entire passages in the Quebecoise dialect and then translates them immediately into English.[2] The passages in French serve to establish the character of the French-speaking Jackie while the English translations (as interventions of the adult writer) are there for our benefit. In the shamanic view, more specifically, this is an attempt at re-creating the lingual and cultural simultaneity of the young narrator's ecstatic adolescence. It is part of Kerouac's overall performance wherein he seeks to deliver his complete experience to the audience and catch them up in it.

Throughout *Sax*, he employs direct address to involve the reader more directly in the story. This strategy presumes (insists upon) the recognition of a written image in the reader's own experience and requires the reader's "partnership" and assent. Direct address in *Sax* is most apparent in "Book Two: A Gloomy Bookmovie,"[3] which becomes, effectively, an interactive screenplay in which the reader is frequently instructed to "look closeup," "see close," and so on. He's insisting that the reader perceive — more than that, "unmistakably" *sense*— his experience. Toward the end of the chapter, Kerouac heightens the identity between the writer and the reader (between the "shaman" and the "tribe") by dropping the second person in favor of the first person plural. Such rhetoric immerses the reader in the story as Kerouac reconfigures memory and dream in the "wild form" of his prose. The effect can be transporting because "when you played with Jack you were in a tree-house, and you closed the curtains, and it was make-believe and it was absolutely safe. But it was quite real; it was high play" (Nicosia 600).

Another important aspect of Kerouac's playful style in *Sax* is the leitmotif. The "wrinkly tar corner" of the first paragraph becomes the central image and root metaphor that is often repeated in the design of the novel. From this single, humble image, the fantastic world of Sax proceeds. Six times throughout the book Kerouac invokes the "wrinkly tar corner" as a pivot in his ecstasy and a mantra to ground the attentive reader in the nostalgic reality of Lowell. It is the insignificant part that leads to the significant whole. Kerouac repeatedly rescues the throwaway detail by making it the catalyst to expansive vision. No moment, object, person, or act is unimportant to the seer in ecstasy. In his preface to *Old Angel Midnight*, poet Michael McClure notes this facet of Kerouac's style, commenting, "Never before has inconsequentiality been raised to such a peak that it becomes a breakthrough" (*OAM* xxi). Beyond reason or, seemingly, even intent, Kerouac randomly freezes the moment in the vision of a mystical detail that, outside of "wild form," would be unremarkable. In chapter four of "Book Three: More Ghosts" Kerouac writes a dream/vision of the physical world of Lowell and Jackie Dulouz's father that begins in a dirty alley, dilates to cosmic realms, and returns to the same alley as Sax looms over it all. The noesis of this vision is that "dreams are where participants in a drama recognize one another's death" (*DS* 110–13).[4] Blake saw the world in a grain of sand; Proust, in a madeleine; for Whitman, it was a blade of grass. For Kerouac as writer-shaman in *Sax*, the alley, the tar corner (in Lowell), or the "nameless little bug" (in Mexico City) — any accident of the physical world — can be a portal to the spiritual ultimate reality.[5] This motif in *Sax* becomes an affirmation of the cosmic import of Kerouac's expanding myth-in-progress.

Kerouac visually embeds the unfolding myth of *Sax* with frequent reference to American popular icons of his day. Even as the landscape of the popular media feeds the young narrator's vision, Kerouac uses it to feed our vision of his performance. This stylistic move has shamanic roots.

As Eliade observes, though the shaman stands apart from his society, he has internalized all the cultural phenomena of his time and place and uses them as an "itinerary for [his] ecstatic journeys" (266). Thus we have Doctor Sax, who, from his laugh to his outfit, is a knock-off of *The Shadow* radio program and comic book. Sax's character is also drawn in the image of and identified with the wise-cracking W.C. Fields (*DS* 29). This allusion complicates Sax-as-hero and shows how he "ignores his own ineptness and takes on the world by sheer force of personality" (Nicosia 397).[6] Figures from radio and cinema abound in *Sax*. Popeye, Isadora Duncan, Humphrey Bogart, Gary Cooper, Alan Ladd, Slim Summerville, Orson Welles, Rudy Vallee, Edith Piaf, Tim McCoy, Hoot Gibson, Tom Mix, and the Marx Brothers all make appearances. The radio serial, the "B" movie, the pulp magazine, the comic book, the popular song — from this palette, Kerouac paints this coming-of-age story in familiar American colors. He doesn't simply invoke the names of his cultural icons, but borrows (and plays with) their tropes. For instance, Kerouac replicates the frenzied bumbling of the Keystone Cops in the action between, and the movement of, the narrator and Sax (*DS* 201). Though the form is wild, the figures are recognizable. Kerouac adopts the idioms of pop culture to set the major figures in his personal, modern American mythology. For Kerouac writing *Doctor Sax*, "the freedom of art, as opposed to the categories and restrictions of society, makes for a silly, Marx Brothers, nobody-gets-hurt slapstick [where] the pain of life gets lost in all the fun" (Nicosia 408). Kerouac's artistic license, playful and humorous, rinses the sentimentality from Jackie's young suffering and initiation.

The problem with *Doctor Sax*, however, according to many of Kerouac's mentors, friends, and critics, is that the reader gets lost in all the play. Malcolm Cowley called it "an exercise in self-abuse" (*JKSL 1940–1956* 68). David Dempsey of the *New York Times* opined that the novel was a "largely psychopathic ... pretentious and unreadable farago of childhood fantasy-play" (*JKSL 1957–1969* 200). A Viking Press staff reader warned against its publication for fear that it would further encourage Kerouac to "take refuge in self-fingering explorations of his childhood and the sources of his own unconscious patterns" (*JKSL 1957–1969* 171). *Doctor Sax* was similarly disparaged by Mark Van Doren, W.H. Auden, Carl Solomon, and, ironically, Allen Ginsberg, who often indulged in such play-

2. The Shrouds of Eternity

ful composition himself.[7] Kerouac was well aware that, even among those who knew him best, the purpose and effect of his fiction were often misunderstood or missed altogether. He had no illusions whatsoever about what he saw as the ignorance of his vehement critics. He figured it would take them a century to figure it out (*JKSL 1957–1969* 200).[8]

The problem (or the opportunity, as I see it) for the reader of *Doctor Sax* is its lack of conventional form, language, and style. "Wild form" proceeds from a need for an absolute freedom of expression that Kerouac worked hard to realize. The critics of his day could not categorize his work according to their own terms, so they mostly accused him of a lack of discipline and not fulfilling the expectations of literary craft. Though Kerouac was certainly guilty of the latter, it wasn't for lack of discipline, but out of the sheer necessity of heeding a call to ecstatic expression.[9] Kerouac's book was a critical failure because he happily dared to forsake any sense of literary convention or decorum and exercise a godly technique.

> I [have] come to the divine tricks of "facetiousness" and "fun" and therefore, anything goes, one point of reference (as in relativity science) is as true as another.... *Take liberties* with your art. Here is the latest full title of Doctor Sax ...—"The Book of the Myth of the Rainy Night; or, the Crazy Book of Doctor Sax; with Varorium Notes and Hints ... Containing Elegies, Riddles, and Roses. etc." [*JKSL 1940–1956* 205].

"*Et cetera.*" *Sax* is many things at once: coming-of-age story, "Faust Part Three," apocalyptic vision, gothic horror, pubescent fantasy, myth, small-town farce, psychological journey, magical performance. Because the nature of this fiction is ecstatic, the list of conventional categories that might apply to *Sax* is extensive. And Kerouac goes for them all in parentheses.

In *Sax*, Kerouac uses parentheses to enact the simultaneous ecstasies of the child narrator and the grown writer dreaming it all again. His parenthetical tangents break the temporal and spatial linearity of the novel so that it tells the complete story from all sides at once. More than a protest against convention, *Doctor Sax* shows Kerouac writing in endless parentheticals because, as a form, it is most faithful to his sense of the human experience, endlessly faceted and existing on many planes at once.[10] "Everything at once," "It's all pouring in"— his early fiction abounds with such ejaculations — this is the ecstatic point of view. In *Sax*, the visions come in telescoping parenthetical thoughts, images, comments, and questions because, as Kerouac asserts in the novel, "in these parentheses sections, so (-), the air is free" (*DS* 88). In the parentheses, past and present often overlap and discrete spaces fold in as one. Using them Kerouac can render the experience of the writer alongside that of the narrator (as on page 92). The parentheses are Kerouac's "divine facetious trick" wherein he attains a simultaneous, ecstatic fiction — a kind of time and space travel enacted on the page for the reader's amazement.

The shamanic quality of "wild form" is much apparent in the blurring and dissolution of such dichotomies as then/now, here/there, and me/you throughout the novel. "Wild form" is the "both/and" style of Kerouac's ecstatic prose technique in *Doctor Sax*. The remainder of this chapter will explore significant aspects of *Sax*'s content that shamanism informs and corroborates. What are the visions of young Jackie Duluoz? What revelation does the grown Kerouac ascribe to those visions? And most importantly, what is Sax's real identity?

Death-Mate: Who Is "Doctor Sax"?

> I sensed he was my friend ... my old, old friend ... my ghost, personal angel, private shadow, secret lover.
>
> — Kerouac, *Doctor Sax* 34

> [A] relation of "familiarity" is established between the shaman and his "spirits" ... [also] known as "familiars," "helping," "assistant," or "guardian" spirits.
>
> — Eliade 88

Consistent with the paradoxical nature of this novel (or any shamanic performance), Sax's identity embraces many antitheses: good and evil, hero and fool, mentor and nemesis, power and weakness, skill and ineptitude, hope and futility. Sax is both frightening and funny, fact and fiction. If he is a hallucination, in a world where dream and wakefulness flow seamlessly into and out of one another (i.e., the shamanic view) he is also quite real — and the novel is proof positive of his existence.[11]

Doctor Sax is a helping spirit and muse who brings on the terrifying initiatory ecstasies of the narrator. In the archaic shamanic tradition, Eliade notes that the "majority of these familiar and helping spirits have animal

2. The Shrouds of Eternity

forms" (89). Kerouac reconfigures this idea to the narrator's world. Jackie Duluoz runs the streets and alleys of pre-war Lowell. He is more familiar with the pop iconography of his time than with the few deer scattered in his Dracut woods. Therefore his helping spirit, as we have seen, takes the form of "The Shadow."[12] Eliade observes that the "relations between the [shaman] and his spirits run the gamut from those of benefactor and protégé to those of servant and master, but they are always intimate" (92). This intimacy is certainly borne out in Kerouac's narrative. Sax is the bridge between the many levels of the boy's evolving experience. He helps Jackie cross over from a world of unconscious play to one of conscious artifice. From the realm of shameful repression, with Sax's aid, Jackie crosses over to a place of shameless expression (in art, on the written page.) From a paralyzing fear of death, Sax makes him face mortality. All three of these journeys are intertwined in illuminating Sax's identity.

James T. Jones suggests that Sax is, "among other things, Kerouac's departed brother [Gerard]" reaching to him from beyond the grave (43). The themes of morbidity, decay, and mortality figure significantly in every book-length manuscript Kerouac ever published. As discussed in the previous chapter, Gerard's death primed Kerouac for a lifelong preoccupation with mortality in his writing that ranged from serene meditation to raving madness. The memory of Gerard started Kerouac staring into the world of death, but it is Doctor Sax who enables him to *tell what he sees there*. Sax serves the role of end-time prophet. The ultimate apocalypse of the world, the local apocalypse of Lowell, and the personal apocalypse of the narrator's childhood are all prophesied and mediated by Sax.

The narrator's morbid imagination, much agitated by his Catholic upbringing, is the birthplace of Sax.[13] Catholicism is not a source of comfort for the boy; instead, it is a looming cause of fear beyond understanding. "A haunted house," Kerouac wrote Cassady in 1951, "is no novelty among Catholic kids" (*JKSL 1940–1956* 270). The statue of St. Therese in his house turns its head to stare at him when he walks by. Jesus Christ (or the Virgin Mary, Jackie can't tell which one for sure) appears to him in glowing profile at night and shakes his bed (*DS* 4). The child is luridly absorbed with the crucifixion. There is a black lacquered cross with a phosphorescent corpus in his mother's room that freaks him out because it has its "own luminosity like a bier, it was like *Murder by the Clock*" (*DS* 44).[14] Nevertheless, Jackie has "a picture of Jesus on the Cross in a horrible oldprint" (85) tacked to the wall of his bedroom. Kerouac raises the image of the suffering, soon-to-die Christ in his fiction as a reminder of our common death. Catholic funeral rituals transfix him (*DS* 43). Sax, who "had knowledge of death," embodies this fear and fascination for the narrator (*DS* 43).

As James Fisher accurately notes, there was no precedent in American literature for Kerouac's "frighteningly direct treatment of many of the darker themes in the Catholic consciousness" (236). The fear of death that drives Jackie's fantasy life also forms the common ground Kerouac establishes in *Doctor Sax*, for we are all "frightened humans of the grave." Of his (and our own) fear, Kerouac writes in *Sax*, "That's where all these things were born" (*DS* 43). As a self-created and self-administered remedy to the paralysis of his mortality, Sax has a "knowledge of death" that he passes on to Jackie. Like the helping spirit of the neophyte shaman, Doctor Sax is able to "carry [Jackie] to the beyond (sky, underworld), reveal the mysteries to him, teach him, and so on" (Eliade 95).[15] The shaman must countenance and conquer mortality by "dying" the ritual death of his initiatory ecstasy. To this end, as it dies to itself, Jackie's identity blurs and fades into that of Sax because the "shaman himself ... becomes the dead man ... in order to demonstrate his real ability to ascend to the sky or descend to the underworld" (Eliade 95). This forms the crux of the novel's metaphorical content. Kerouac fashions a personal mythos in *Doctor Sax* as a creative (active, Faustian) response to his most deep-seated fears wherein he trades the passive unconsciousness of childhood for the dark artistic fascinations of maturity.

Doctor Sax is a product of those fascinations. Kerouac's wild form yields a sequencing of events, images, and themes that reflects and reconfigures a shamanic experience. "Book Four: The Night the Man with the Watermelon Died" thoroughly traces an initiatory incident. In it, Kerouac describes an actual (and defining) event from his childhood. A close reading of the chapter and analysis that attends to the sequence of the writer's spontaneous composition best illustrates the shamanic drama that unfolds throughout the novel as it reveals the relationship between the writer's experiences of death and his artistic recreation of those experiences.

2. The Shrouds of Eternity

Morbidity and Death Ritual on the Moody Street Bridge (Book 4, Chapter 1)

The first two paragraphs of this chapter immediately posit the lesson Jackie learned when a man died before his eyes on a nighttime bridge: the boy now had a full realization of the ubiquity of death (*DS* 117). By way of preface, the narrative backtracks to the hours before this defining moment on the bridge. We are shown Jackie's Uncle Mike, who is dying slowly from respiratory illness. (Uncle Mike's daughter, Blanche, plays an important role in this key sequence, as we shall soon see.) High on medicinal marijuana, Uncle Mike would often wheeze out his somber, fatalistic wisdom to young Jackie. Mike is the long-suffering, intelligent, poetic death mentor of the Duluoz family (*DS* 118). He warns the boy that he is destined for a life of suffering more than any other Duluoz. He proceeds to give the woeful Duluoz genealogy before tearfully proclaiming the doom of the entire family. Jackie has nightmares about Uncle Mike that he doesn't dare share with his mother because her outlook is equally gloomy. She is no great comfort to him, and as this preface to the "main death event" resolves, our narrator is preoccupied with mortality beyond any comfort.

Significantly at this point, the narrative telescopes parenthetically ahead to an incident where Jackie's dog, Beauty, is struck and killed by a car. This news comes to him (shouted through the transom) as he is in bed discovering the pleasures of masturbation (*DS* 121). The moment is blackly comedic and marks the coupling of sex and death that would pester Kerouac's psyche (and frequently appear in his writing) for the rest of his career. Finally, Jackie is ready to explain the particulars of the fateful night that leads to the Moody Street Bridge, where his ritual death and shamanic initiation are fully engaged.

Every aspect of *mise-en-scène* in this night is tinged with mortality and loneliness. Jackie and his mother (Angy) walk cousin Blanche home "to the horrible brown glooms of her dying father's house" (*DS* 123). Hospitals and funeral homes scroll by. "Black lawns" and "grand darkness" lead down to the foaming, anomalous Merrimac River.[16] The summer night domed in by countless stars coexists, in Jackie's perception, with his death obsession. They cross the Moody Street Bridge that always, according to Jackie, afforded the people of Pawtucketville the perfect opportunity to kill themselves (*DS* 127). (Even Blanche attempted to commit suicide there once.)

Blanche's faith is a formality at best and no safeguard against her hopelessness. She's a lonely spinster of classical tastes who is still hoping to find "the ideal man." While the ladies discuss the "irony" of Blanche's predicament, Jackie is scanning the night for Sax. He knows nothing yet of the romantic dramas between men and women, so Blanche's love-troubles mean little to him. While the ladies talk, Jackie frolics in a kid world of action, oblivious to the thoroughly depressing atmosphere of this night.

They arrive at a grotto that is behind an orphanage. In this grotto are "the Stations of the Cross," fourteen scenes that depict the passion and death of Jesus Christ in marble statuary. The orphanage concretizes the human crisis of abandonment. (Earlier, Jackie's mother "charmingly" reminded him that he wouldn't have parents one day.) We have already discussed the narrator's timorous relationship with Christ crucified. To Jackie, the grotto with its "Stations of the Cross" is a fetishistic monument to suffering, a death parade. The faithful Catholics kneel at altars before each station to contemplate the Passion of Jesus. His mother often takes Jackie there "to get some praying in. 'Wishing, I'd call it more,' Blanche said" (*DS* 123). The first station faces the side of a funeral home such that, like the orphanage, "your reflections on the subject become mirrored" (*DS* 125).

The arrival at the grotto ratchets up the mortal fright that is so characteristic of the boy. Although Doctor Sax and Jackie have yet to communicate directly in the novel, Jackie "knows" (parenthetically) that Doctor Sax is present and, somehow, contextual to this scene (*DS* 122–23). Up to this point, Jackie has only caught fleeting glimpses of Sax — heard his laugh, felt his dark presence. Now, at the grotto, Sax is beginning to manifest his interest in Jackie Duluoz more fully (*DS* 126). It is the first time we get the inkling that Doctor Sax might be able to offer Jackie a blasphemous reversal of his mortal Catholic fears and be a friend to this "frightened human by the grave." In Sax, Jackie begins to spy an alternative perspective to his boyhood Catholicism.

The late-praying trio makes its pilgrimage through each of the stations. The gruesome scenes of flagellation, assault, and mortification climax

2. The Shrouds of Eternity

with the ghastly crucifixion (*DS* 123). Though frightened by the sight, Jackie savors a faint note of sympathy. In his dark imagination, Jackie can identify with the fear and desolation of the dying Jesus under the summer stars of Lowell as the Merrimac roars in the background. The "poor dog" is suffering and alone on the cross, thrust into a night that is electric with death. At least Jackie has Sax. The Doctor is circling in, a savior from his own imagination, preparing Jackie for a fantastic discipleship.

His mother makes her way to the foot of the cross on her knees to show Jackie how the old-school Catholics did it. Thus ends their visit to the grotto: Angy with her grim faith, Blanche with her fatalistic doubt, Jackie with his eyes and imagination peering into the darkness for Doctor Sax (*DS* 126). When Blanche departs, Angy and her son walk on under a full moon "of death" (*DS* 127).

The two find themselves again on the Moody Street Bridge, this time walking behind a man carrying a watermelon. Jackie wonders briefly where the man came from, registers the river below, and discusses the "mysteries of life" with his mother (*DS* 127). He is happy. But this illusion is broken when the man with the watermelon collapses and dies quickly in front of them. Jackie is shocked, but also absorbed by the man's glassy death stare. As they both (he and the dying man) eye the river below, Jackie is united with the man (and with death). They both perceive "the long eternity we have been seeking" (*DS* 128).

As in a dream, though, Jackie realizes that the perishing man is experiencing "something private." While we all might seek eternity, only the dead realize it, one at a time, and alone. When a stranger at the scene offers to call an ambulance, Angy bluntly announces in French that he's "finished" (*DS* 128). Like Sax, Angy possesses a knowledge of death that is "uncanny" and mystical (*DS* 129). Here again Kerouac's spontaneous prose yields a major shamanic motif when Angy cries, "Look, the face of a skeleton in the moon!" (*DS* 129).

Eliade notes and comments on the mystical significance of skeletons, bones, and skulls across a wide range of shamanic traditions. Kerouac invokes such images fourteen times throughout the *Doctor Sax*. In shamanic ritual "deaths," skeletal visions signify "a passing beyond the profane human condition and, hence, a deliverance from it" (Eliade 63). In shamanism, bones signify the life source and the skeletal condition is at once a reminder of mortality and "equivalent to re-entering the womb of this primordial life that is to a complete renewal, a mystical rebirth" (Eliade 63). For the shaman, when the flesh of the profane human condition is stripped away, so too is the illusion of death (which only applies to the body). Thus, the shaman recovers "the very source of spiritual existence, which is at once 'truth' and 'life'" (Eliade 64). The death ritual on the Moody Street Bridge enacts this dual significance of the skeletal vision (the paradoxical interdependence of life and death) and indicates that the shamanic journey within *Doctor Sax* (and, accordingly, in Kerouac's career as writer) has been fully inaugurated.

After the "watch beside a corpse" and "the ordeal of fear" (both of which have been described thus far in this sequence), the next step in this initiation scenario is "the terrible apparition of the initiatory master (or) mythical ancestor" (Eliade 345).

Building the Myth: The Snake, the Castle, and the Sax Scripture (Book 4, Chapter 2)

Only after Jackie's initiation, his fearful watch with the dead man on the Moody Street Bridge (itself described in skeletal terms), can the legend of Sax fully come to life in the imagination of the narrator, the memory of the writer, and the experience of the reader. The narrative now fully delineates the archetypes and histories of Jackie's dream world that have only been alluded to thus far. A paradisal vision shows an eighteenth-century pre–Lowell with its Pawtucket Indians and lone settler, Epzebiah Phloggett, the retired seafarer and slave trader who is ensconced in a "Castle" modeled after an actual (and rather common) Lowell residence of Kerouac's childhood. Yet Jackie with his new skeletal vision sees it as "a ruinous old bones of a house" (*DS* 130). Phloggett's death from snakebite and the consequent infestation of the entire hill with snakes cause the house in its abandonment to be renamed "Snake Hill Castle." Here, Kerouac borrows the "World Snake" legend from the Aztec myth of Quetzebiah and introduces it as the embodiment of evil worming its way to an apocalyptic showdown with Doctor Sax. The Snake will emerge from this Castle. Though the significance of the Snake remains consistent, the metaphorical

2. The Shrouds of Eternity

meaning of the "Castle" evolves as the myth builds throughout the novel, as reality and fantasy embrace.

In the nineteenth century, the Lowell property was purchased as a summer residence for an out-of-town affluent family and renamed "Reeves Castle." Eerily, the genteel and sophisticated family grew bored, got sick, and died. The house, thought to be cursed, lay derelict until 1921, when it was purchased by an eccentric neo–Transcendentalist named Emilia St. Claire who turned it into a salon for the dilettante art set (*DS* 133). The progression of owners of the Castle is noteworthy. The primal Phloggett, the evil slave trader, then the civilized, though contemptuous, Reeves family were both purged from the place in nature's course. But when Emilia St. Claire opened the Castle on weekends as a cultural experiment in liberal thought and *ars gras artis*, when she renamed it "Transcendenta," "Mwee hee hee ha ha, Doctor Sax was ready for them all" (*DS* 133).

Even as the "terribly rich" St. Claire pursues her indulgences in the castle on the hill, down below in a poor Lowell tenement, a young mill worker (Amadeus Baroque) finds a discarded sheaf of papers in the gutter. It is the original scripture, a portentous seminal document, from the pen of Sax himself (though written under the pseudonym of "Ghoulens") (*DS* 134).

Baroque retires to his furnished room and reads the "snaky mysteries" of the document.[17] The form of the novel now shifts (in font and format) to an embedded account from the found text. Sax ("Ghoulens") asserts that St. Claire, due to her excessive wealth, can afford to be culturally "whimsical," and that she has become a "tyrant" in her sprawling Transcendenta. Sax's dwelling, on the other hand, is shown to be a humble (though mysterious) wooden shack that is perfectly square and indistinguishable in the rising mists. Sax scornfully reports on how Emilia St. Claire fills her castle with actors, artists, pianists, poets, sculptors, dancers, critics — intellectuals, poseurs, and ersatz barbarians of every stripe — simply because she feels "the need for something different" (*DS* 138).[18] Doctor Sax bides his time alone with his "alchemies" in the weird Yankee *Ka'ba* of a shack (*DS* 135). He will soon freak out the feckless Transcendenta crowd, and bring them to an end.

In another linking of sex and death, Ghoulens reports that just as the party is leering at the fulsome body of a guest named Polly Ryan, Sax appears. Precisely at this moment so charged with sexual tension, the green-eyed Sax with his knowledge of death emerges, looking in the window *exactly* where Polly is looking out, and worlds collide. She screams and faints. Sax's materialization has a similar effect on the rest of the partygoers. He gleefully watches one after another of the new "Transcendentalists" swoon and fall. His bizarre physical presence, coupled with his "secret wisdom" and "huge malevolent humour," confound the roomful of posers. Sax is the real thing, shamanic and bizarre. "He knew something that no other man knew; a something reptilian; pray, was he a man?" (*DS* 142). Sax knows that the Snake is coming into the world through this very Castle that has been inhabited by the villainous, then the elite, and now the intelligent. (The full meaning of the Castle has yet to be revealed to the reader.) Doctor Sax is ready for war.

Emilia St. Claire moves out in 1932, symbolically ending any Transcendental hopes for Lowell. Now the Castle fills up with characters from Jackie's imagination only: wizards, monsters, vampires, gnomes, ghouls, and huge spiders — all the forces of darkness, all nemeses of Sax, all there to prepare the way for the Snake's apocalyptic arrival. They set off an earth tremor.

Jackie's dream has finally and unmistakably cracked through his waking life. His ability to distinguish between the two is so frayed as to be nonexistent. Fact and fiction, art and life, are no longer at odds. They never would be again in Kerouac's life as a writer. *Doctor Sax* records this singularity. Local records show that an earth tremor did, in fact, rock Kerouac's childhood Lowell after the flood of 1936. Jackie intuits some evil cause behind it. He's sure of this.

Gathering Power (Book 4, Chapter 3)

Fleeing from the bridge (where the "watermelon man" died) with his mother and returning home, Jackie indulges in his old fears. He recites a virtual litany of death images from the novel thus far (*DS* 145–46). He hears an ax strike, and feels its thud. Though his mother explains it's only the neighbor, Marquand, chopping wood in his cellar, Jackie knows it's "the voice of doom coming to prophesy [his] death" (*DS* 146). He feels

2. The Shrouds of Eternity

pursued by the dead man on the bridge later when Marquand throws a loud moaning fit. Like Doctor Sax, Jackie now has "knowledge of death." He's convinced that Marquand only put up his moan after receiving a communication from the realm of the dead and (significantly) from himself (*DS* 148).

But after a week in bed with his mother, both quarantined with the flu, Jackie gains an insight into the affinity between life and death, even as he earlier detected the interplay of dream and reality, and will soon witness the apocalyptic dance between good and evil. Jackie, without yet fully understanding why, has attained a growing shamanic viewpoint that banishes his fear: "so secure did I become that death vanished into fantasies of life ... I had conquered death and stored up new life" (*DS* 148). In the last line of the chapter Kerouac clearly addresses the reader directly in a voice free of mortal fear: "Beautiful music, regale me not in my bier heaps" (*DS* 148).

Twin Prophets (Book 4, Chapter 4)

The brief and wild final chapter of this fourth book solidifies the relationship between the narrator and Doctor Sax. After facing death in visions and rituals, they now share a sense of the coming apocalypse. When Jackie sees the movie *Trader Horn*, he perceives the invading hordes depicted in the film in terms of his own developing myth-imagery. That is, the invaders wear dirty bones, have hair like black snakes, and "hung people upside down on crosses in fires" (*DS* 150).

Furthermore, in this chapter, Kerouac for the first time identifies *himself*, not his narrator, with Doctor Sax. The following quote describes Kerouac at work on this novel as well as Doctor Sax investigating the origins of the combatants in the final conflict. They are one and the same. Kerouac dons the literary mask of Sax to write out this apocalyptic ecstasy. "Doctor Sax made a special trip to Teotehuacan Mexico, to do his special research on the culture of the eagle and the snake—Azteca; he came back laden with information about the snake" (*DS* 149). Kerouac goes on to describe a vision he has ("just now") of a human sacrifice atop the Pyramid of the Sun transported across time to his Mexico of 1952. There is no more prying apart apparition from ocular sight or dreams from the waking consciousness — no separating Jackie from Sax from Kerouac. Book Four of *Doctor Sax* shows us that Kerouac's (and his narrator's) response to the essential fear of death is to prepare a mythic arena (the page, the imagination) where the ultimate destination of the human soul will be determined. This myth replaces the paralysis of mortal fear with the ecstasy of literary expression. As Gerald Nicosia notes,

> Because the knowledge of death continually dissatisfies us with life ... Sax embodies the will in man to interfere with natural process, to direct the cosmos, and as such he is the type of the artist [404].

Sax/Jackie/Kerouac are now a kind of shamanic trinity. Having peered through the shrouds of death, soon they will encounter the soul in a way no conventional religious ideology can. Book Four closes with a scene reminiscent of Jesus' lamentation of Jerusalem (*DS* 151). Doctor Sax's mission is to save Lowell from destruction by the World Snake. He is a messiah with only one disciple. All that remains before the final ecstatic confrontation is the flood.

What the Flood Washed Away

> Get off the raft — the rope's cut off — you're floating away!
> —*Doctor Sax* (Kerouac) 170

In March 1936, the Merrimac River flooded its banks, swamping many of the neighborhoods of Lowell. Throughout Kerouac's Legend, March is the month of disastrous calamity.[19] In *Sax*, he portrays this flood as a period of physical and spiritual tribulation on the Lowell landscape. Sax is still somewhat aloof, biding his time on the edges of Jackie's imagination and fantasy. Again Kerouac identifies Sax's voice with the incessant rumble of the river. The repetition of this motif reminds the reader that Doctor Sax is born in large part from the boy's fear and awe of the river now purging Lowell for its apocalyptic moment. Even as the narrative in Book Four details the history of the Castle in fantastic shifting forms, Book Five (for five pages) abandons the prose narrative entirely to present the full genealogy of a Merrimac flood. Kerouac depicts the archetypal river

2. The Shrouds of Eternity

in two poems, "The Poems of the Night" and "The Song of the Myth of the Rainy Night." This isn't just any river, or just any flood.

For Jackie, the Merrimac cuts through Lowell as the single maw of life and death. Foaming brown and reptilian, it dances through town, foreshadowing the Snake's arrival. It dawns on Jackie that the river is a metaphor for the unconscious processes he seeks to verbalize. Most importantly, perhaps, the Lowell flood describes a rite of passage for the narrator and his friends. To the youth of Lowell, the flood proves that "something huge and independent had come into their lives" (*DS* 167).

Much expository prose in this book is spent with Jackie and friends standing transfixed and dreaming on the edge of the river. Jackie, especially, sees the whole episode of the flood as an opportunity to dive into the great mysteries. In a telling scene, he is playing with his friend Dicky Hampshire at the water's edge, where they have snared the intact roof of a chicken coop from the current. After securing this "raft" to the shore, they begin playing on it, and Jackie falls into a dream and has a series of visions. He sees that the flooding river *is* a Snake, an emissary of Satan. He spies a shamanic cosmology where a sacred locus, "an arcade shaft," offers flight from this world to heaven. He has a vision of a dove delivering a mystical herb to Doctor Sax.[20] Finally, Jackie sees Doctor Sax receiving the message from the dove. He dreams all this in a few moments from the roof of the chicken coop that serves as a tethered raft in the ripping current of objective space and time.

Jackie is so caught up in this reverie as he spies the secret significance of the flood that he doesn't notice the raft has torn loose from its makeshift mooring, and that his friend has already jumped off and is screaming for him to do the same. At the last possible second Jackie does jump. Safely back on the shore (of reality), he reflects knowingly that he could have gone "farther" (*DS* 171). It could have been his one-way ticket to the full vision of eternity, the endless unadulterated dream. Though the flood is only a cleansing preamble to a new world, Jackie's tone reveals the near-fatal episode on the raft as an opportunity lost.

The flood wreaks havoc on the adult world of Lowell. With one part of the city cut off from another, and many places of business (including his father's print shop) flooded beyond use, the "grown-ups" have nothing to do but line the riverbanks and watch for the waters to recede. However, for the children of town, it is all great fun. Jackie and his friend G.J., in their Saxish play, seek to augment the destruction by poking holes in the sandbag walls, hoping the flood will destroy the grown-up world of Lowell for good (*DS* 171–72). They wish blasphemously for a new world of play (instead of the work-a-day routine). Aligned with Sax, Jackie is realizing the power of his dreams.

The next morning, Jackie and G.J. find that the flood has indeed overrun the same sandbag wall they poked at just the day before, wishing it would crumble. The role of their imagination in the disaster is confirmed. Again, the real world and Jackie's dream of it become one. Aside from the kids of Lowell, the only one having any fun in this catastrophe is Doctor Sax, laughing in the background and proclaiming his readiness for the end times from high above the catastrophic scene. Sax pulls an inflatable rubber boat from his slouch hat and paddles off (*DS* 172).

Interwoven with the mystical narrative of the disaster, there is a note of naturalism in Kerouac's portrayal of the rising water. This force of nature causes Lowell to come unhinged. The flood is unaffected by the faithful who daily fill the churches to pray novenas for some relief from the tribulation. Jackie's family, literally, stands on the brink of destruction. Rats are flushed out in the open and the whole town is inoculated against typhus, shots that make Jackie and his friends very ill (*DS* 177). An Irish woman named Mogarraga, a boarding house owner, hysterically proclaims that the flood is a punishment of all Lowell's profligate characters, starting with her own boarders (*DS* 178). Even time itself yields symbolically to the cataclysm and, in so doing, Lowell is opened up to eternity. But when Jackie sees that the clock in city hall has stopped working, he pivots in his attitude toward the flood. "I began to dislike the flood, began to see it as an evil monster bent on devouring everyone — for no special reason" (*DS* 179).

The flood replaces routine with imbalance, complacency with discomfort, and order with chaos. The whole modern structure of the world of Lowell is purged by this disaster. Only now, it seems, are Jackie and his childhood Lowell ready for the strange world of Sax. Whereas the man with the watermelon privately confronted Jackie with death on the Moody Street Bridge, the flood makes that vision public and ushers in the apocalypse.

2. The Shrouds of Eternity

The Meaning of the Castle and Imagination's End

> Antichrist Kerouac, the SNAKE came for him alone, no one else.
> — Kerouac in a letter to Neal Cassady, December 28, 1950[21]

The sixth and final book of the novel, "The Castle," opens with an idyllic review of the most telling images of Jackie's childhood dream. A new and brief Eden emerges in Lowell when the flood recedes. Jackie and his sister dance over the Moody Street Bridge to the library (*DS* 183). (As a boy, Jackie reads books, but soon, with Sax's manqué help, he will be a writer.) The narrative rapidly touches upon memories of movie theaters and onscreen heroes, tender recollections of little Lowell girls who have died, the image of a young priest genuflecting, scattered scenes of the Lowell adults returning to their routines, and food. During the flood, Jackie and his friends had forgotten their hunger in the terrible excitement. Now, in this lull before the arrival of the Snake, Kerouac describes Jackie's hunger in a gustatory prose worthy of his dear Thomas Wolfe. This recollected paean to his real life before the flood ends abruptly in a twelve-line second chapter when the phantasms return in broad daylight. Jackie sees a gnome perched high atop the Castle on Snake Hill. And, though it has always spooked him, Jackie is attracted to the hill with the Castle (*DS* 190). Why?

Eliade tells us that a shaman, after his ritual death ecstasy, is "the great specialist in the human soul" (8). Only the shaman can really see the soul. The Castle in this novel evolves into a metaphor for the soul. When Jackie passes through the end times with his helping spirit (Doctor Sax), he too will apprehend the soul directly and be able to perform it in his art. For now, he only has inklings and intuitions of the Castle-as-soul. As far as everyone else in Lowell is concerned, the Castle has been empty for years, save for a groundskeeper named "Old Boaz" (*DS* 191). But Jackie knew that "the Castle was Totally occupied," that is, the soul of Lowell, his soul, was full of dark specters (vampires, gnomes, "black priests," evil attendants, and the like). Furthermore, Jackie had long intuited that the Castle was hiding a shadowy secret because it was close to his birthplace (*DS* 191).

In a narrative that has been looking forward, backward, and sideways from the outset, we now see that this is the same afternoon of Lowell's earth tremor, first mentioned in Book Four, but now, after the purging flood (and its apocalyptic portents), the import of the event is intensified considerably. Jackie senses that Satan is curled beneath his Lowell waiting to get him (*DS* 192). But Jackie doesn't react with fear. Instead he spends all afternoon singing songs.

In the shamanic context of the narrative, the time for Jackie's first face-to-face meeting with Sax is now ideal. Up to this point, his childhood experience of Lowell has been characterized by maternal security, game-playing, repressed sexuality, morbid Catholicism, a fearful preoccupation with death, a loathing of adulthood (which appeared to be a boring prelude to death), and the flood. But now, thanks to the strange and, thus far, peripheral presence of Sax in his imagination, Jackie has gained some perspective on these issues and stands ready for the final vision quest and the lesson it will reveal.

After dinner at home, Jackie walks out in the dusk. He is standing on a sandbank when he meets Doctor Sax (*DS* 192). Unlike the guests of Emilia St. Claire's "Transcendenta," Jackie hides his alarm and simply asks, "What do you want Doctor Sax?" Sax's first words to the youth, crass as they are, indicate a key aspect of his mentorship. Doctor Sax, it seems, has observed Jackie masturbating, and he chides him, saying,

> You didn't read a book today, did you, about the power of drawing a circle in the earth at night — you just stood here at nightfall with your mouth hanging open and fisting your entrail piece [*DS* 193].[22]

James Jones expounds on this important aspect of Sax's mentorship of the narrator. "The word 'Sax,'" he notes, "is too close a homophone of 'sex' to obscure Doctor Sax's basic function: to help Jackie win the 'pubertical war' of the second phase of his childhood" (44). Throughout the novel, sex is an abhorrent mystery for the young Jackie, made all the more disturbing, no doubt, by the repression and prescribed morality of his Catholicism. Therefore, for Jackie, Lowell at night is a chimera of sexual stranglings (*DS* 14). Though Sax immediately and frankly recognizes Jackie's adolescent obsession with sex, he doesn't shame him for it. Sax is more concerned with the boy's study of mystical rites and the activity of his imagination, which he commends. Standing on the sandbank that night, Jackie knows that Doctor Sax is his friend (*DS* 194).

Sax's actions and dialogue from here on are loaded with shamanic allusions. Holding a mask to his face, he explains the meaning of the flood

2. The Shrouds of Eternity

to the boy. "The understanding of the mysteries," says Sax, "will bring forth your understanding in the maples" (*DS* 194). Though it might be difficult for the reader to understand all Sax says and does, Jackie comprehends him intuitively. Mask-wearing is common in shamanic rituals, as is the tree motif (the "World Tree") that represents the summit of the world where shamans are hatched by a giant bird (Eliade 38). Although "a great dark eagle of the night" does swoop low over Sax and Jackie, it is only a foreshadowing of the giant bird that will intervene in the novel's climactic final pages. Nonetheless, "the shaman ... has a tree on whose life he is in a manner dependent" (Eliade 70). In this view, Jackie's "understanding in the maples" can be equated with shamanic wisdom.

Sax now encloses Jackie in his flowing black cape. They melt "in a black statue of ecstasy" and embark on a flight through the Lowell night with strange visions, such as a huge fiery eye and bats that drop fireballs. But Sax, as if speaking in tongues, remains unshaken and prophesies the coming of the Snake. Again, Jackie intuits that Sax's secret language masks a revelation. "I know that Doctor Sax is speaking to the bottom of my boy problems and they could all be solved if I could fathom his speech" (*DS* 197).

Mystified, the boy sees that Sax, though weird, is entirely secure in his own identity and somehow the hub of activity (*DS* 198). Doctor Sax is actualized in the human experience, even as the imagination, the spirit, and the soul can be actualized. As these mysteries unfold for Jackie, his shadow (his Sax) goofs around and laughs (*DS* 199). Doctor Sax has got the big medicine, the shaman's magic. Chapter five ends in a vision rush that simultaneously shows Jackie everything from the women of Lowell ironing and laughing at jokes to an older friend who stops at church after having had sex in a dirty barn — everything from piles of "kidshit" to the image of a brooding God figure in this expansive apparition (*DS* 199). In this way all the secrets of Lowell are delivered up to Sax and Jackie in their ecstasy.

They now move like shadows through town. The visit to Gene Plouffe's window illustrates the transporting, hence ecstatic, possibilities of reading (possibilities that are integral to Kerouac's writerly myth). The fifteen-year-old Gene is in bed engrossed in a pulp Western magazine. Sax prophesies the joys but mostly the rigors of life that await the likes of Gene and Jackie and all the youth of Lowell. "You'll come to rages you never dreamed," he explains (*DS* 202). Sax prophesies that maturity brings sex, loneliness, unrequited love, employment, and nightmarish paranoia about world politics. Old age brings on the messy decrepitude that ends only one way. Though the future looks bleak, while spying on Gene Plouffe joyfully reading, Sax concludes, "You'll never be as happy as you are now in your quiltish innocent book devouring boyhood immortal night" (*DS* 203).

The ghostly duo moves on, significantly, "under immense roars of the huge tree above" (*DS* 203). Sax's next prophecy would be incongruous to any but a shamanic reading of the novel. Under this tree (again, the World Tree, the center of the universe) Sax offers Jackie his bizarre prediction on time, death and a "vegetative" afterlife (*DS* 204). In other words, the soul remains eternal as the life essence reemerges from death.

Jackie is now beset by myriad visions. He sees his mother, father, sister, and a great variety of Lowell characters all going about their normal Saturday-night business. All at once, Jackie hears conversations, voices, greetings: the polyphony of the Lowell night (*DS* 207). Like the funeral procession scene in *Visions of Gerard*, this sequence is evocative of Joyce's "Wandering Rocks" in *Ulysses*, and the simultaneity of Jackie's perceptions shows his experience to be ecstatic.

No sooner does Sax proclaim that this is the night of his showdown with the Snake in an oratory so inflated that even Jackie is confused, than the boy's eye falls on the original image-object of the novel, "the old wrinkly-dinkly tar corner" (*DS* 209). In this novel, time is a bone-yard of memories and images repeatedly revivified by the power of Kerouac's spontaneous recollection and writing. *Doctor Sax* remains in a constantly fluid state of becoming each time Kerouac breathes into his memory horde. The shamanic journey began with this image of Jackie and his friends loitering on the wrinkly tar corner. In the crescendo of the novel, he returns momentarily to this image that he had figuratively walked away from in order to piece together the legend of Doctor Sax. Now, quickly, Jackie sees his characters again on the corner, or approaching the corner, or leaving the corner: G.J. ("Gus"), Scotty, Vinnie, Charlie, Lou, Normie, Lucky, and the Bergeracs — the whole kid world that is soon to pass away is transfigured on the tar corner one last time.

When Gus sees Jackie ("Lousy") approach, he says, "Whenever I see

2. The Shrouds of Eternity

Lousy coming, I know I'll go to heaven" (*DS* 210). Precisely at this moment, the narrative ecstasy (the shamanic journey) significantly pivots again as, with Sax's aid, like the shamans of old, Jackie flies above the world (*DS* 210).[23] Though he doesn't understand it yet, Sax is spiriting Jackie away from his childhood passivity (from his reliance on religious convention, for instance) and on to a realm where he will actively filter all external experience through himself, an essential predisposition for the artist. Sax tells him, "Listen to your own self— it ain't got nothin' to do with what's around you, it's what you do inside at the controls of that locomotive crashing through life" (*DS* 211).[24]

With that they descend to the netherworld of Sax's lair, where he has been preparing alchemical powders to battle the Snake. Jackie is amazed by the clanging forge, the fire stoked by "batwing" bellows, and Sax's animal attendants: a four-foot-tall black cat and parakeets that speak Spanish. There are vials and jars of different colored powders in the forge. In his increasingly convoluted language, Sax announces that the encounter with the Snake will be at dawn. When a "balloon" rises out of one of the vials, explodes and turns everything blue, Jackie becomes overwhelmed with a soul-centered intuition (*DS* 213).

Sax now performs for Jackie in the lair. He dances, screams, jumps up and down; all this by way of preparing Jackie for the fateful meeting at dawn (*DS* 213). Sax expounds upon the fellahin origins of the powders with which he hopes to conquer the evil Snake. The remedial powders and the disease (i.e., the Snake) are from the same place (South America). Similarly, the affinity between good and evil in Doctor Sax himself (who has been shown to be both benign and malevolent, both a shaman *and* a sorcerer) clearly foreshadows the novel's climax and the full ecstatic import of the narrative.

The outcome of this Armageddon is in no way assured (*DS* 216). Having pocketed his vials, Sax and Jackie leave the shack. Again they fly through the air toward the Castle (soul). All of Lowell is now bathed in blue light, and the night sky is crowded with disembodied eyes (*DS* 217).

Shamanic and Catholic imagery blend again in an interlude that recalls Christ's "Agony in the Garden." (This is another of Kerouac's favorite tropes, which he visits often in his work, as we have seen, for example, in *Visions of Gerard*.) Journeying to the Castle, Sax and Jackie tarry at the river's edge in a rainstorm. Sax voices his trepidation that his lifelong mission may have been futile. Jackie can only watch and listen as the "blue era" ends and the night turns into "a horrible red suede red." Sax bemoans the essential crisis of the apocalypse: Who will win?

Sax is ambivalent on this account mainly because he suspects that his participation in this Armageddon might not even be necessary. Also, "it seems" to him that the problem of evil should be taken care of in the "organic tree of things" where shamans are born of mighty birds and able to travel beyond notions of good and evil. He intuits an apocalypse without a final judgment. Although the prospect of facing the evil World Snake is terrifying, and even though the value of his presence at the event is in doubt, Sax embraces his fear in a gesture of "not my will but yours be done" (Luke 2:42). How will all this be rectified?

They move on to the very "Pit" of the Castle where the Snake will enter the world through the soul of mankind. As they approach this threshold Jackie thinks, "I feel like I did on the raft, I can jump or I can stay" (*DS* 219). Here, he decides to keep on dreaming with the unfolding mysteries. An array of bizarre creatures delays their trip to the Pit: Blook, a monster with 20-foot-long arms, huge "Mayan spiders," weird birds, and giant scorpions. With the world bathed now in red hues, Jackie, in true shamanic style, has a skeletal vision of paradoxical images (*DS* 221). The night is multifaceted and alive with bones, blood, and the vital, nonmaterial orgones that Wilhelm Reich (Kerouac's "pet" philosopher of the time) believed could cure every human deficiency from impotence to the common cold. The bones are black, yet alive. Life and death, decay and regeneration meld as Sax and Jackie enter the Castle of the soul. Kerouac depicts this paradox in "a long file of gnomes pointing spears alternately at us and then at themselves in a solemn little ceremony" (*DS* 221). Jackie and Sax push past them easily, for paradox poses no obstacle to the shaman in ecstasy. In a flash, they are in a golden room and then, just as suddenly, cast into a dark cave-like realm. Jackie is in the cellar of the soul now. He looks out a high window to a world absolutely soaked again in red.

Now Sax is transfigured before Jackie's eyes even as Jesus was transfigured before the eyes of his chosen disciples. The Gospel of Luke tells us that while Jesus "was praying, his face changed in appearance and his clothes became dazzling white" and he was soon beheld in the company

2. The Shrouds of Eternity

of Moses (archetype of the Law) and Elijah (archetype of the Prophets) (Luke 9:29–30). Kerouac again spikes the biblical trope with the shamanic imagery as Doctor Sax appears dressed in stunning white, in a white tree, and is welcomed by a group of spirits (*DS* 223). The Transfiguration episode in Luke's gospel edifies the disciples in order to steel their nerve for the trials that lie ahead. It solidifies their faith and shows them that Jesus had the big medicine, that is, the sanction of the Law and the Prophets.[25] However, the transfiguration of Sax doesn't have nearly the same effect because, outside of his pocketful of powder and the bewildered Jackie, no formidable allies appear on his behalf. In fact, it is the "Wizard" (his archenemy) who welcomes Sax. Further affirming the affinity between good and evil, the Wizard also dresses all in white.

In the Pit of the Castle-soul, Doctor Sax and Jackie are the lone advocates of good, while the attendants of evil, allies of the Snake, range in countless ranks upward and out of sight. The boy can sense Sax's fear and doubt. The Wizard says, "Bring your boy to see the Plaything" (*DS* 224). Peering far down into the Pit, they finally see the Great World Snake. It is enormous — two lakes for eyes, a river for a mouth and a mountain for a head. Jackie's terror increases as the Wizard explains that the Snake has been mining its way toward the Castle an inch an hour since the beginning of time and that millions of gnomes, at his dark behest, have been digging down to hasten its arrival (*DS* 228). The ground below the cave is shuddering and heaving in spasms. The world all around this event persists in transfigured, whitened shades.

The Wizard prophesies that the Snake will bring the unstoppable destruction of civilization as we know it. Sax pats his pocketful of powders and sweats it out. Jackie wonders again, now more certainly, if this Snake was the cause for the crack in the earth he had seen in the park or the source of his apocalyptic dream of the *Trader Horn* movie. His moment on the brink of the Pit is the ecstatic culmination of his very own imagination. In this sense, the novel is a self-administered apocalypse.

Now it's Easter Sunday morning, resurrection day. Hot, rank air is shooting out of the pit ahead of the Snake. Chaos reigns in the quaking Castle-soul. At this crucial moment, as Sax makes his final refutation, he seals the bond between good and evil by revealing that he and the Snake come from the same place (*DS* 234).

Jackie now has a vision of the Castle-soul that is complex and complete. The range of imagery with which he describes this experience of ultimate reality is vast, exploding in a simultaneous vision of the panoply of human action. When Jackie hears the word "dawn," a crack opens up in the Castle to make way for the hundred-mile length of the Snake. Sax and the Wizard are at opposite sides of the Pit. Here, Kerouac reveals in dialogue a crucial distinction between the two, and by extension, an essential distinction that remains between good and evil in this peculiar apocalypse. The Wizard represents the waking, rational, empirical mind; he's eaten of the Tree of Knowledge. He can offer persuasive arguments based on evidence, and can prove that the Snake is nigh. The Wizard is the unrepentant proxy of evil, and it looks like he's going to win. Doctor Sax, on the other hand, born of a boy's dreams and "little ideas," represents the intuitive unconscious. He is the protector of the human soul from its scoffers. His cause is ineffable, and he's holding a single untested vial to fend off destruction (*DS* 237). The Wizard is a "knower"; Sax is a "believer."

True to the monistic character of the mystical experience, as the narrative speeds to its climax, events in *Doctor Sax* merge in an essential singularity. Jackie looks into the Pit and instead of seeing the Snake, he sees himself. That is, he perceives the Snake but not his difference from it (*DS* 238). The evil of the world is not separate from the individual, even as evil does not enter the soul, but originates there. The horror of this apocalypse boils down to Jackie (and by extension, to you) having to face this realization, this "both/and" oneness. This comes as a shock in all this "western wrath," where the mind can only operate on dichotomy and phenomenal distinction, where allies and enemies must be perceived as discrete from one another. Although he wrote the novel about two years before embarking on his extended study of Buddhism in 1954, the essential unity of the ecstatic experience in *Doctor Sax* suggests a revealed but as yet undefined Buddhist point of view.

Finally, Sax produces his magic powders and tosses them into the Pit. Almost comically, the Snake is only momentarily stunned and Sax disappears from Jackie's sight. At this moment, before the event horizon of the Snake, Jackie looks past the night that enfolds the Castle and out into the light to see Lowell on Easter Sunday morning, oblivious to the final chaos.

2. The Shrouds of Eternity

When the mountainous head of the Snake bursts forth from the Pit, Jackie is alone in the anarchy of imagination, in the upheaval of his soul. The Castle crumbles and all its inhabitants either flee or perish.

Now Sax reappears *sans* cape and slouch hat, looking quite normal and in no way like the superhero-savior of the world. He stands behind Jackie and simply says, "Goddam, it didn't work." Yet Sax is somehow relieved in his defeat and glad that he doesn't have to run around on this day keeping up the act "the Lord prescribed" for him (*DS* 240). Of course, "the Lord" Doctor Sax speaks of is Jackie Duluoz. Jackie imagined Sax to protect him from all his fears. But Sax's final take on the situation is simple. "Nothing works in the end," he says (*DS* 241).

As Jackie's innocence and playful imagination are about to be left behind, sick at heart, he asks the defrocked Sax why they can't have another chance and why they have to go through this. All the while one hundred miles of Snake keeps ripping out of the Pit and shooting up into the sky. Then, as foreshadowed (yet to everyone's surprise except those familiar with the myth of Quetzalcoatl), a great bird comes out of the sky (*DS* 242). It snatches the Snake up in its beak and carries it off in a "grand ecstatic flight ... unto the Unknown" (*DS* 245). Sax now offhandedly reveals the final lesson of the novel. It was as he thought it should be. "I'll be damned.... The Universe disposes of its own evil!" (*DS* 245). When one recognizes his own soul and explores that Castle in all its terrifying facets (as Jackie has done), there is no need for a savior, divine or human. The capacity for salvation coexists with that of damnation or, as James Jones notes, "evil rectifies itself when individuals face it in themselves" (54).

That all of Doctor Sax's preparations against this day were utterly pointless doesn't minimize his intervention in Jackie's world as shamanic mentor. In terms of shamanism, the mock performance of the ecstatic experience is no less legitimate than the experience itself. It's all a show, a performance and ritual re-creation of that mystical condition all human beings share, but rarely access. That's the message and the medicine. When Doctor Sax's medicine becomes Jackie's, his mentoring role in Jackie's life ends, as does the primacy of imagination in Kerouac's fiction.

Never again did Kerouac apply his imagination to his novels in such depth and complexity as in *Doctor Sax*. If childhood was marked by his playful life of imagined events as shown in this novel, then adulthood brought the hard, fast recording of the autobiographical experience, "the veritable fire ordeal ... the discipline of making the mind the slave of the tongue with no chance to lie" (Kerouac, *Desolation Angels* 229). *Doctor Sax* marks Kerouac's departure from an imagined existence and his passing into an actual world of real events he re-creates through shameless autobiographical fiction. In *Sax*, he works out the myth of his ascent to his own mature style, his own writing soul. Perhaps that's why Kerouac said of *Doctor Sax*, "It's the greatest book I ever wrote, or that I will write" (Nicosia 410).

3

Visions of Cody
"Kidnapped, Shanghaied, and Orphaned"

Written between October 1951 and May 1952, *Visions of Cody* is a project of "word incarnate" in which Kerouac seeks to reenact Neal Cassady ("the complete Cody") on the page. In a letter to Ginsberg dated May 18, 1952, he refers to it as "a big multi-dimensional conscious and subconscious character invocation of Neal in his whirlwinds" (*JKSL 1940–1956* 356). *Visions of Cody* is a post-shamanic performance in words, a vision of a life (many lives), all objects of Kerouac's ecstatic attention, written out for the reader's participation. Like Gerard before him, Cody is an ideal surface on which Kerouac projects the full range of his fantasies in ecstatic biography. Evoking the phenomenon of spirit possession, this novel implies a complete identity between the two while Kerouac retains control over his own consciousness in the writing. This "Neal Book" (as he called it for a time) sets out to re-create the free-wheeling individualistic soul of Cassady for his own sake and that of his deadened age. *Visions of Cody* reveals Cassady as a Beat shaman who, to Kerouac, accesses each of the cosmic regions — God in his heaven, Satan in the nethers, and the imbecilic saint (the "holy goof") of the contingent world around us. In this son of a wino, Kerouac sees a twentieth-century "son of Man" for postwar America. Shamans always come from the edges in opposition. From Kerouac's perspective, *Visions of Cody* traces the arc of Cassady's rise and fall as a Beat messiah.

Cassady's life stands as a thoroughly ecstatic and countercultural response to his day. As biographer Dennis McNally astutely notes, "Only in the historical context of a bland oppressed culture could Neal Cassady, a carjacker from Denver, have become an icon in populist mythology" (355).[1] In his introduction to *Visions of Cody*, Ginsberg observes that

Kerouac wrote the book "as an explanation and prayer to his fellow mortals, and gods" (*VOC* xi). *Visions of Cody* is a multivalent *apologia* that explores the many meanings of Neal Cassady (or "Cody," as I'll refer to him from here on) in the life and work of Jack Kerouac.

Not published in its entirety until three years after Kerouac's death, *Visions of Cody* is, as Tim Hunt notes, "his first mature text and the paradigmatic text for his career" (xxxvii). As might be expected, *Visions of Cody* is not a novel in any conventional sense. Rather, it is an experimental text spontaneously written (for the most part).[2] *Visions of Cody* foreshadows numerous subjects and points of style that are evident in Kerouac's other work. As a piece of modern hagiography, it anticipates *Visions of Gerard*. Its nonsensical passages of raw glossolalia predict the "writing in tongues" we see in *Old Angel Midnight*. The extended passages that blur the boundary of dream and reality augur his reveries catalogued in *Book of Dreams* and *Doctor Sax*. The "love story"—the "bromance" of *Visions of Cody*—forecasts the anxious adoration of Leo Percepied for Mardou Fox in *The Subterraneans*. Significantly, the final section of *Visions of Cody* contains a condensed, speeded-up version of *On the Road*, which he had just completed. In this fast, stacked re-envisioning of *On the Road*, Kerouac executes "a vertical and metaphysical study of Cody's character and its relationship to the general 'America'" (*JKSL 1957–1969* 209). While Kerouac's visions are subjective and varied, they also speak to his time, and they don't begin with Cody anywhere in sight.

The Cody Context

As in *Doctor Sax*, the spontaneous form of *Visions of Cody* often shifts associatively from section to section (there are three), and within the sections themselves. Part 1 begins with brief word sketches of seemingly disparate scenes and moments. They are rendered in extreme detail and don't involve Cody at all. As always, Kerouac consistently asserts the universality of what he sees. What he feels, you (the reader) have also felt. For example, that "in-the-city feeling that I first dug (and all of us) as an infant" (*VOC* 18).[3] It soon becomes clear that, for Kerouac, to remember Cody, to re-create what he calls "the Cody constellation," is to dig *everything*, to trance

3. Visions of Cody

out on the surround and write it down (as in *Old Angel Midnight*). In this way, scenes of diners, men's bathrooms, movie theaters, employment agencies, New York streets, cafeterias, subways, backyards in Poughkeepsie, grocery stores, St. Patrick's Cathedral, St. Jean Baptiste Church and tenements of Lowell — and the skies above all of them[4] — as well as the myriad characters he sees in these places show the ecstatic context from a wide angle that will, at length, telescope in on and eventually become Cody. Kerouac observes all of these visions with a mystical eye. They all "breathe," he notes, and "want to tell something intelligible to me" (*VOC* 10).

A remarkable number of these opening sketches have to do with food. The smell and taste of food provide Jack with a vital link to Cody. Kerouac's initial visions of Cody in Part 1 are, in many instances, diffused in what he sees when he is hungry for food, and avid, as well, for the soul sustenance that he intuits in Cody Pomeray. The imagery grounds Kerouac's metaphysical portrait of Cody in the human physical condition. Communion with Cody is food for body and soul. As a Catholic, Kerouac believes in the Eucharist, the body of Christ transubstantiated into bread that is consumed by the faithful. The nature of this sacrament, and of Jesus' or any other shamanic career as a whole, is to erase the divine distance, and make the spiritual reality present to the senses.

In fact, sensual imagery of all kinds predominates in the spontaneous sketches of Part 1. (See, for example, the exclusively aural "vision" that happens as Kerouac contemplates Cody in Jamaica, Long Island [*VOC* 9].) For Kerouac, to contemplate Cody is to hear, see, feel, and taste *any* moment of existence in its entirety. If you keep the antennae of the senses up and out long enough with disciplined attention, and couple that with memory — which is the premise of the spontaneous prose technique here — then it will "all pour in," as Kerouac says. (Therein sets my claim that spontaneous prose is an ecstatic technique.) Kerouac confirms this idea in a letter to Gary Snyder, dated June 24, 1957. "I want ecstasy of mind, nothing else ... and I only have it when I write or when I'm hi or when I'm drunk or when I'm coming" (*JKSL 1957–1969* 46).

Another characteristic motif that appears early on in *Visions of Cody* is the frequent allusion to the cinema and movie stars. W.C. Fields shows up four times in Part 1 and occasionally throughout the novel. In films, particularly the common cinema of the B-movie, Kerouac appreciates the possibility of escape, and the ecstatic capacity of film to transport the viewer to an alternative reality. It is a genre on which he, in part, models his visual writing style (i.e., "the bookmovie"). In W.C. Fields, Kerouac sees an antecedent for Cody himself, an unapologetic outsider who keeps his own counsel and chronically grates against the status quo. (I'll discuss the lure of cinema as Kerouac sees it in greater depth later on.) All the pop culture references in *Visions of Cody* provide a common experiential ground and work to connect Jack with Cody, and Kerouac to his audience, in this opening section (Tytell 178).

While his hometown Lowell continues to provide Kerouac with the universal "solvent" for his visions, *Visions of Cody* is mostly opened out to other locales. Still, Part 1 sets a scene that introduces two important themes in the Duluoz Legend that are filtered through his hometown. In it, Kerouac's deep and complex relationship with Catholicism becomes apparent, as does his troubled relationship with women (who are often associated with a form of "dying").[5] Sitting transfixed in St. Patrick's Cathedral in New York City, Kerouac is equally reverent of the divine ("Lord, I scribbled hymns to you") and dubious of the modern Catholic ("People come to church for guilt now") (*VOC* 28). He contemplates St. Joseph's side altar (and the statue thereon) with a depth of understanding that outstrips formalistic piety. He sees St. Joseph in the dark holding the Christ-child, keeping the faith though mystified, and describes Jesus' ostensible father as "a humble self-admitting and truthful saint ... without glory, guilt, accomplishment or charm" (*VOC* 29). It is a scene that demonstrates Kerouac's profound feeling for, and perception of, his religion, all of which becomes part of this constellating overture of Cody.

When a group of devout women in the cathedral intones a novena,[6] his reverie flashes back to his childhood church in Lowell where his experience of Catholicism was mostly characterized by a sense of mortal dread. What happens next is more characteristic than coincidental in Kerouac's work. The funereal image is, if not linked, then certainly juxtaposed with the image of, not an individual or particular woman, but a female "type" that equally attracts and frustrates him through no intention of her own. In this case, immediately, spontaneously, Kerouac sees and writes:

> Always this kind of girl in church: unbearably pretty, unbearably neat ... I always think: "You're too unbearable for anything — the least or most of which

3. Visions of Cody

is love or the house of the real dying God —..." I know what she's up to, who she's really trying to drive away (me I guess) [*VOC* 30].

The allure and equally deep suspicion of women are a dual dynamic throughout the Duluoz Legend, often crudely so. Early on in *Visions of Cody*, he confesses, "As far as young women are concerned, I can't look at them unless I tear off their clothes one by one" (23). This raw tension often adds up to a blind male chauvinism exposed in the transparent confession of Kerouac's spontaneous prose. The sexist language and scenarios in more than some of these sketches are highly offensive from numerous points of view. Yet the tone of these lusty passages is all straight-on and unapologetic, somehow innocent and free of malice. As Kerouac writes on the fly, there's no time to recriminate, so, like Cody himself, this book exhibits an automatic honesty that is often self-incriminating and never retracted. (I'll elaborate upon this automatic or blindly confessional aspect of Kerouac's ecstatic technique in the next chapter on *The Subterraneans*.)

These personal confessions are pertinent in building the "Cody Context" in Part 1. Though Cody is bisexual, he doesn't suffer from Kerouac's brand of ambivalence when it comes to women. Cody is renowned for his female conquests. Supposedly "horrified" by Cody's bisexuality (as in a scene excised from *On the Road* that appears in *Visions of Cody*, page 358), he mostly ignores it in the rest of his Legend. Jack admires Cody's prowess with women and probably envies it as an attribute he never possessed, being, in the end, freaked out by women, as shown time and again in his work. For the most part, women are necessary and maddening adjuncts in the "Cody constellation." He loves Cody.

In this "bromance," Jack perceives a complete identification of mind and soul that surpasses being bonded to a wife or girlfriend. It is only with Cody that he can communicate completely (*VOC* 39). This becomes clear in the sequencing, style and content of a letter to Cody that concludes Part 1 of the book.[7] This sincere impassioned missive, quoted in full, starts with a lot of locker-room bluster, sex talk, and spontaneous goofing about typos and such, all of which, Jack notes, are imitative of Cody, an invocation of his voice. Cut to a flashback of Kerouac jamming on drums (*a la* shaman) and beheld by a naked negress in some primordial hipster pad. This poses a critical moment for Jack, as discussed above. So immediately he cuts to his confession of friendship and love for Cody, their intimacy, and the soul they share. He drops names of literary greats they've both read and the secrets they know on account of that. Jack has a moment of lucidity in this letter: he's grown tragically static—drunk, stuck, self-absorbed, and doomed. This indicates the big-picture crisis, and the soul sickness that begets his ecstatic response. The language of Jack's yearning for Cody's company is highly charged and thinly veiled in erotic metaphor as the letter ends (right before a postscript to Cody's wife, Evelyn).

This letter provides something that might pass for plot development in the ecstatic vision of Cody thus far. Jack will visit Cody and his family in California. He'll stay in the attic, and idly boasts of bringing a girl of his own, as form requires. He'll set out on a journey to commune with this strange tutelary figure who means so much to him (which is what he's been doing since page 1 of *Visions of Cody*). He'll go across America to find the Cody-essence and return, as he later notes, magnified, enhanced, and wise (*VOC* 94). Thus ends Part 1, an overture of the Cody "surround." The stage is set for this performance to focus on the individual Cody.

Cody: The Childhood "Narrative"

A shaman can be called by heredity, supernatural calling, or personal choice.[8] Cody attains distinction as shamanic figure by a blend of these (as does Kerouac). Part 2 of *Visions of Cody* reveals Cody's place in a shaky marginal heritage characterized by the circumstantial extremity that often begets ecstatic response, high or low. In this vision (early 1930s) we see his father, former tinsmith, now part-time barber and skid-row drunk with a six-year-old Cody at his side on Larimer Street in Denver. Old Man Cody knows the low road to ecstasy in the bottle (*VOC* 51). Cody's mother is portrayed as a tragic figure who died when he was quite young. He holds an image of her in his memory, an interior portrait of an imagined pre–Depression domesticity that exploded with her passing. Cody eventually joins Dad on the bum. Mom remains a mystery. Kerouac summarizes our hero's Denver childhood as a nadir "where little raggedy Codys dream" (*VOC* 8). Cody's upbringing makes him ripe for ecstasy.

On Larimer Street, among his father's "cronies," the boy finds many mentors. One named "Rex" in particular exemplifies a Peter Pan-ish imper-

3. Visions of Cody

ative that Cody would internalize and later manifest in his own way. "Rex who was no king but just an American who had never outgrown the boyish desire to lie down on the sidewalk which he did year round from coast to coast" (*VOC* 51). Do what you want, whenever you want, and don't reproach. The hobo as free and somehow holy, this is part of what Kerouac thought would come to be known as "Beat."

Kerouac sees (repeatedly) how the boy Cody deeply registers all his experiences and how he perceives in them many faceted and multiple realities. (See, for example, Cody's vision of the tile floor in a barbershop [*VOC* 53].) Even as a child, Cody is extraordinary because of his fantastic power of perception. "Cody knew, he knew everything like mad" (*VOC* 49). This ability to "dig deeply" in the derelict characters and setting of Denver, coupled with his "training" in comic books such as "Major Hoople" (which he finds mystical), as well as a stay in a reformatory, all prime Cody for a more rigorous reading of Schopenhauer and *The Lives of the Saints* (*VOC* 56). Cody is now prepared for his final emergence into the pool halls of Denver, where his progress as a self-elected shamanic figure evolves and "the heart of Saturday night" becomes holy hour in this nascent Beat myth.

Watson-as-Mentor

Tom Watson is a hunchbacked pool shark who lives with his grandmother in Cody's boyhood Denver (*VOC* 57). The shaman is commonly defined by some type of physical malady. Cody embraces this aspect of Watson. Furthermore, he admires it, intuiting that Tom Watson is privy to some fundamental human understanding because of his infirmity. Cody sees him as a dreaming Assyrian King (*VOC* 59). Later, he becomes "the only one who'd ever put his arm around the hump of Watson's sorrow" (*VOC* 64). To Cody, Tom Watson, "diseased and beautiful," represents the "great American Image of beautiful sadness" (*VOC* 59). He finds the nonchalant Watson irresistible, perceptive and wise. Watson, as a pool hustler, is also a con man from whom he can learn (*VOC* 58). One Saturday afternoon in 1942 (when Cody was fifteen), Kerouac describes a mutually telepathic moment between the two characters in a Denver pool room that

Cody busts wide open to a bigger con that will further his progress in the unfolding mystery. His first words to Watson are a proposition: "Do you want to learn philosophy from me?" (*VOC* 59). Cody offers this dubious service in exchange for pool lessons from Watson but, more than that, "to establish a blood brother loyalty in [their] souls" (*VOC* 59). As Kerouac sees it at this point, souls are what Cody is most after in the ecstasy of this book (even as Jack is most after Cody's soul). There is a kind of "soul snatching" all about this project. Knowledge of the soul, familiarity with its ways, being and indicating the soul — this is the shamanic underpinning of *Visions of Cody* and the emerging Beat impulse it delineates.

Cody accessorizes this breathless introduction with a strange dance, an entranced rocking on his feet, the whole show. Watson finds the performance hypnotic. Cody pitches his ultimate automobile skills, and throws them into the deal. He can fix them, steal them, even get in one and drive Watson to the Notre Dame game that weekend a thousand miles away (where Watson can watch the game while Cody rounds up girls for after!). Cody promises all of this, experience actualized on a whim, in a car. "I be your chauffeur, you teach me pool, snookers, anything else that comes in your mind, be my big brother, I be your helper. ... What say?" (*VOC* 61). It is a dazzling fugue and come-on. Watson thinks he's crazy,[9] but accepts Cody's proposition, and takes him in.

Cody luxuriates in the comfort and plenty of Grandmother Watson's home and careful attention. This is a wondrous event for a boy like Cody, who's gone without for so long. Cody takes it all in voraciously, food and setting alike. He gets a glimpse of that domesticity he's only fantasized about and it launches him to a new stage of development. Watson's tutelage begins with a lesson on how to cheat at cards. After digging in his closet, Watson gives Cody his first suit to replace his street clothes. Ill-fitting as it is, like a Charlie Chaplin outfit, Cody is honored by the gift. He's prepared now for a "second phase" that will begin with his entry into the mystical "all-of-it-pouring-into-town Saturday night" (*VOC* 63).

Kerouac's vision of Watson and Cody together (as are many of the visions that precede and follow it) is deftly portrayed as a trick and play of reflected light. This time around, their images reflect on the fender of a new car (*VOC* 63). Cody crosses that threshold spouting more of his own stories and circumstances, and finds himself able to speak on "several levels

3. Visions of Cody

to express himself to Watson" (*VOC* 64). Already (or still) entranced, Cody's excitement is agitated by the world he sees now, in clean clothes with his eyes up and out. Now it's girls, cars, lights, iconic redbrick walls and flashing neons. Cody is no longer scouring gutters for dropped change looking like a bum (*VOC* 64). In an earlier vision of Cody in reform school, he vowed to never to be a bum like his father. Now Cody is seeing more.

Kerouac shows Watson playing Virgil to Cody's Dante and they arrive at the pool hall. Kerouac's description of this scene (with backdoor open to reveal another pool hall also with doors open across the alley) evinces a double world. A chaotic hellish illusion, it will be where Cody realizes his ecstatic technique.[10] Whatever the pool hall means to most of the people crowding in there, it means more to Cody. Everything means more to Cody, except those things he doesn't care about, all of which Kerouac will chronicle by the book's end. The Beat impulse in general is defined as much by one's "not caring" about certain things as it is by one's enthusiasm for others. Kerouac's repeated intonation of the phrase "He didn't care" in *On the Road* is sometimes directly stated, and always implied, in *Visions of Cody*. Watson doesn't care about his hunchback, Cody doesn't care about his too-small suit. They are a self-validated and potent duo on account of that. It's Cody's debut.

Even (especially) before anyone notices him, Cody is both in perfect tune with the scene and hopelessly gone at the same time. Watson introduces Cody to his gang, and the boy's vision deepens on all they say and do. Cody sees it as "all part of one great three-dimensional moil that was all around him now instead of just flat in front of his face like a canvas prop, he was up on the stage with the show now" (*VOC* 66). The world has gained yet another dimension for Cody, and he sees it from the absolute center. In his first throes of connection, Cody appears quiet and shy, also "hilarious" and "dumb," but he's secretly excitedly thinking how to best impress these people, so they will eventually "turn to him for love and advice" (*VOC* 67). Essentially Cody is planning how to con them and, in a sense, replace Watson in their estimation.

Nothing in the tone of Kerouac's vision of this implies any malice in Cody's "ambition" to be the hub of an even bigger show. It already seems to be his destiny. All this is revealed as they shoot pool and Cody plays his own con. He's already won over Watson. Soon, Slim Buckle (Watson's right-hand man) displays an affection for Cody that becomes "hero worship" (*VOC* 67). Only one of the crew is wary of Cody's charisma, warning that "Cody wasn't everything he seemed to be" (*VOC* 67). Nevertheless Cody goes on to solidify his leadership position by demonstrating his extraordinary driving and athletic skills. Kerouac alludes to his budding "messiah-ship" by comparing Cody to a crucified Christ shot out of a cannon (*VOC* 70). In Part 2, he also devises a modern American metaphor to house the meaning of this hero on his journey to the Beat essence.

The Meaning of a Tabernacle

In *Visions of Cody*, Cody Pomeray is the personification of the Beat ethos. The "redbrick walls behind the neons" are its objective correlatives (*VOC* 82). Saturday night is its holy hour. Kerouac establishes this central image and time frame as a metaphor for the Beat impulse that's at the root of the mystery that is Cody (and America at large). This is where Kerouac enshrines the collective American soul of his time. I'm not sure what Bartleby saw, but for Kerouac this was no "dead wall reverie." Like a tabernacle, this metaphor obscures and indicates something at the same time. Hidden there is the essential, private yearning of the individual to be recognized, to make contact. (The secret of America, Kerouac notes, is "*the memory of love*," not being in it (italics in original [*VOC* 19].) Even as the sky hangs like a holy-card proscenium over so many of Kerouac's visions in all of his novels, in *Visions of Cody*, the anonymous redbrick walls and neon signage of American movie theaters, drugstores, auto shops and diners signify a closer heaven that is no less meaningful for its proximity. Only the lonely can see it (*VOC* 82). The redbrick wall flashed upon by beckoning neon is the ideal tabernacle door of the longing American soul — hidden in plain sight, furtive, secretive, and (like Cody) at once sacred and profane. In shamanic terms, "the poor hidden brick of America" becomes the center of the universe that Cody (via Kerouac) recognizes as a locus of ecstasy (*VOC* 87). Kerouac's use of the "poor hidden brick" here and elsewhere, like his visions of Cody as Beat icon, likewise reflects a "mysticism of image" (also post-shamanic) that expressed itself in early

3. Visions of Cody

Christianity. It is the highest reality in symbol, secreted away, the unspeakable mystery. Is it even there at all?

Visions of Cody does not portray this "wall ecstasy" (this Cody, this America) as a "happy trip," or, in the end, as even being more substantive than Bartleby's vision (which is the perfect secret). Emblematic of many later novels in his Legend, as a post-shamanic performance, *Visions of Cody* shows that ecstasy-as-nadir is as meaningful as the ecstasy of bliss. In Kerouac's Beat scripture, sadness is beautifully potent, and happiness pales in comparison to the intensity of being and awareness that Cody embodies. In form, *Visions of Cody* wanders like the Beat road where it's not the destination but sheer movement that matters most—where the conscious search is more important than any actual attainment. The manifestation of the "IT" essence that possesses Cody (that once possessed America, as Kerouac dreams and laments) is the spiritual grail of anyone's Saturday night in *Visions of Cody*. It's the thing people want most but can't find (or, on finding it, can never keep). To Kerouac, this pursuit is an act of American faith he sees stashed behind the redbrick walls and lit by neon lettering nationwide every weekend. "That poor hidden brick of America, the actual place you must go if you must bang your head to bang it at all, the center of the grief and what Cody now saw and realized from all that time [as] the center of ecstasy" (*VOC* 87). Like all ecstatic techniques, this is wholly subversive to a normal perspective, banging your head against a brick wall.

Part 2 of *Visions of Cody* is the word-incarnate performance more fully engaged. Kerouac describes Cody's heritage, and in it, sees the robust pioneer spirit of the Old West, the rugged individualism of the Whitmanic "yawp." The mastery of Cody's mystical bent over his mundane circumstance makes it so. We see Cody the seducer, the driver, the thief, the focal point, the con man and shaman. Kerouac proclaims Cody to be "the archetypical American Man" (*JKSL 1957–1969* 209). Cody is also the hub of Kerouac's highly personal and fantastic creative wheel. Part 2 of *Visions of Cody*, in a comparatively straightforward and concrete style (for this book), re-creates the world in the image of Cody's face. The long beginning of Part 3 transcribes the words from Cody's own mouth.

Goofing on Tape

As noted earlier, as the centerpiece of *Visions of Cody*, Kerouac inserts 130 pages of tape-recorded conversations between Cody, himself and a few others while high on marijuana.[11] "Frisco: The Tape" is a very conscious and conceptual artistic move in this otherwise spontaneously written performance. Although these are actual transcriptions, they somehow lack the substance, excitement, and immediacy of the rest of the book. In other words, as John Tytell discerns in his analysis of *Visions of Cody*, they lack the interface of Kerouac's *art* (183). Ironically, there is a pretense here that is absent elsewhere in *Visions of Cody*. I appreciate the numerous critics who cite the archival value of "The Tape" as a specimen of Beat talk and actual speech rhythms, or see it as a subversion of traditional narrative line. Ginsberg eventually grasped the Tape as a kind of literature *verite* that he called "the God-worship in the present conversation" (McNally 144). But even Ginsberg, at the time, was "worried" by this manuscript. Thinking it unpublishable and "crazy in a bad way," he suggested shortening the Tape section (*JKSL 1940–1956* 373).

In the final analysis, my view is that "Frisco: The Tape" is a shaky conceit. Numerous times I have read these conversations, in various conditions and dispositions, all in the hope of discovering a profanely inspired scripture revealing a treasure trove of Beat insights. Unfortunately, I can't get past my impression that "The Tape" presages our Twitter phenomenon. It does serve to highlight the agility of Kerouac's prose in the rest of the book and, in general, to reaffirm the role and efficacy of art in heightening reality, not recording it. "The complete Cody" as buddy, muse, "lover," hero, God and Satan — the full shamanic shot of it — is eventually played out in the modern ecstasy of the final titled section of the novel. But first we must explore another aspect of *Visions of Cody*.

"Imitation of the Tape"

This section is not an impersonation of *what* or *who* Kerouac hears in "Frisco: The Tape," but an expression of how he mediates the spontaneous impulse behind it. This imitation is more authentic than the original

3. Visions of Cody

and more engaging for its visionary performance. Here we see Kerouac again in a continuum with the shamanic tradition (where the technique of ecstasy = ecstasy). "Imitation of the Tape," in form, shows Kerouac afoot in the characteristic dilation and collapse of his apparitions. (See his "nation of monkeys" vision for a concise example of collapsing imagery [*VOC* 14].) Like Part 1, this section barely mentions Cody at all, and by the end, indicates only minimal direction and focus (just like the taped conversations it imitates). Still, it is more interesting and engaging.

An excerpt from Jack's sixth-grade composition about American pioneers starts it off, then there's a direct address (to whom?),[12] some kind of mental hang-ups on the fly, and Barney Google starts talking, then a would-be peyote "tell-all" that never gets started is left behind for further anarchic minutiae. Actor James Mason, jazz geniuses Bud Powell and Miles Davis, the mythical "Endeemion," a newspaper, a speech and a guy named "Roger Buttock" all show up in the spontaneous bedlam. Numerous false starts that dash (—) into other remembrances and moments all come and go at a vigorous pace.

Kerouac finds a brief eddy in the spontaneous stream when he happens upon thought of "all our B-movies" (*VOC* 251). He recognizes film as not only a modern portal of escape, but as the source of a modern discontent and paranoia. (An enigmatic aside for now, Kerouac will elaborate upon this in the next titled section of the novel.) His description of the B-movie house as a haven for thousands of children (a place that is both safe and mysterious) is one of the more coherent passages in this section. This quickly elides into a declamatory lament of America at large, more interrogatory dialogue, the burial of a body with a mystical clock, and a sweeping critique of hipsters because they don't show the proper respect toward figures "like Abraham Lincoln or even plain Abraham" (*VOC* 252).

Soon *Visions of Cody* breaks into column format and looks like a newspaper. Nominally this is an "essay on Cody Pomeray," but the "article" is more about the imaginary baseball games Kerouac played alone as a child. These games were incredibly complex and involved a league of teams, whole rosters of players with individual statistics, team uniforms and so on — stories within stories — all created, compiled, and maintained in his imagination. This multilayered sports mythos was an early alternative reality Kerouac explored and reported on in great depth in *Doctor Sax*.

As *Visions of Cody* returns to its "normal" formatting (huge blocks of text with little punctuation besides dashes), numerous other images flash by, including exquisite descriptions of the sky and visions of a boyhood tree rocking in a 1938 hurricane (*VOC* 256, 258). After an abrupt break in mid-sentence, the text takes on an aspect of social commentary.

He critiques college for sapping our youth of what little common sense they have and, in general, seems to question the "sophistication" of our idea of intelligence and the disillusion we suffer as a modern society on account of it. It's a common "grown-up" lament that Kerouac summarizes here. He writes, "I feel as though everything *used* to be alright; and now everything is automatically — bad" (*VOC* 260). His nostalgia for the "good old days" is not only a primary motivator of Kerouac's creativity, but is also brought about, as he sees it, by the closing down of the American soul. He illustrates this diagnosis in a parable where two personified fears meet on the street and avoid contact because of their suspicious natures (*VOC* 260–61). This is a compelling appraisal of our atrophying humanity in the Land of Plenty that is symptomatic of the modern American sickness. This is the decaying soul-sense that Kerouac responds to directly in all of his writing.

His subsequent complaint over the loss of the rogue American male "who used to slap all the asses of the women, including your mother," however, is not as convincing (*VOC* 264). It is, conversely, an effective segue to the dark and riotous conclusion of this section that, at this point, begins with an essay of sorts on the caveman. If the caveman serves as a metaphor of the lost virility Kerouac mourns in his post-war America (as well as the conventional notions of masculinity about which he is personally conflicted), then it's no coincidence that we see Hemingway ("Ernest Hummingbird") in this vision being ejected from a party by a "flunk" he could easily "flatten" (*VOC* 266). Not only is Hemingway our poster boy for troubled machismo, but he was arguably (in 1951–1952) the alpha-male in the modern American writers' club. America, it seems, is a place where "a man's man" no longer gets his due. This is, of course, a dubious reflection of America in the Fifties that doesn't impress one as a society in the process of refining or cleansing its "caveman" instincts. It does comment, however obliquely, on both Cody, who is a "man's man" in more than the common understanding of the phrase, and Kerouac, who is nostalgic for the era of

3. Visions of Cody

traditional gender roles, and aspiring at the same time to be a great writer like America's top-dog, Ernest Hemingway.

The block text rolls on, and this "Imitation of the Tape" briefly shows "you" as a stoned Huck-type on the creeks and rivers of America. Then, as happens occasionally in these long passages, the voice of an editor, critic, or consciousness itself emerges and asks, "Ladies and gentlemen, are we still supposed to communicate?" (*VOC* 267). It's a good question for the spontaneous prose writer.[13] In response, Kerouac immediately shifts to a more familiar, if not archetypal, scene: the crucifixion of Jesus Christ. But he does so in such a shocking manner, so spiked with sexist and racist imagery, as to make it practically unreadable. That being said, as a mélange of the sacred and profane, this re-vision of Golgotha in "Imitation" shows the ecstatic writer's capacity to link antitheses and to operate full-speed ahead with zero regard for social convention or political correctness.

Only six pages of text remain in this section. A couple of them look like a film script. There's an altar boy and "SR" (who is presumably a priest). They intone some phonetic Latin to each other. "Aderiadne," a man on a soapbox, Gary Cooper, a ski instructor, and Moldy Marie also figure in the script. Two unidentified characters briefly search for a roach pipe (that's been stolen by that recurring character in the Duluoz Legend, the "shroudy stranger"). There are further allusions to Yeats, Milton Berle, Danny Kaye, Eddie Arcaro, and Ted Williams. Passages of raw scatology and glossolalia abound.

As this bewildering rush of pages approaches its conclusion, an eight-line litany about "cracking your head" shines through because readers have heard it before. It evokes the redbrick wall metaphor of America that Kerouac established earlier as the ecstatic center where "you must bang your head to bang it at all" (*VOC* 87). This is a kind of prayer in *Visions of Cody*, and perhaps a reader strategy, too. You must bang your brain open on "Imitation of the Tape" and crack your head free of all reason to let in language exonerated of rational meaning in order to sense an ecstatic spontaneity that is often strange and disturbing. Though the content of this section has little to do with him, its chaotic form and lack of decorum is an homage to Cody. Throughout *Visions of Cody*, Kerouac's search for Cody is revealed as the search for himself. While composing *Visions of Cody*, Kerouac writes to Carl Solomon in December 1951, "[The] latest things

I wrote and have been writing 'about Neal' suddenly and curiously are really about myself" (*JKSL 1940–1956* 329). His visions of Cody are necessarily visions of himself. Both are a quest for a mystical essence and Big Bang whose background radiation crackles on the *avant garde* pages of "Imitation of the Tape."[14]

"Joan Rawshanks in the Fog"— "This Debacle Spectacle"[15]

In San Francisco 1952, Kerouac famously witnessed an outdoor night shoot for the filming of *Sudden Fear* starring Joan Crawford (as Myra Hudson) and Jack Palance (as Lester Blaine). This film was a comeback of sorts for Crawford. She portrays a successful playwright whose husband (Palance) and girlfriend (Gloria Grahame) are conspiring to kill her. It earned Crawford an Oscar nomination and bombed at the box office. It is purely coincidental that a tape-recorded conversation (and the playback thereof) plays a major part in *Sudden Fear*, as it does in *Visions of Cody*. Or that Myra Hudson's description of the perfect leading man could apply as well to Cody Pomeray: "He has to be the kind of charm boy that makes every woman in the audience go MMMM! the instant he walks on that stage." Perhaps it is less coincidental that the evil mistress, Gloria Grahame's character, is portrayed as such a beatnik. She smokes a lot of cigarettes and listens to jazz up loud in San Francisco hotel rooms while she plots murder. Kerouac despised the "beatnik" stereotype of brooding, brimming violence.

The powerful seduction of film in Kerouac's estimation is never in doubt in this or any of his books. But here he has a darker vision of the industry whose powers of illusion have gone beyond the theaters. In this way, "Joan Rawshanks in the Fog" is a Beat echo of Nathaniel West's *The Day of the Locust* (1939). We see a Hollywood dystopia, only from Kerouac's "don't care" high perspective and satirical distance. On the streets of Russian Hill, all the movie artifice and Hollywood fakery is in plain sight, yet the crowd who watches the filming of this scene has a difficult time separating the illusion from the reality (*VOC* 279). Kerouac, like West, sees the audience as complicit in the con. This is no hanging matter when it

3. Visions of Cody

come to shamanism (or faith-based religions, for that matter), except that here the audience collusion is cynical and adoring at once. They are fogged by the performance, not enlightened. This vision of the scene behind the scene doesn't portray the Hollywood con with much sympathy.

Kerouac watches take after take of a single scene in *Sudden Fear* that, in the final cut of the film, lasts about a minute. Crawford is past her prime. The illusion is blown, at least for Jack. He refers to her as Joan "Rawshanks," "Ashplant," "Clawthighs," and "Crawfish." By any name, she epitomizes modern celebrity. She is trapped, pinned down by the lights of the industry, and taken by the eyes of onlooking strangers that fix on her "in all kinds of ways" (*VOC* 275). The star is the slave, publicly adored and secretly loathed by the faceless masses. Kerouac's take on the whole scene shows Hollywood stardom to be a killing sport, comparing it to a bullfight, "the actual moment, the central kill ... the Take" (*VOC* 281). Yet the kill doesn't satisfy. Each of the multiple takes of this simple scene in *Sudden Fear* with its limited action becomes sinister in this light, but for reasons not in the script.[16] Jack feels sorry for her, as he intuits that she's being treated badly because of her age by the young director. He also notes that the crowd is also being treated somewhat harshly, herded from here to there for some fascistic Hollywood reason no one in the crowd can understand.

In "Joan Rawshanks," the characters in that crowd rarely emerge as individuals but rather as types: adoring onlookers, confused policemen, disgruntled onlookers, dotty old ladies. However, when the shoot is over, Kerouac spots a "subsidiary love affair ... going on in the audience itself" (*VOC* 278). The romantic triangle between "Susan," "James" and "Barbara" is a stock story, too. He sees it as "the play-act going on simultaneously" with the movie shoot (*VOC* 290). He is, nevertheless, incredibly attentive to the rehashed romantic details of this tired scene, and puts it on par with "Joan Rawshanks in the Fog." These characters in life, as on film, are equally flat. Yet Jack tries to love all the actors, on screen and off, for their flat fakery. Everybody's just doing what they think they should be doing. Besides, Kerouac was too self-consciously fallen for cold satire, or as biographer Dennis McNally notes, his "innocent eye could never develop a saving shield of cynicism" (374).

During all this, Cody (the "Multi-Dimensional") is "at home not letting anything happen but himself" (*VOC* 277).

"Harken to Cody's Face"[17]

Perhaps the most sexually charged sequence of crass obscenity in the book acts as a bridge between the film imagery of "Joan Rawshanks" and the incrementing raw revelation of Cody. It's been a while. Kerouac's letter of intent to visit the Pomerays is on page 38. It's not until page 293 that he embarks on his trip to Denver to find Cody in the summer of 1949. He will start and restart the narrative several times from this point in the associative stream. *Visions of Cody* gets kaleidoscopic, and treks, like Jack, toward the final close-up and singular wonder of Cody.

Kerouac senses Cody in everything about Denver when he stops there on his trip. Cody, as Whitman might say, "is in the float of the sight of things" (139). An intiatory shamanic cycle of death and vision ensues. Jack intones a refrain, "Down in Denver, all I did was die," then "suddenly" comes upon a softball game in his roving (*VOC* 293). Alone and wandering, Jack is "dead," and the Denver world becomes transposed into Cody, the apple of his mystical eye. He sees the "poor little Mexican hero Cody's of the Denver night!" (*VOC* 294). Omnipresent, or "hugening" (to use Kerouac's term from *Doctor Sax*), Cody becomes each of the boys playing ball. His first wife, Joanna, becomes all the girls in the stands. Cody is possessing Jack's consciousness, and the apparition of Cody's face (like the redbrick and neons earlier) has become an icon of his vision. As is Kerouac's imaginative wont, Cody is everywhere and everyone in the stadium. Cody is in the heat of the game and the marrow of life. Significantly, this image is framed by a simultaneous perception of the surrounding neighborhood, with porches, lawns, streets, traffic lights, and cars waiting to go. This is a close echo of the "Great American Intersection" Kerouac saw in Part 1 (*VOC* 37), and like it, this aside prepares the reader for movement to another level of vision. The portraiture is growing more acute.

Kerouac flashes back to show Cody as a prodigious boy, a neophyte who performs marvelous feats with his pink rubber ball and delivers newspapers on his "soul bicycle." Then, emerging from some dark Rembrandtian interior, we see Jack himself shot out into the open, heading west in the backseat of a travel bureau car. There he receives a shamanic call of his own. On the move, in this pilgrimage, Jack is singled out and commissioned by God to make a "report" of Cody to the world. Kerouac's motif

3. Visions of Cody

of the sky has finally spoken. God with indicating forefinger is set in the sun-shot clouds like the stained glass windows that have transfixed Jack elsewhere in the novel. He commands Jack to "go moan for man ... go groan alone go roll your bones" (*VOC* 295).

A genuine moan is not a conscious act; it is not melodic, not a song. In America's youth, Whitman sang out. He can't be blamed; the whole American experiment bode well in his day. It looked good, and, as in "Song of the Open Road," sounded even better. Perhaps God pointed to Whitman in his day and said, "Sing!" (Maybe He pointed to Bartleby and said, "Stare!") But in the Fifties, Kerouac is told to moan for an America that, in many ways, has grown old before its time. The wording of this divine mandate indicates that "reporting on" Cody will be a primal task, a dolorous and chancy trial (a roll of the dice.) But his visions of Cody will be the "bones," "pods," and "seeds" of the regenerative ecstasy. (At least that's what God thinks.) In terms of absolute visual clarity, musicality of language, and the stunning implosion of vast imagery to minute detail to nothing before your very eyes, this nine-line sentence ranks among the most dazzling in all of Kerouac's work.

Now it's on! Kerouac's rendering of Cody from here is redolent with marijuana incense, even more deeply meditative, and, to varying degrees, "blown away." "Harken to Cody's face," he commands, and gets down to it (*VOC* 296). Kerouac's portraiture this time is nearly pixilated in detail and hyper-focus. Cody, and Kerouac's visions of him, now embrace and evince multiple paradoxes, and his résumé as a shamanic figure assembles.

Cody is a Master-of-Time, yet seems to be driven mad by "the cataclysmic import of the here and now" (Tytell 176). Cody is acutely aware of time passing, yet his mantra is "everything's always alright." For all his frenetic behavior, it is the patience of "old continuous Cody" that most exhibits his mastery of time (*VOC* 300). Cody will recognize this quality in other figures he and Jack encounter on the road, especially jazz musicians. Time flies, but Beat characters endure.

Cody is a "Man/Woman." Cody is a macho man, yes, but he enjoys mimicking women and wishes he was one. (More likely, it is Jack who wishes Cody was a woman. The silver bullet for the demon of his psyche, perhaps.) In any case, Cody is firmly in the both/and mystery, beyond category.

Cody is angelic America. Kerouac envisions Cody as American archetype in an expatriated moment of apotheosis. Mexico, as John Tytell notes, signifies an "encircling timelessness" (70). Cody and Jack are high on the fellahin Mexican plateau when they both become ecstatic, that is, "so completely and godlike-ly aware of every single little thing trembling" when it happens (*VOC* 298). Whereas, at the beginning of this novel, Kerouac mapped out the "Cody constellation," here Jack sees him grow big as the sun. Cody is the greatest man Jack has ever known. He is as magnificent as Franklin Delano Roosevelt. Cody is America deified.

In the very next paragraph, however, Kerouac portrays Cody as his demon and "greatest enemy" (*VOC* 298). The timing of this revelation is purely associative in *Visions of Cody*. (The linear style of *On the Road* pretty much saves this realization until the end.) What the visions reveal are not what the visionary hoped for. The ecstasy here is one of nadiral disappointment. Cody is an abstraction, "an ominous motif of failure in American life" (Tytell 176). Kerouac reaches for him in mind, heart, and prose, but while seeing everything for the effort, he touches nothing. Cody's is an elusive hyper-reality that ultimately doesn't care. He is not Gerard.

Along with his robust individualism, Cody is an equally hearty and profligate narcissist. He empties himself at the center of the attention he demands, but gives nothing. Cody saves no one. He is not the Beat messiah Kerouac prophesied and grimly demystified in his Legend. By the time of his writing *Visions of Cody*, Kerouac had accepted this for years. Yet Cody abides in Kerouac's visions until the end (as we'll see in *Big Sur*). Jack loves Cody still and always. He writes on. "Everything's alright." That's Kerouac's victory in all this Cody-disenchantment: "the love is to the lover, and comes back most to him" (Whitman 193). The visions intensify.

"Stooge Ecstasy"[18]

The second best vision in the entire novel, according to its author, is the one that shows Cody transfigured with the Three Stooges. In this fantasy *reductio ad absurdum*, we spy Cody's greatest shamanic significance (and Kerouac's, as well). Although Cody is no savior, the "Stooge Ecstasy" reveals how and why he evades the modern American soul malaise.

3. Visions of Cody

The Three Stooges were a vaudeville act known for their slapstick physical comedy. They went on to make mostly short subject films from the Thirties through the Sixties. The heyday of the Stooges coincided with Jack and Cody's 1930s B-movie youth. I also watched a lot of the Three Stooges on TV in syndication as a schoolboy in the Seventies. Every day after school, Channel 48 out of Philadelphia ran an hour of the Stooges that I never missed. As "old-fashioned" as these comedy shorts were, they were very popular among us boys. We took Moe, Larry and Curly in with our first rock 'n' roll, and like rock music, the Stooges made us kind of wild and reckless. Every day we spoke "Stooge" with one another at recess as we slapped, poked and tweaked ourselves about. Curly's "nyuk-nyuk-nyuks" with fingersnaps and cheek-pops would often happen behind the nun's back as she wrote on the blackboard. It should have come as no surprise when one day in seventh grade (1975) the homeroom nun gave us a long cautionary lecture, warning us against listening to the glam-rockers KISS *and* watching the Three Stooges. Both of them, as Sister saw it, were subversive to everything normal and decent. She was right about the Stooges. The "subversive Stooge essence" proves to be the object of Kerouac's greatest exultation in this vision of Cody.

It is interesting and maybe significant to note that, as Kerouac begins to write it, he dissembles the novel's major metaphor (or removes half of it). The neons (now "pretty pink" in San Francisco) remain, but the red-brick wall is gone and replaced by a "modernistic front," a less concrete image (*VOC* 301). It's as if the tabernacle door is gone, and this is what Jack sees. He sings a litany of the dive bars of the city to intone the mystery.

This section, like other parts of the novel, is an impersonation, a repeat ecstatic performance. It is also a full-blown fantasy trip of the Stooges that is woven into Jack's mind by Cody, who bridges the worlds of illusion and reality. Cody imitates the Stooges, and Kerouac imitates their interaction in writing. Like most of his visions, Kerouac asserts the universality of this reverie by a looping train of association. The afternoon San Francisco streets that Jack rambles with Cody (in the adult present tense of this sequence, for now) are "just like" the afternoon streets Jack wandered with his pal G.J. in boyhood Lowell. And later, in further flashbacks, the streets of Cody's childhood Denver are the "same" as the main streets of Charleston, West Virginia, and the dusty thoroughfares of nameless Southern railroad towns (populated by "nations of Negroes"), and the Depression-era streets of Los Angeles rolled over by families of Okies (*VOC* 302). The string of associations goes on to show the boy Cody walking with his father on a May afternoon in Denver as the boy Jack walks with his father on Massachusetts streets near the ocean, where he glimpses alleys that remind him of avenues in Germany scented with Chinese food that spawns additional visions of Cody in which Jack gets caught up, "kidnapped, Shanghaied, and orphaned ... in the interesting old void" (*VOC* 302). (This phrase works as a kind of shorthand or synopsis of Jack's role in his relationship with Cody throughout this novel and the entire Duluoz Legend.)

As the vision returns to its founding context (what I've called its "adult present tense"), we see Jack and Cody high on the San Francisco streets. They are ready for a breakthrough, "noticing everything, talking everything" like Homeric heroes transported to modern America. When Cody begins "to imitate the stagger of the Stooges," the scope of Jack's insight expansively blurs semblance and fact (*VOC* 304). Before it's over, this whimsy will radiate outward to implicate all of America, and flaunt a seditious alternative to its status quo.

This ecstasy of Cody and the Stooges is initiated by a hypothesis that Kerouac eventually states three different ways: "What if the Three Stooges were real?" (*VOC* 304). Each time he invokes this supposition, Moe, Larry, and Curly appear at Cody's side as the scene starts, shoots off in associative tangents, and restarts. The fantasy is vivid and rolling as the Stooges become an unorthodox trinity with whom Cody "interallies" in plain sight. As Jack studies the vision, he begins to make out its revelation.

The trademark antagonism of the Stooges was always a ruse, a con for laughs. They are really *compadres* whose ferocious and often vicious interaction is a three-partnered dance, a performance perfected where each offense is parried by an equal and opposite defense. They do no harm to each other. Conventional standards and practices, on the other hand, take a beating when the Stooges start cuffing one another. High society tea-parties devolve, laws are broken, kings of industry grow weak, dictators crash and burn, dresses fly up and toupees fly off. Like Rex, the hobo from Cody's boyhood, the Stooges do what they want. Furthermore, the Stooges

3. Visions of Cody

are savage, barbaric, and absurd. Like Cody, they are iconoclasts who destroy the status quo by sheer force of their goofing performance.

Kerouac's individual introductions of Moe, Curly, and Larry are brief, evocative and entirely authentic in language and imagery. Soon their dealings with each other result in Larry having a huge nail embedded in his "eyebone," which causes Jack to trip into his version of the prophet Ezekiel's vision of the dry bones (*VOC* 304). After all, the Lord has called them both; Ezekiel to prophesy and Jack to "report." And, in each of their visionary books, the Lord leads them to the "bones." The skeletal vision, as noted elsewhere, is characteristic of the ecstatic experience in widespread shamanic traditions (and is a frequent motif in Kerouac's work). Bones exhibit the both/and dynamic of *solve et coagula* ("falling apart and coming together"). Bones signify both death and regeneration. The bones in Ezekiel's field belong to the slain Israelites who will reassemble in body and spirit once he prophesies as commanded by the Lord. Jack's vision is more figurative, pop-inflected, and fun. In this aside, Jack's chant (in the style of the much-recorded spiritual "Dem Dry Bones") describes a miraculous reconstruction of awareness. The order of assembly for the "bones" in *Visions of Cody* is notable in that it expresses a perceptive cosmology through a series of connections:[19]

"Eye" → "Shadow" → "Luck" → "Foul" → "High"
"Air" → "Sky" → "Angel" → "God" → "Bone"

Sight ("eye") bonds to darkness ("shadow") that ties in to fortune ("luck") that joins with calamity ("foul") that links with the series of transcendent connections ("high," "air," "sky," "angel," "God") before cycling back to the original image. This chant adds a heavenly counterpoint to the unfolding vision of these imbecilic saints carrying on "in an underground hell of their own invention" (*VOC* 304). What if they were real?

Before Cody's face (in yet another apotheosis and iconography of the novel's central image) again shimmers over the day of this vision "like a sun," Jack flashes back to his beloved B-movie houses and the magic spell the Stooges wove there (*VOC* 305). But he makes sure to clarify that this vision of Moe, Curly, Larry, and Cody (these "crazy kids") is no Hollywood illusion, but the ecstatic breakthrough and realization "that life is strange and the Three Stooges exist" (*VOC* 306). Jack has seen their reality and meaning in and through Cody. Like the archetypal America, Kerouac shows Cody to be self-appointed and realized with no need for outside validation of any kind. Like the archetypal Beat, Cody cannot be compelled to conform to (or receive) the values of any status quo other than his own individuality and will. Kerouac sees that this "barbarity," this "silliness" — all these "goofs" and visions — though chaotic in the "now," will be justified in time. This raucous alliance with the Three Stooges against the serious preoccupations of modern America shows Cody at his shamanic height, world-hopping, defiant, and, for the fleeting moment, even invincible.

But, in a subsequent series of visions, as Jack goes on to contemplate Cody as his lost brother, as arbiter of his thoughts, as father, worker, hero, champion, and muse, Cody's diminishing trajectory comes quickly into focus. (We've known this for a long time in *Visions of Cody*.) As he studies the objects in his Frisco attic, Jack glimpses the "still-life" of Cody's mundane existence (*VOC* 327). Finally, trancing out on the sun setting over a park, Jack announces, "Cody is dead." (It is more accurate to say that Cody "dies" to Jack's expectations.) I think it's indicative that before Jack says goodbye to Cody in the last line of this novel ("Adios, King"), Cody (as a Beat messiah, a superhuman mythical figure) has already said farewell to Jack, and left him with a final word of encouragement. "Adieu, sweet Jack, the air of life is permeated with roses all the time" (*VOC* 328).

Shamanic Denouement: Return of the Average

At the outset of his visions, Jack saw that the secret of Cody's transcendence was a child-like soul-centered perspective that didn't entertain any distinction between the ridiculous and the serious, the repulsive and the attractive. As Kerouac notes, it was all a project of "loving the soul of man" (*VOC* 307). This articulates a kind of worldwide vocation. Perhaps it is not so curious, then, when Jack completes his journey to Cody and sees him domesticated in San Francisco, married with children, holding down a job and so forth, that he qualifies his friend's obituary: Cody is *not* dead, only average (*VOC* 329).[20] Jack sees him for the first time in this light and, as if Zeus had taken a day job, struggles with the strangeness of this diminished status. Though he spies hints of mystery in Cody either

3. Visions of Cody

because of his middle-class domesticity or in spite of it, it's not the same. *This* Cody believes in money, while Jack believes in the Church (*VOC* 330). Each loves the other, yet curses and could kill the other. In a novel whose last third has been rolling from strength to strength, the final four entries leading up to the retelling of *On the Road* (which concludes the novel and celebrates the zenith of Jack and Cody's relationship) establish Cody as yet another archival figure of Jack's lost paradise, an object of his nostalgia that, like his Beat vision, never turned out as he had wished. Just like the road itself, though the trip to Cody described in *Visions of Cody* in the most roundabout and discursive series of visions has promised much, it has disappointed in the end. Kerouac finally comprehends that, not only has Cody become a ghost, but also that Cody has always been a ghost, a phantasm of his own desire. That settles it. This is the quietus, the finishing stroke, that releases Kerouac from these *Visions of Cody*—a realization that kills Jack, and gives him dead eyes to regressively see the events and mysteries of *On the Road* all over again (*VOC* 336).

Conclusion

Seventies rock critic and gadfly Lester Bangs once wrote, "It's tough having heroes. It's the hardest thing in the world. It's harder than being a hero. Hero-worshippers ... must live with the continually confirmed dread of hero-slippage" (161). When it comes to the relationship between Jack Kerouac and Neal Cassady, *Visions of Cody* (like *On the Road* before it, and *Big Sur* after it) represents this notion entirely. Perhaps, from the perspective of Kerouac's orthodox Catholicism, it is the fate of the hero worshipper, the idolater, the saint-maker, the pot smoker or peyote eater — the destiny of anyone who presumes to attain the divine mystery of godhood — to be let down or even go mad. (As Cody describes it, this is what happened to someone he knew named "Harold Jew" [*VOC* 315].) From the shamanic perspective, though, *Visions of Cody* embodies a successful vision quest that establishes both Cody (in his being) and Jack (in his writing) as post-shamanic figures. Cody's shamanic "deformity" is an unhinged individuality that stands out in glaring relief against the backdrop of his time. Shamans can display both curative and deadly powers, and over the course of this book, Cody is the soul of such a paradox—sick and healthy, crazy and sane, self-destructive and self-promoting, man and "woman," extraordinary and average, living and dead. Cody is a transgressor of boundaries and Kerouac's written visions of him are necessarily innovative and conventionally subversive. In *Visions of Cody*, Kerouac confronts the uncomfortable truth of hero worship. The ideal Cody, like the ideal America, never really existed anywhere but in his mind—a bleak vision, but an epiphany nonetheless. "Sadness," Kerouac writes, "is inexplicable and creative" (*VOC* 379).

4

The Subterraneans as Nadiral Ecstasy

> ONCE I was young and had so much more orientation and could talk with nervous intelligence about everything and with clarity and without as much literary preambling as this; in other words this is the story of an unself-confident man.
> — *The Subterraneans* 1

In the opening lines of *The Subterraneans* (*TS*), the narrator laments the loss of immediacy in his life. Kerouac, as we have seen in *Visions of Gerard* and *Doctor Sax*, always looks to childhood as his paradise. Here, the word "ONCE" indicates a time before he became a writer, before his actual existence became intertwined with his literary existence. The move from the lived experience of the child to the written (artificial) experience of the adult writer marks a crisis in his confidence. In *The Subterraneans*, this crisis initiates a shamanic response wherein he has to re-think, re-feel, and re-create what he has undergone in a recent relationship in order to enshrine it in this novel.

Kept awake by benzedrine, Kerouac wrote *The Subterraneans* in 72 consecutive hours in October 1953. Set in bohemian post-war San Francisco (though the events upon which it is based took place in New York City), the novel is an extended monologue about the love lost between the autobiographical narrator, Leo Percepied, and a younger woman (half African American and half Cherokee), named Mardou Fox. Though it is patently nonlinear and spiked with the author's comments on anything from the view outside the window to his thoughts about writing the novel itself, the narrative is an extended complaint and loosely coheres to a jeremiadic cycle.

The abandonment of conscious craft in literature makes Kerouac as writer-shaman a conduit for unconscious forms that are paradoxical and often ecstatic. In *The Subterraneans*, the three-part profile of a Beat jeremiad is discernable in the promise of new love, the fall from that promise (due to the narrator's ambivalence), and finally, a peculiar type of redemption through writing. Over the course of this cycle, Kerouac reveals his mostly disappointed view of the "hipster" subculture that he, along with Ginsberg, Burroughs and others, unwittingly spawned. His portrayal of Leo Percepied's private struggle with issues of race and gender comments upon similar tensions in post-war America-at-large. Furthermore, the rambling narrative embodies the conflict between the immediacy of experience and the artificiality of writing, a tension that consistently fueled Kerouac's career. The point of view in *The Subterraneans* is nadiral, and the technique, what I call the "loathe-confessional," is ecstatic.

The "Loathe-Confessional" as Ecstatic Technique

> [In] fact I wanted to be hurt and "lacerate" myself— one more laceration yet and they'll pull the blue sod on, and make my box plop boy.
>
> —*The Subterraneans* 14

A one-sentence synopsis of *The Subterraneans* might read like this: "I am a bigot, a misogynist, an egomaniac, a paranoiac, an alcoholic, and a repressed homosexual." Not a pretty portrait of the autobiographical narrator; so why did he do it? Like many of Kerouac's contemporary critics, Norman Podhoretz saw such confessional musing as the pose of a braggart and condemned him for it: "[T]his notion that to be hopped up is the most desirable of all human conditions, lies at the heart of the Beat generation [which is] hostile to civilization [and] worships primitivism, instinct, energy, 'blood'" ("Know-Nothing Bohemians"). Robert Brustein scorned the writing of Kerouac and other Beats as "belligerently exalting [their] own inarticulateness" ("Cult of Unthink").

While their reaction to the Beat poetics is negative, mine is positive for the same reasons. The variety of "all human conditions" in the post-war cultural landscape had been much depleted. As Kerouac saw it (via Oswald Spengler), America made a Faustian bargain by severing the indi-

4. The Subterraneans *as Nadiral Ecstasy*

vidual from a cosmic sense of self and casting him adrift, puny and isolated, in a modern and monolithic status quo where individuality wasn't much encouraged.[1] Is it any wonder, then, that one might consider the "hopped-up" condition to be more desirable for at least some of the generation coming of age? In an altered state one might get a glimpse of a mystical shamanic truth — what Kerouac calls "the lesson you forgot," namely, that "God is not outside us but is just us" (*SOGE* 29). The re-creation of any ecstatic experience in writing is liable to fall short of a reader's traditional expectations of what novel-writing should do and be.

To cut through the cultural fuzz of his readers and to "circumvent the machinations of the Faustian social filter," Kerouac needed to write in a manner more akin to Whitman's "barbaric yawp" that exercises a primal poetics both instinctive and elemental (Lardas 153). Podhoretz and Brustein reduce the significance of Kerouac's confessional mode to the infantile histrionics of a self-aggrandizing drunk. But Kerouac's project is never bragging or self-enhancing in nature. In *The Subterraneans*, it is more like an exorcism of self-loathing. Viewed in the light of ecstatic technique, Kerouac's spontaneous prose confession in this novel marks a shamanic journey to the bottom of his life in modern America, and the lesson of this voyage is neither boastful nor flattering.

John Lardas, in his excellent study of the Beats called *Bop Apocalypse*, sees in Kerouac's confessional style a strategy "to realign the self with the cosmos through the drama of introversion" (153). Many times for Kerouac (as for the Vedantic Whitman before him), the cosmic sense of seeing through the subjective lens pointed inward reveals the grand vista of a universal common ground. In a letter dated August 30, 1951, Kerouac writes, "I want to re-visit the mysteries of my past, which is my job; the mysteries of my source, my soul, the things that now teach me the meaning of universal love" (*JKSL 1940–1956* 322). So much of Kerouac's fiction (until his work in the Sixties beginning with *Big Sur*) embodies (even preaches) the universal resonance of individual experience and the possibility of love. The shamanic scope of Kerouac's confession in *The Subterraneans* comments on the struggles within his own soul as well as those within the soul of the American tribe. Lardas expounds on this notion:

> [Kerouac] proposed that by confronting the most intimate aspects of one's personality it was possible to not only release the self from the bonds of Faustian

constraints but also catalyze the American soul. The confessional strategy became a way to speak openly about [himself] ... while simultaneously addressing social issues [137].

Full loathe-confession, then, for Kerouac, becomes a rhetorical performance that will exorcize the shame of his own "emotional congestion, poor American folly, fear and self-horror" (*VOC* 92). The goal is redemption through admission of guilt. The process is written masochism. Kerouac's confession in *The Subterraneans* is no cool, formalistic (hence empty) ritual, but an orgy of self-laceration at the bottom of his existence wherein he re-creates his wounds and perfects his pain (*TS* 25).

Leo Percepied, the romantic mystic, applies this confessional style as a way to mortify his male ego, and, by shamanic extension, *the* male ego. His ego drives him, as a writer, to produce "great erected constructs" of his experience. It is Leo's ego, as manifested in his writerly ambition, that overrides his heart throughout the novel and, in the final analysis, costs him the love of Mardou. The primacy of male artifice prevents the narrator from actualizing a wholeness of experience and scuttles any notion of a salvation through "onelove" with a woman. (In this aspect, the novel proves to be, oddly enough, prescient of the *l'écriture féminine* impulse of the Seventies feminists Hélène Cixous and Luce Irigary, who exemplify a similar indictment in their criticism.) And it is only through the full confession of his nadiral experience with Mardou that Kerouac can achieve a kind of redemption of her loss. In the ecstasy of spontaneous prose, his pain sings for the sake of his art.

Fascination Street: Gender Mess and Racial Taboo on Heavenly Lane

> [Leo Percepied is] a glaring example for anti-racist and feminist critics of the attitudes they decry in American culture and its mainstream literary tradition. Far more than television's famous Archie Bunker, Leo Percepied is the fictional embodiment of the woman-degrading, male chauvinist, racist, and homophobic attitudes that have engendered some of the ugliest controversies in the United States since World War II.
>
> — Warren French 112

4. The Subterraneans *as Nadiral Ecstasy*

The relationship between Leo Percepied and Mardou Fox, in terms of gender and race, originates in ambivalence and devolves in repeated vortices of fascination, apotheosis, and revulsion. As we have seen in *Visions of Cody*, in *The Subterraneans*, Kerouac's narrator aligns himself with what he perceives as the heterosexual (and chauvinist) mainstream: "I am crudely malely sexual and cannot help myself and have lecherous and so on propensities as almost all my male readers no doubt are the same" (*TS* 5). At the same time, he sees sex ("making it") as "the key to pain" (*TS* 9). Nevertheless, Leo's attraction to Mardou is immediate, and he admits his initial desire has much to do with her being a woman of color (*TS* 3). Leo's fascination with the opposite sex in general and Mardou in particular is agitated and ambivalent because of the latent homoerotic and racist leanings he does not confess until much later in the monologue. Leo Percepied's gender orientation is, in a word, troubled.

The preoccupation with death has followed Kerouac's narrator from his childhood with Doctor Sax into his dissipated adulthood. Percepied explains that his positive self-image has been burnt out "under years of drugtaking and desiring to die, to give up ... to die in the dark star" (*TS* 9). Perhaps the most indicative of the narrator's earliest confessions in the novel (and most telling, in shamanic terms) is that he is "nervous and many leveled and not in the least one-souled" (*TS* 3). It is this soul sickness, this spiritual schizophrenia, Leo seeks to cure by entering into the ecstasy of the "onelove" with Mardou Fox (*TS* 9).

Besides this carnal attraction, Leo's fascination with Mardou has much to do with the shamanic ramifications of her being a woman of color. Marginalized and repressed by the patriarchy in both the dominant culture and the hipster subculture, Mardou responds in an ecstatic manner that is a product of her improvisation on her nadiral moment. This capacity, as Matt Theado observes, is a legacy of both her past and present circumstances. "Mardou is a mixture of the ancient high civilizations and the emergent new one, the one populated by bop children" (Theado 117). Throughout the Duluoz Legend, Kerouac champions the African and Native American as alternative models to a WASPish status quo.[2] In this novel, Kerouac expands this critique to include the hipster ("subterranean") culture that he sees as insincere and incapable of comprehending Mardou's inherent value.

The "true love" between the two begins not with the drunken sex of their first night together, but the morning after when Mardou curls up on Leo's lap and reveals her life story. This sequence initiates their relationship on a deeper level and has a transporting effect on Leo (*TS* 29). In extended blocks of narrative, Kerouac performs this revelation by combining, interspersing, and overlaying Mardou's words with Leo's visions and extrapolations. This simultaneity makes it difficult at times to tell who is "speaking." This blurring and transference of identity displays Kerouac's self-perceived kinship with Mardou. John Tytell contextualizes Kerouac's affinity with the Native American in particular:

> Kerouac ... believed Indian blood was mixed in his French Canadian past [and] felt deep sympathy for Indians, a feeling which was to find its fullest articulation in a long Faulknerian eulogy in *The Subterraneans* for Mardou's father [168].

This eulogy for Mardou's father as fellahin archetype serves as a prelude for Leo's retelling (or re-presentation) of Mardou's ecstatic "flip." Kerouac's rendering of Mardou's experience takes the form of a shamanic sequence that locks Leo into a deeper, more comprehensive state of fascination that approaches worship.[3]

Mardou's Flip: The Ecstasy of Integration

> She's lost her mind, her usual recognition of self, and feels the eerie buzz of mystery.
> — *The Subterraneans* 32

"Flip," the hipster term for a temporary state of insanity or mental breakdown, lends itself well to exploration of the nadiral ecstasy. As Norman Mailer writes in *The Deer Park*, "You drop to the bottom only to gain momentum for the leap to the top" (246). This is certainly the case with the encapsulated narrative of Mardou's flip. Like the novel as a whole, this subplot shows the triadic form of the jeremiad (promise, decline, and redemption). As Mardou "dictates" this story, the narrator/author reenacts her ecstasy in a variety of prose styles that appear and fade spontaneously (i.e., dialogue, interior monologue, expository prose, descriptive prose, and reverie).

4. The Subterraneans as *Nadiral Ecstasy*

The tale begins with Mardou in a state of weakness, always seeking but never finding love and satisfaction among the men of the hipster circle. In *The Subterraneans*, she rises naked from Ross Wallenstein's "loveless" bed while he is on a heroin nod. She stands frozen in her existence for long moments, then experiences a "calling" to move away, and to proceed into the unknown (*TS* 33). Called away from this subterranean tribe, Mardou leaves the room. She is now engaged in a shamanic initiation in which she will suffer and die to her previous state of weakness and, in isolation, gather her powers. Naked, alone, and washed in the rainy night, Mardou senses in herself an Edenic state of innocence. She climbs up and stays perched on a wooden San Franciscan fence to await her next instruction (*TS* 34). Here the image of Mardou is like that of Jesus on the cross: innocent, exposed, vulnerable, and hung up on a wooden threshold between existence and oblivion, between a sense of self and the utter loss of self. (To further this Passion analogy, before long, Mardou is coldly looked upon by a group of leering witnesses who make no move to help her.) Enraptured with the picture of Mardou perched naked on the fence, Kerouac underscores the mystical aspects of this moment with a rhapsody to its universal significance (*TS* 34). In Kerouac's vision, Mardou is an archetypal Indian Madonna who personifies the entire history of her people back to their Asiatic roots. She exists poised astride space and time in this moment before she comes down off the fence to seize her ecstasy and realize her divine aspect. Even as she is intuiting "visions of truth" (*TS* 35), she (like Gerard in *Visions of Gerard*) bemoans her powerlessness and raises a complaint to the God who made her (and all human existence) "so decayable and dieable and harmable" (*TS* 36). She receives an oracle of sorts atop the wooden fence that encourages her independence and self-sufficiency until the final apocalyptic moment (*TS* 36).

This realization marks a turning point in Mardou's flip (i.e., her ecstatic initiation). She has faced oblivion. Perched on the existential fence, she has internalized the lesson of mortality and knows, now, that time returns us all to a transcendent origin. Transfigured, Mardou is emboldened and able to take action now. She gets down off the fence and moves back into the world.

She borrows some clothes from a stranger, then some money (two dollars) from a friend in order to buy a brooch, which she explains will be "the first symbol" in her new life, an outward sign of her inward journey. Mardou's reincorporation into the tribe is marked by a new power and confidence. (Later, as part of the "same flip," she describes how she'd contend with men on their own physical terms by fist-fighting Jack Steen and arm wrestling Julien Alexander.) She waits for the stores to open in an all-night cafeteria where, before her flip, she would have been preyed upon, but now the roles are reversed because she is empowered. Now it is Mardou who stares at everyone, and they are afraid of her, sensing "some living danger in the apocalypse of her tense avid neck and trembling wiry hands" (*TS* 38). When the stores open, Mardou buys the brooch, and, with the ten cents she has left, two carefully selected picture postcards she adopts as "personal omen emblems" (*TS* 39).

Besides being able to neutralize the masculine threat and power of the male gaze, Mardou's new ecstatic impression of herself features a heightened sense of connection with everyone she sees (*TS* 40). This is followed by a surreal episode in a pet store wherein she "communicates" telepathically with the animals and the store attendant. By attributing a cosmic awareness to her, Kerouac portrays Mardou in shamanic terms that are shaded, as always, by his own Catholicism. After her night on the fence, after liberating herself from Wallenstein's bed, Mardou wanders San Francisco on Easter morning, resurrected (*TS* 42). Having attained her vision, she has managed a "safety and salvation" (*TS* 43). She has become aware of her integration in the cosmic design. Furthermore, she is intuitively compelled to spread the word of her ecstatic experience (her "vibration and new meaning") to others (*TS* 44). The "flipping Mardou," like Dean Moriarty in *On the Road*, is now a charismatic outsider who returns from the depths with a message of hard-earned optimism. She has become, in Eliade's terms, "the great specialist in the human soul" (8). She has become a shaman.

Mardou resolves the story of her flip by describing an expansive vision through a pane-glass window that dilates to include all of San Francisco before focusing on the central image of the fence upon which she perched the night before (*TS* 45). She intuits the "mystical unity" in the bop music that pours out of neighborhood jukeboxes (*TS* 48). Here, as in other novels in the Legend, Kerouac invokes bop jazz as a motif for expressing her triumph over her personal anguish. She is free and powerful. Before long,

4. The Subterraneans as Nadiral Ecstasy

though, there is a shift, during which Mardou recognizes and laments the transience of the mystical experience. She says, "God it was all the most beautiful thing that ever happened to me in its own way—but it was all sinister" (*TS* 46).

"It was all sinister." The tale of Mardou's flip implodes when she returns to her family in Oakland. They call the police, and she is hospitalized for her erratic behavior. Such is often fate of a shaman in the modern world. She is shuttled off to the margins, and her ecstasy is written off as madness. If, as John Lardas asserts, "madness [is] a way to cast off Faustian influence and ... reconnect to the universal macrocosm" (95), then sanity is a means of renouncing the legitimate identification with the universal macrocosm by which Mardou can reconnect to the rational and compartmentalized norm. The stay in the hospital shakes Mardou's faith in the experience of her flip as revelatory ecstasy, and she soon denies the whole thing to speed her release to the mainstream, where she will escape scrutiny (*TS* 49). She was out of there in two days.

Nevertheless, the noesis of Mardou's flip ecstasy—namely, her realization that she must be a woman who is independent and self-reliant—remains with her. (This highlights, by way of contrast, Leo's flip of dissolution, which comes later in the novel.) Furthermore, and significantly, Mardou's telling of this tale makes her equal in Leo's eyes to the great male heroes of his experience (*TS* 50). Leo's fascination with Mardou is now complete. He will now glorify her through great mental constructions and assignations in *The Subterraneans*. He will crown her in his confessional art.

But you can only be fascinated by something or someone that you don't really understand or fully know. Leo has listened to Mardou's story and is moved by it, but he doesn't understand it in the least. So, in another confessional moment that is darkly comic (and unintentionally so, I think), our narrator resolves to "show her more sexuality" (*TS* 50).

Apotheosis on Heavenly Lane: Mardou-as-Essence

> I don't want to be adored for what I merely represent to you.
> —Alanis Morrissette, "I'm Not the Doctor"

Shortly after their first sexual encounter and before recounting her ecstatic flip, Mardou informs Leo, "Men are so crazy, they want the essence, the woman is the essence, there it is right in their hands but they rush off erecting big abstract constructions" (*TS* 23). Leo agrees with her and, apparently quite unconscious of his chauvinism, assures her that the concept of "woman-as-essence" is an "old" idea of *his* own. Nevertheless, he remains characteristically ambivalent toward Mardou. Though he can savvy this female essence in theory, in his mind, he cannot embody this recognition, nor abide by it intuitively in his actions. Many tensions along these lines drive the narrative in *The Subterraneans* where it is the male "dingdong essence" vs. the female "bangtail essence," the mind vs. the soul, cognition vs. intuition, art vs. experience, mother-woman vs. lover-woman (*TS* 66). Such deeply rooted conflicts cause Kerouac to present the relationship between Leo and Mardou as a series of crises from the bedroom on out. In Mardou, Leo initially sees pride, beauty, beatitude, and sensitivity, while in himself he sees her from the perspective of a would-be macho man whose attitude toward women is admittedly limited (*TS* 12).

Leo objectifies the vagina as the female essence (*TS* 103). He sees Mardou's sex as a saving wellspring from which he can strengthen and rejuvenate himself. He initially worships at the altar of her body (*TS* 54). But later in the novel, after Mardou spurns him, his sense of worship is exposed as sense of ownership. Most of Leo's erotic memories of Mardou are self-serving to his bruised, sexually insecure male ego and barely veil his feelings of inadequacy in her presence. He consistently skirts explicit description of sex, waxes briefly metaphorical, then proclaims her as a goddess (or even a sister) to the reader (*TS* 71).

Sister, goddess, *campesino* bride "padding wifelike Ruthlike" after him in Mexico — such are the fantasies Leo constructs about Mardou (*TS* 40). If woman is the essence, then, for Leo, Mardou is the quintessence; such is the myth of love he lays on her. This is what he seeks and needs from her. In the end, however, Mardou asserts her authentic existence in the world independent from Leo as a lover and free, as well, from the contextual myths imposed on the female by the male. "'Look man,' she'd said ... 'don't call me Eve'" (*TS* 149). Straight out of a Lacanian paradigm, Leo is always trying to lay his story (and his body) onto Mardou. But in the purity of his confession, this doesn't fly in *The Subterraneans*.

4. The Subterraneans *as Nadiral Ecstasy*

Mardou's story caught in the web of the narrative is especially evident in the second part of *The Subterraneans* where Leo simultaneously reads, critiques, and sometimes cruelly scrutinizes a letter from Mardou while constantly interrupting her letter's narrative for the purposes of self-indulgent complaining (*TS* 75–83). Though Leo does little to justify his self-pity, he does seek to intellectually refine his "crudely male sexuality" by couching it in terms of Reichian analysis. Wilhelm Reich, an Austrian-born psychoanalyst and contemporary of Kerouac, theorized in his book *The Function of the Orgasm* that the fragmentation of the individual in modern society could be resolved by spontaneous sexual expression. The orgasm, "the little death," is the key to this breakthrough of sex-as-ecstatic-technique. This secularized mysticism of the body appeals to Leo, who, in his relationship with Mardou, consistently proceeds from a comprehensive state of confusion, weakness, and lack. He sees fullness and completion in Mardou, in the "onelove," but she wants no part of it. She tells Leo, "Oh don't pull that Reich on me in bed" (*TS* 64).

In the final analysis, Leo's fascination with and apotheosis of Mardou (what he calls his "love" for her) is always solipsistic, a product of his romanticized vision of minorities and his heroic self-image (*TS* 96).[4] Leo's apotheosis of Mardou does not lead them to any love of real substance, but casts the couple into a frightening emotional landscape where relationships must crash and burn and head toward the nadir.

Revulsion on Heavenly Lane: Crucifying the Madonna

> Mardou becoming the big buck nigger ... and I the little fag.
> — *The Subterraneans* 67

> Then it became abominable.
> — Frank Norris, *McTeague* 288

In *The Subterraneans*, Leo is constantly pulled between his "lived" experience and his re-created life on the page, between his carnal encounters with Mardou and his "asexual work" of writing (*TS* 57) where he retreats to his mother's house to build the "big abstract constructions" of his fiction. As Matt Theado notes, "Leo is split between discovering essence in a woman and discovering essence in his own mind, and for him one precludes the other" (114–15). In the end, the mind essence wins out. Mardou is long gone, but the novel remains.

The reader has known from the beginning of the monologue that the relationship between Leo and Mardou is doomed and, in fact, has already ended. Until the second part of the book, however, the nastiness of the particulars and the full confessional details of Leo's deeply troubled character are not fully revealed. His post-coital revulsion of Mardou is rooted in the same feeling that compels his fascination with her in the first place, namely, her race and her sex. The confessional mode here becomes pathetically frank and indicative of the darkest facets of Leo Percepied. In the first part of the novel, Leo's racist reflexes are alluded to in passing. Twice he mentions waking up with Mardou and being repulsed by the sight of her still asleep with the flecks of white pillow stuffing in "her black almost wiry hair" (*TS* 53). And the opening lines of Part 2 make this issue clear as Leo confesses that he "had doubts" about Mardou "because she was Negro" (*TS* 59). What ensues is a rhapsody of racist and sexist revulsion, ambivalence, and paranoia that is, at times, shocking, and always nadirally indicative.

Whereas Leo initially harbored fantasies of domestic bliss with Mardou beyond any racial concerns, now he's dubious. He concludes that his family, living in the South, would disapprove and that a long-term relationship with her would fragment his life beyond repair (*TS* 62). His disgust with Mardou's negritude (and her body) waxes bizarre as he makes a confession about seeing her naked and seeing a penis between her legs (*TS* 63). When Mardou submits to closer examination, Leo realizes that this was some kind of hallucination and swings back to his initial fascination with her that is less a matter of sexual attraction than cheap ego boosting. He consoles himself that she is quite the hipster-trophy on his arm, and that their being together is a constant barb to the other subterraneans who have always treated him in a suspicious and unfriendly manner, a fact that he resents (*TS* 64).

But when Charles Bernard (legendary hipster in *The Subterraneans*) wrongly accuses Mardou of stealing a pornographic picture from his apartment, Leo, in a telling loyalty crisis, cannot raise himself above the basest of racial stereotypes to defend her. Repeatedly he asks Mardou about the missing picture, convinced that she did it. Repeatedly she not only explains

4. The Subterraneans as Nadiral Ecstasy

that she didn't take the picture (which showed a homosexual act), but also that she wouldn't even want it in the first place, and couldn't have taken it if she did as there were no pockets in her outfit. This is all for naught because Leo confesses to the reader that his "deepest doubt" is that Mardou was out to steal his "white man heart" and sacrifice him in a ritual (*TS* 67–68).

Though Leo admits that he's locked in a paranoia fueled by alcohol, marijuana, and jealousy, what he cannot consciously admit (though it is clear in his spontaneous confession — so what's the need?) is that he's also patently racist and misogynist. As the monologue rolls on, he swings erratically and with incrementing frequency between loving Mardou and loathing her. He can no longer regard Mardou as a Beat Madonna and "essential woman" (as he could in the first stages of the affair). Now she is a thief, a social pariah, and, when she eventually forsakes Leo's madness for a tryst with subterranean newcomer Yuri Gligoric (based on poet Gregory Corso), she is a "whore" and a "bitch" (*TS* 131). Even the "essence" of Leo's initial sexual devotion to Mardou takes on strange and threatening overtones of castration (*TS* 104–5). Clearly these confessions reveal substantially more about Leo than they do about Mardou. He is repulsed by her strength and injured by her because of his own weakness, dependency, and, as we shall see, sexual ambivalence. He has internalized the malignant glare cast by white America on mixed-race relationships and, furthermore, abides by its censure (*TS* 93–94). For all his progressive sympathetic rhetoric as a Beat, Leo Percepied is not immune to the racist legacy of this culture.

Finally, Leo is of two minds toward Mardou's womanhood because of a self-hatred caused largely by the closeted homoerotic leanings he cannot hide from Mardou or the reader. In this context, "making it" with Mardou becomes the key to Leo's revulsion and flight. Leo's nadiral logic works like this: "Mardou is dirty and hateful because I am dirty and hateful and we've had sex." Instead of love, tenderness, and respect, Leo now transfers all of his anguish and psychological violence onto Mardou in order to torment and mortify her, to try to pull her into his schizophrenic vortex, to destroy their relationship in the "dark star" of his jealousy and self-loathing. And Kerouac writes this confession, not so much to secure forgiveness (from whom?), but to redeem the human catastrophe he's become in the ecstasy of art, in this spontaneously composed monument to his self-caused pain, for whatever it's worth.

Leo's Flip: Disintegration Suite, the Aberrant Technique, and Mardou-as-Man

> This is the confession of a man who can't drink.
> —*The Subterraneans*, 77

Mardou's ecstatic flip, though terrifying, renders her, for a time, strong and confident. But in *his* flip, Leo sinks to a more perfect nadir where nightmares and hallucinations become indistinguishable, and he orchestrates his own misery and loss. It happens in a dream. Leo dreams that he and Mardou are naked in bed in the midst of a crowd (*TS* 86). Leo, in the dream, gets up from the bed to pour some wine from a bottle suspiciously hidden in Mardou's dresser. When he turns to the bed, he sees that the new subterranean poet, Yuri, has taken his place with Mardou. Leo will obsess on this dream until it becomes a self-fulfilling prophecy by the end of the monologue.

Mardou is forced to share Leo's obsession with this dream. These lovers in *The Subterraneans* re-create their own world. Leo and Mardou now move through an emotional terrain fraught with opposition. Leo's impulse in the relationship, as detailed earlier, swings between Reichian breakthroughs and sheer disgust with Mardou's sex and race. Tired of Leo's ambivalence, which she at once internalized and seemingly overcame in her flip, Mardou sets herself on a course of self-reliance. Try as she might, she cannot love this man who so loathes himself (and her much of the time). However, they are now locked in the affair, and the sway it holds over them, the changes it puts them through, is toxic, to say the least. Their relationship transforms the external world as Leo's delusions bleed into reality. In this tale of ersatz, neurotic, lopsided, and darkly confused love called *The Subterraneans*, the external world mimes Leo's emotions and hang-ups. They are "lost in the actual physical manifestation of the mental condition [they'd] been in now together for two months" (*TS* 128).

4. The Subterraneans as *Nadiral Ecstasy*

Although verbal communication between the two is consistently stunted and overlayed by Leo's "problems," Mardou, after her flip, exhibits a telepathic understanding of Leo thoughts. He can hide nothing from her. She's well ahead of him, empowered with a kind of empathic X-ray vision (*TS* 125). Even though Mardou can now see into the black hole of Leo's schizophrenia, it becomes a threat to her own sanity. She drinks more than she ever did before and skips appointments with her analyst. Leo, as Mardou sees it, is trying to "erect" a two-souled schizophrenia and trap her in it.

Adding to the downward spiral of this whole affair is a constant binge of alcohol and marijuana, with entire nights spent in bars until dawn listening to jazz. It all melds into an aberrant ecstatic technique that cannot be maintained. They drink and "blast" at the homes of Leo's (mostly gay) writer-acquaintances and talk literature. Leo insists to Mardou that these are "important literary moments" (*TS* 72). However, all these subterranean happenings, in their sheer excess, become pseudo-events in Mardou's eyes. Soon she waits them all out in silence, often suffering from her telepathic awareness of a general scorn.

Selfishly, Leo drags Mardou on his own bumbling trip day and night. When Yuri Gligoric becomes part of the scene, Leo spies him as an immediate threat to his own identity as a lover and a writer. (Throughout the Legend, it's so often the crisis of discrete worlds colliding for Kerouac, really.) Yuri, like Frank Carmody (William Burroughs) and Adam Moorad (Allen Ginsberg), is a writer of great talent in Leo's estimation. Unlike Carmody and Moorad (and perhaps Leo himself), Yuri is young, handsome, and simply heterosexual. But Leo's greatest fear, even more than Yuri cutting in on his relationship with Mardou, is that the new interloper wants to replace him as a Beat idol (*TS* 90–91).

In his nadiral ecstasy in the subterranean realm, Leo is no longer the young lion, and warily eyes the next generation. Therefore, Leo takes Yuri under his wing as a "young brother" more as a defensive strategy to protect his literary and sexual territory. But he can't save himself from his own delusions and the self-destructive instincts of his nadiral appetite. He can't let go of the "cuckold dream" though Mardou truthfully denies, at this point, any romance between herself and Yuri (*TS* 118). This dream comes to dictate and realize Leo's fatalistic view of his relationship with Mardou.

The "cuckold dream" necessarily evolves into a self-fulfilling prophecy with a little help from Leo's drunken forays into the gay fringes of his disintegration.

Leo's massive alcoholic intake often relaxes the guilt of his homoerotic impulses. Leo confesses that he has gained a reputation "as a big fag" (*TS* 84). The description of his meeting with Arial Lavalina (Gore Vidal) shows an inebriated blurring of his literary and homosexual attractions (*TS* 73–74). In this episode, Leo sends Mardou home while he returns to a bar called The Mask for another of his "important literary moments." It is a troubling sequence full of paradox, contradiction, and confusion that marks Leo's descent into a full loathe-confessional made in the nadir. Is Leo boasting or is he humble? Is he titillated or sickened? Guilty as charged, simultaneously, on all counts, it seems — the singularity of his darkly ecstatic realization stands forth in the depths of this confession.

In another instance of drunken infatuation, possibly the very night after the meeting with Lavalina cited above, Leo falls all over someone he describes as a "beautiful faun boy." On this night, Mardou gives Leo an ultimatum — choose between him or her (*TS* 76). Receiving no answer, she leaves Leo to his questionable dalliances in The Mask. Even though Mardou returns to The Mask and they eventually spend the night together in her apartment, the tone of Leo's admission is perplexing, to say the least. "[Once] more I'd been a bad boy and again ludicrously like a fag" (*TS* 77). So far now from the female essence, this "Heavenly Lane-of-a-book" has become a confession of repressed homosexuality.[5]

Later in the monologue, a handsome young writer named Harold Sand catches Leo's fancy. Again (as with Lavalina and "the beautiful faun boy") the language of Leo's confession betrays a clear, though confused, attraction that's at once literary and physical. This dalliance causes him to spend even less time with, and pay less attention to, Mardou (*TS* 113). Throughout *The Subterraneans*, the male (i.e., Sand and Lavalina) is linked to the artistry and literary ambition that are the narrator's primary turn-ons. Now Leo, in his drunkenness, often finds himself "avoiding Mardou's womanness" (*TS* 116).

As further testament to Leo's sexual confusion, it is conversely notable that the three occasions in the monologue where he is *most attracted* to Mardou — and explicitly confesses his "love" for her — are instances where

4. The Subterraneans *as Nadiral Ecstasy*

she acts out and impresses Leo *as a man*. The first instance is the forceful impact of Mardou's flip-story. As discussed, this puts her in the company of that which, truth be told, Leo desires even more than the female lover — the male buddy:

> I had never heard such a story from such a soul except from the great men I had known in my youth, great heroes of America I'd been buddies with ... the boys beat on the curbstones seeing symbols in the saturated gutter, the Rimbauds and Verlaines of America on Times Square [*TS* 49–50].

The significance of Kerouac's choosing Rimbaud and Verlaine, players in one of the most pathological gay love affairs in all literary history, to epitomize these "buddies" of his can't be minimized. No sooner does Leo sense this forbidden affinity than he declares that his feelings toward Mardou were "like love" (*TS* 50). In the second example of this "Mardou-as-man" phenomenon, she imitates the stride of Jack Steen, another surly subterranean (*TS* 69–70). Again, Leo confesses his love for her in this impersonation. And the third instance of Leo's love for Mardou gushing to the top of his confession occurs when she's wrestling with Adam Moorad (with Leo's encouragement). Here, Leo sees her as "so great, buddy like, joining in, humble and meek too and a real woman ... I suddenly loved her" (*TS* 90). Wrestling with men, imitating men, suffering like a man — if only Mardou had *been* a man, it seems, Leo might have found the salvation of his "onelove."

Significantly, when Leo's worries about Mardou and Yuri are still only a hypothetical torture, he wishes he could see "old Carmody somehow" (*TS* 130). So, depressed with his "woman troubles," Leo leaves Mardou to eat her dinner alone. He wants to see his homosexual friend because, as he figures it, "I know he'll understand how sad I am now" (*TS* 131). Leo is going all to pieces, diving into the depths.

The key to the dissolution of Leo Percepied's personality is his many-souled confusion. The only identity that congeals to him from this nadiral flip is that of "writer." That is what he bargained for, after all, in *Doctor Sax*, what he sold his soul for, wasted his love for; and in *The Subterraneans*, it's what he mortifies his ego for — the story of his life, nothing more. What lesson could there possibly be in that for him or us, shamanic or otherwise?

Darkness on Heavenly Lane: Mother's Face, Feet of Clay, and Agony in the Railyard

> I don't want to live in this beastly world.
> —*The Subterraneans* 9

Through his doom-regimen of alcohol and narcotics and its attendant paranoia, it becomes clear to Leo that, at some point, Mardou is going to bail on him (*TS* 140). Respectfully, almost funereally in *The Subterraneans*, he again quotes Mardou's letter, this time without any overlaid scrutiny or comments. Leo's engaged in the end game now, closing in on the nadir of this affair.

The fitful night of drunken forgetfulness spent wrestling with Adam and Frank at their place is followed by the hung-over morning scene so often described with anguish throughout Kerouac's Legend. This was a "final hangover that said to [him], 'Too late'" (*TS* 141). The world becomes a hostile and jagged place for Leo. He cannot eat. He cannot rest. His loss magnifies and becomes phantasmal: "[C]ouldn't stop, had to walk as if someone was going to die soon, as if I could smell the flowers of death in the air, and I went in the South San Francisco railyard and cried" (*TS* 141). What happens there, second only to the three-day composition of this work a few months later, is the shamanic crux of the novel: the dark ecstasy of vision, ritual death, and noesis.

Though Mardou's infidelity hasn't even occurred yet, Leo's convinced of her loss beyond any illusions (*TS* 141). Under a newly risen moon in the railyard, he finds himself in a personal Gethsemane-like agony. In the Gospel of Luke, an angel appears to Jesus in the garden to comfort him the moment he gives himself over to the will of the Father, a surrender that makes his Passion and death inevitable (Luke 22:43). Here, Leo, like Jesus, is alone, crying, when he faces the inevitability of his own loss and sorrow. In the railyard, Leo acquiesces to a fate he himself has predestined. The object of his paranoia has been fulfilled. Utterly incapable of consoling himself, for Leo the nadir shines, as it always will, with vision: "[Seeing] suddenly, not in the face of the moon, but somewhere in the sky as I looked up and hoped to figure, the face of my mother" (*TS* 141).

The lover-woman is replaced in Leo's tormented consciousness by

4. The Subterraneans as *Nadiral Ecstasy*

the mother-angel who brings a message of asexual doting care, speaking in French (*TS* 142). This provides a maudlin prelude to Leo's inevitable confession of his responsibility for what has happened in his relationship with Mardou, and the just condemnation of his crimes against her female essence. Only after the merciful vision of his mother's face leaves Leo broken and cracked in his unworthiness does he access the metaphorical import of this nadiral ecstasy.

> Something fell loose in me — O blood of my soul I thought and the Good Lord or whatever's put me here to suffer and groan and on top of that be guilty and gives me flesh and blood that is so painful the — women all mean well — this I knew — women love, bend over you — you'd as soon betray a woman's love as spit on your own feet, clay [*TS* 143].

Like Mardou earlier in the novel, like the biblical Jeremiah and Job, here Leo complains about his suffering humanity and God's responsibility for that condition.

His allusion to the Old Testament Book of Daniel ("clay feet") introduces the prelude to Leo's full and final confession. The prophet Daniel's interpretation of King Nebuchadnezzar's dream of the giant statue with a golden head, silver chest and arms, bronze hips, iron legs, and feet "partly of iron and partly of clay" is particularly echoed in Leo's nadir in a few respects (Daniel 2:31). In the biblical dream, a stone breaks loose from a cliff apparently of its own accord ("without anyone touching it"), strikes the statue at its alloyed feet, and destroys it. In context of *The Subterraneans*, as Leo might see it, the gold head is the "mind essence," while the torso's arms and legs, less refined by degrees, are the "crudely male essence." The alloyed feet become the weak foundation of this great construction for a particularly telling reason.

Daniel interprets the statue in terms of a succession of increasingly decadent and fractious empires that are to follow Nebuchadnezzar's rule. Of the statue's feet, the Book of Daniel says, "You also saw that the iron was mixed with clay. This means that the rulers of that empire will try to unite their families by intermarriage, but they will not be able to, any more than iron can mix with clay" (Daniel 2:43). The analogy belies the primary reason why his love for Mardou was always fated for a catastrophic end. The mix of a white homoerotic man playing at heterosexual devotion to a black woman made their relationship ripe for destruction from the outset, not from a rock thrown by an invisible hand but from Leo's own ignorance, sexual ambivalence, and loathing. Leo realizes this in the railyard.

In a spasm of self-recrimination, he speaks to himself "in the bottom" of this episode (*TS* 143). He recognizes himself as "a bum, a drunkard" who is unworthy even of his mother's love. Leo is fully conscious now (as is his mother) of his utter impotence in the world to

> take care of yourself and even find and hold the love of another protecting woman — and all because you are poor Ti Leo — deep in the dark pit of night under the stars of the world you are lost, poor, no one cares, and now you threw away a little woman's love because you wanted another drink with a rowdy fiend from the other side of your insanity [*TS* 143].

The lesson for Leo, and the fruition of his nadiral ecstasy in *The Subterraneans*, is "know thyself." After that, *consumatum est*.

Leo leaves the railyard having given himself over to his own latest apocalypse. Though it's doubtful that Leo really repents of the sins that have dropped him in this nadir, repentance along those lines was never the goal here. The redemption of Leo's confession in *The Subterraneans* is *artistic*, not moral. His individual experience, no matter how flawed, is, at its roots, ecstatic and worthy.

Orphic Joker

> The greatest key to courage is shame.
> —*The Subterraneans* 29

> The process is one of redemption, not of mere reversion to natural health, and the sufferer, when saved is saved by what seems to him a second birth, a deeper kind of conscious being than he could enjoy before.
> —James, 157

After all the offenses to Mardou's dignity and affection, after the crimes against her gender and race, too many to mention here (though exhaustively and swiftly confessed in the novel), as Leo has "prophesied" all along — one night, he goes to see her and, ominously, the light is out on Heavenly Lane. The monologue unwinds quickly from there. He soon

4. The Subterraneans *as Nadiral Ecstasy*

learns that his cuckold dream has come true on the very night he was crying in the railyard having his nadiral moment of lucidity.

On their way to a movie, Mardou confesses that she and Yuri have slept together (*TS* 148). Her tone is unapologetic and indicative of the self-reliance and independence achieved earlier in her ecstatic flip. She asserts and marks this independence by purchasing a purple bandana, yet another emblem of her evolution and growth. She is a queen, above the mess that was her relationship with Leo. She pays his way into a movie called *Brave Bulls*. Leo empathizes with the bulls because he sees (and has known since his vision in the railyard) that his love with Mardou has been an event where he's been tortured and killed, though by his own doing. Again he weeps.

Back at Mardou's, the couple reprises their symposium on woman-as-essence and the male cathartic impulse to forsake that essence in order to rush off and "build big constructions," but it's an empty refrain (*TS* 151). Leo now has a Freudian sense of having been "pierced" by her "adultery" that he prophesied in the "cuckold dream" (*TS* 151). But when Leo falls into a reverie of exacting violent, masculine revenge on Yuri, something unexpected happens. Instead of falling further into the lacerating coil of his loathing, he experiences, in the novel's last line, an expansion of consciousness.

> [But] I continue the daydream and I look into [Yuri's] eyes and I see suddenly the glare of a jester angel who made his presence on earth all a joke and I realize that this too with Mardou was a joke.... And I go home having lost her love. And I write this book [*TS* 151-52].

Throughout the monologue, Leo has been blinded by his own confused, selfish interests, remaining unable, for the most part, to see any humor in his and Mardou's devolution as a couple. But from the nadir of his loss, this vision of Yuri as a jester/joker/trickster seems to come to him as a gift. It marks a redirection upward toward a salvific moment that is enabled by the relieving sense of the absurd. At the nadir of his entire journey with Mardou, this ability to laugh, to countenance the trickster at play in his pain, breaks Leo from his paralysis. And something of the trickster stance remains in his re-creation of the whole mess in this novel. As Lewis Hyde notes, "[The] Trickster starts out hungry, but before long he is master of the kind of creative deception that, according to a long tradition, is a prerequisite of art" (17). The creative deception of *The Subterraneans*, the reader discovers, is the book in hand, which is the single artifact rescued from a house burned down.

Throughout his career, Kerouac's ecstatic vision is so often a hybrid of various and often antithetical approaches. In *Doctor Sax*, for example, we saw him interweave Catholic tropes, archaic shamanic symbolism, Aztec myth, Faustian legend, and American pop iconography to establish the earliest portion of his Legend. In the loathing confession of this novel, albeit perhaps unconsciously, he again taps into a paradoxical shamanic narrative that reveals the nadiral aspect of his maturity. By simultaneously rendering Mardou's empowerment and Leo's disintegration, Kerouac lays claim to a wholeness for his narrator that is impossibly beyond his grasp by adding key elements of the Orphic myth to the narrative performance.

In Orpheus, we find a figure with whom Kerouac might well have compared himself, even as he so often perceives an affinity between his life and that of Jesus Christ, as we frequently see throughout his Legend. Orpheus, the primal voice that precedes and is contextual to the oral and written forms, embodies "the great freedom to embrace all things without being lost in confusion, the freedom to accept each life and everything and to renounce a world inhabited by fragmentation and division" (*TEOR* vol. 11, 112). Kerouac might similarly claim that his spontaneous prose technique is one that precedes and is contextual to traditional literary craft, and yields a fiction of singular integrity and freedom. For instance, the firstborn of the Orphic myth, Phanes, has two pairs of eyes, two different voices, and, most significantly, both male and female sex organs. In *The Subterraneans*, Leo Percepied (with eyes for the boys and the girls) is a type of dual character who can only realize his "onelove," complete and undifferentiated, in his spontaneous written confession. Mardou could not effect this wholeness in Leo even as Orpheus could neither enchant nor restrain the wild women sent by Dionysos to tear him to shreds.

> [Orpheus is] destroyed by what he most deeply despises: the feminine which brought to humankind the disease of birth and death. [Orpheus] embodies the purely masculine ... but he does so via the multiplicity of forms and by the roundabout path of polymorphism [*TEOR*, vol. 11, 114].

Kerouac adapts this strategy and view in *The Subterraneans* as Leo recognizes in himself a "womb" of creative potential, where before he had only acknowledged an agitated and incomplete maleness. And so, over three

4. The Subterraneans *as Nadiral Ecstasy*

consecutive days and nights in October 1953, he sat down at the typewriter to perform this mysterious fulfillment in which he resolved the tension between the male "dingdong" essence and the female "bangtail" essence. In other words, he wrote this novel because he was "[so] mad as to show I GOT MY OWN LITTLE BANGTAIL ESSENCE AND THAT ESSENCE IS MIND RECOGNITION" (*TS* 66–67). So, like the hermaphroditic Phanes, or the Zeus of the Orphic myth who impregnated himself by devouring his firstborn, Leo purports to be a pregnant god who brings to life a second creation of his own experience in writing. While this is a hilarious move, really, to a facile and entirely implausible summation of this modern American novel, his realization of an identity with the gods, from the shamanic perspective, is sound.[6]

Most of Kerouac's novels end on a winsome, hopeful note, regardless the proof of their nadiral content. We tend to laugh at that optimism because, when it comes to modern romance, Joseph Campbell aptly notes,

> The happy ending is justly scorned as a misrepresentation; for the world as we know it, as we have seen it, yields but one ending: death, disintegration, dismemberment, and the crucifixion of our heart with the passing of the forms that we have loved [26].

5

"In-stasy" and the *Book of Dreams*

In a letter to Malcolm Cowley, dated February 4, 1957, Kerouac describes his *Book of Dreams* as a "300 page tome of some excellence, spontaneously written dreams some of them written in the peculiar dream language of half-awake in the morning" (*JKSL 1957–1969* 9). Published in 1961, it contains more than 200 entries written between 1952 and 1960. While his novels show Kerouac in the ecstasy of his conscious experience written out, these transcriptions show us the subconscious "in-stasy" of his dreams.[1] Road-tripping through a haunted dreamscape that is often violent and frequently paradisal, the dreamer shows up, disappears, and slides unhinged through dimensions of space and time, knowledge, perception, and identity. In terms of his deep Buddhist interests, *Book of Dreams* is like a mandala, a wheel of his inner time. And his primary challenge (as always, I have contended) is shamanic: how can he translate these ineffable visions for himself and communicate them to the tribe? More specifically for Kerouac, the question was how to authenticate all that into language and still retain the eidetic quality of his dreams in the narration.[2] *Book of Dreams* is a written performance of Kerouac's most interior, subconscious life played out in the secret language of dreams in entries that range from wildly complex sagas to concrete single moments. Its tone can run from sacred to profane, bewildering to hilarious, often at the same time. He wrote these dreams down in pencil and they appear in the book (undated, untitled) in type, including a foreword, preface, and the author's "Table of Characters," which cross-references the names of recurring dream characters with their names in his other novels. This dream journal is an odd duck in the predominantly novelistic form of his "Legend of Duluoz," yet it is an integral and revealing complement *to*, and in many ways, source

5. "In-stasy" and the Book of Dreams

of, his novels. It provides a rewarding "participation mystique" to any serious reader of Kerouac in particular, or of dreams in general. Like Endymion, Kerouac finds everlasting sleep and knows a type of immortality under the lunar face of his *Book of Dreams*, only he wakes up to perform it on the page and reveal an eternity shot through with freight trains, ghosts, sex, chimeras, and, perhaps, "some excellence."

You Must Be Dreaming

We all dream, and, for the most part, know the difficulty of successfully putting our dreams into words (i.e., with a vivid of sense of detail, if not meaning). Though he admits that "the greatest deepest dreams are unrecoverable to the ordinary waking brain," Kerouac didn't fit that description (*BOD* 116). The years represented in this book show him at the disciplined height of his spontaneous prose practice that begins, always, in the "tranced fixation dreaming upon the object before you" (*GBO* 72). The dream is the fading subconscious artifact to be rescued, and the ultimate testing ground to be tried with his spontaneous prose technique. The alternative reality presented in dreams and the transient impressions they leave on the waking mind, for Kerouac, was the ideal landscape in which to race around and word-sketch like hell before the wipe-cut of consciousness. In the foreword and preface, he makes no pretense about interpreting the dreams and only claims to fish them out from the deep pool of the subconscious, in real time, once and for all (that is, spontaneously) in words, before they disappear. His project is to transcribe, as eyewitness, the weird nocturnal terrain in the minutes before it fades for good.

The interpretation of this book, or any book, is up to the reader. A person who thinks dreams are significant and revealing is liable to appreciate *Book of Dreams* on an initial reading, if not for its content, then perhaps for its style. A person who thinks dreams mean nothing significant at all either in themselves or in their interpretation will find *Book of Dreams* unreadable. What is a dream? What can it communicate? How to tell it?

Dreams present all of us with what Karl Jaspers calls "limit situations," which are fleeting experiences "in which the human mind confronts the restrictions and pathological narrowness of its existing forms, and allows itself to abandon the securities of its limitedness, and so to enter a new realm of self-consciousness" (Thornhill). To a shaman, a dream can be an initiatory experience, a source of calling and premonition, or a means of communicating with helping spirits in the trance of sleep.[3] To a holy man of any faith, a dream can be a mystical encounter with God.[4] To a Freudian, a dream is the theater of our waking repression.[5] To a Jungian, it is an archetype authenticated.[6] To a neuroscientist, the dream is a play of brain chemicals. "Theories shmeories!" (*BOD* 165). Among the seven modern Western approaches to dreams (some of which I've mentioned) Kelly Bulkeley notes in *The Wilderness of Dreams*, there is no consensus as to the definition and significance of dreams and dreaming. I agree with and can only be thankful for the different perspectives offered by each.

My writing about *Book of Dreams* here is more like a meditation and topical overview than an analysis. My approach will be syncretic of various notions about dreams and their possible meanings, even as Kerouac demonstrated an eclectic combination of spiritual approaches, ideologies and styles in his writing. I will discuss the techniques he uses to render dreams on the page. I hope to place some of these entries in a cultural context and show how they reflect the conscious "real" world that Kerouac, perhaps, sought to escape, reflect on, and/or resolve in his sleep. (Without shamanism in the interpretive mix, there is little resolution in *Book of Dreams*.)

As in all of Kerouac's work, I'm at least as interested in *how* he writes (his ecstatic technique) as *what* he says (its content and meaning). I found *Book of Dreams* baffling on both counts when I first read it in January 2000. However, reading and rereading this (or any book, of course) is like playing an instrument: the more you do it, the better you'll get at it, the more possibilities you will realize, and the more you will hear. Reading *Book of Dreams* and considering the prospect of its meaning is more like play — playing and replaying this book-instrument that's ecstatically fun, intellectually rigorous, and, here and there, unbearable. It's taken me ten years and four reads to "get it," at least this far.

"Secret Language" and Mystical Style

Eliade's claim that the innovative archaic "secret languages" used by the earliest shamans are responsible for the allegorical language we use today

5. *"In-stasy" and the* Book of Dreams

places Kerouac (as a modern dreamer/writer) in the shamanic continuum that, from the beginning, has always been tasked with communicating the fleeting and ineffable experience that is ecstasy (511). It's the same challenge and crisis that begets and tortures every art form: the mind outruns the medium. Language developed over time to represent the consensus objective reality is pushed beyond its sensible limits vis-à-vis the highly subjective dream experience. Therefore, Kerouac uses specific language strategies and styles to perform his dreams to the reader.

Like Joyce and other spontaneous writers before him, at times Kerouac will fabricate words, a kind of writing-in-tongues, to goof the limits of language in *Book of Dreams*.[7] Also, as is characteristic of all his work, these dream entries are necessarily confessional, though of his subconscious mind, not his deeds. They are often raw and amoral in tone, sometimes uncomfortably so.[8] Consistently, as a way of translating the subconscious process Freud calls "condensation," Kerouac writes many of the dream characters and settings in aggregate, which results in a simultaneous signification and plurality of identities, places and times. Kerouac explains that this is an accommodation to the limited capacity of the conscious filter "for the poor brain yearns" (*BOD* 24).[9] He encodes this composite nature by often using quotation marks to distinguish the plural characters and places in his dreams from their singular (conscious) referents.

Book of Dreams shows Kerouac watching/writing the "in-stasy" of his dreams in a simultaneous and self-referential narrative style that's complex and fluid throughout. There is no story traditionally told here (no plot, linear or otherwise). However, since dream episodes do overlap, intersect, dialogue with each other, and magnify themselves, there is a sense of an elastic narrative nonetheless. The style displays a quantum aspect of superposition, and proposes possibilities where the dream narrator can be both boy and man, lover and son, father and son, alive and dead, and (as in one entry) man and train (*BOD* 61). Like a shaman, the dreamer is "the *border crosser* who is able to be in different places at the same time, and who is domiciled in various worlds" (Mayer 94).

Of course, as commonly understood and used, language is a definitive art aimed at expressing specific meanings in sequence. However, dreams are artless, replete with unlimited meanings all at once that patently defy language. The idea of *writing down* your dreams is like showing up at a chess match in a catcher's mitt. If a dream is a kind of ecstasy, and (along with death) our common mystical experience (so impossible, it seems, to communicate), then the dream has meaning, a sense of its own, what William James calls the "noetic quality." To put dreams into words, part of Kerouac's strategy involved taking language built for the "one-or-the-other" world, and making it show the "both/and" world.

Metaphor is best fit for this purpose because "by being and not being the thing, by referring always to something other than the thing-in-itself, it is capable of bringing together the image and the referential gap of the linguistic elaboration" (Marozzo 703). Metaphor is the language marker of "both/and" we're most comfortable with, and an essential instrument of Freudian dream analysis. Besides the manifest meaning in many of the entries (of which there is no lack),[10] root metaphors recur in *Book of Dreams* that enable the reader to orient himself in the dreamscape, and perceive, if not exactly the story, then at least the themes revealed there.

The major Freudian dream symbols abound in *Book of Dreams*. Snakes, airplanes, knives, and guns for the male. Ships, caves, cellars, and houses for the female. Movement in and out, ascending and descending of stairs, and so forth, for the sexual act. The latent meaning of these metaphors reveals the dreamer's general sexual anxiety that is well documented in the rest of Kerouac's Legend and biography. I count no less than 37 entries that exhibit either manifest or latent sexual content in *Book of Dreams*. But Kerouac, based on his Buddhism, it seems, didn't think much of Freud's take on dreams. "[D]ream analysis is only a measurement of the maya-like and has no value — Freudianism is a big stupid mistaken dealing with causes & conditions instead of the mysterious essential, permanent reality of Mind Essence" (*BOD* 158). Suffice it to say that anyone who's ever shown up naked in high school (or anywhere) in a dream will share some humorous sympathetic moments with Jack in this volume. For now, I'll focus on the dreams between the narrator and the major recurring characters, living and dead, real and imagined, and see where that takes us.

Dad Dreams

"LAST NIGHT MY FATHER WAS BACK in Lowell — Oh Lord, O Haunted life" (*BOD* 11). Kerouac's father, Leo, who died in May 1946,

5. "In-stasy" and the Book of Dreams

shows up early in *Book of Dreams* (the fourth entry), and frequently reappears thereafter. As in his novels, Lowell remains the object of Kerouac's nostalgia for paradise (as I'll elaborate upon later). In the "dad dreams," Lowell is a place to cavort with the dead and gone, an especially strange, ambivalent paradise. Leo is dull, listless, and dying (again). A ghost-in-waiting, he loafs around Lowell in a kind of limbo half-life. Jack mostly wishes Leo would just die (again). He'll eventually see Leo hung for making anti-fascist remarks on page 89. But before (and after) that entry (because Leo continues to pop in every so often after his hanging, anyway), there is no joy in these encounters with his father, simply the resigned understanding of death that is part of the shamanic skill set. For the shaman, death is a known and familiar state (Eliade 510). Kerouac's conscious familiarity with death in *Visions of Gerard* and *Doctor Sax* is matched by a subconscious affinity with it in *Book of Dreams*. In these dreams, death is the object Kerouac stares at, transfixed. Leo becomes a root metaphor that expresses Kerouac's ultimate existential concern.

The noesis of the visions in these dreams can seem bleak. Leo's bloated posthumous presence is no promise of an afterlife according to Kerouac's Catholic upbringing, nor is it a Buddhist nirvana[11]; it's just extra time on the clock to contemplate our common death. Leo is a real drag. In a later visitation, after Leo's been hung, Kerouac laments, "This is our sweet Papa of starry night pasts when we grow up and grow old in this world the least of which you can say is that it leaves a bad taste in your mouth" (*BOD* 106). In the variety of shamanic myths about "The Difficult Passage" (i.e., death), simply put, you don't want to be "overweight" because that indicates you didn't make it through the initiation to the spirit world. Eliade explains that he who makes this passage in "lightness" and "swiftness" has transcended the human condition and become a spirit (485). *Book of Dreams* presents no resolution (as yet) to the existential dilemma-made-flesh as personified in Leo's corporeal ghost.

So, in a characteristic move, in the initial dream of his father Kerouac condenses Leo's identity in this "overtime" failed passage with his own. "I think I see his true soul — which is like mine ... or I'm my father myself and this is me" (*BOD* 12). Here, in dream and on the page, Kerouac is spying the soul and communing with the dead, an essentially shamanic performance. Though he later claims (in one dream only) that everything we lose in this life will be regained in heaven (*BOD* 40), the prevalent sense in this volume often makes you wonder if this is so. His trademark tone of sadness (and frequent invocation of the word "sad" in *Book of Dreams*)[12] throws a shade of doubt on it.

In the second father dream, Kerouac merges Leo (the biological father) and Cody (Neal Cassady, the Beat father) "into the One Father image of Accusation [that] is mad at me because I missed my local, my freight, I fucked up with the Mother Image down the line, I did something childish (the little boy writing in the room) and held up the railroads of men" (*BOD* 13). This dream is indicative of Kerouac-as-writer in a few significant ways. First, it shows his middle-class preoccupation with employment. (The first few lines of most entries in *Book of Dreams* contain at least a passing mention of the narrator and/or other characters having secured this or that job.) In this dream (as often in the period before his literary fame), he is working on the railroad. Trains will get you absolutely anywhere in Kerouac's dreamscape. All told, trains are mentioned in more dreams than are cars, ships, or planes. Apropos of the "in-static" experience, houses, bungalows, cottages, attics, apartments, and myriad interiors (especially cellars) predominate over open vistas in the *Book of Dreams* terrain. But even when his dreams manifest a honeycomb of interiors, the access of the trains is complete. Trains become the metaphor for the real "get 'er done" masculine ethos that was always problematic for Kerouac. The trains, in this and other dreams, are going so dangerously fast that he's afraid to jump on. In *Book of Dreams* Kerouac is often hiding, protecting, or otherwise sort of freaking out over his "culpable revealing manuscripts" that identify him as a writer, and a screw-up (20).

"Screwing-up" is a prominent theme in *Book of Dreams*, as is the dreamer's recurring ambivalence toward writing as an immature (or "unmanly") career choice. (Both are standard throughout the Duluoz Legend.) The narrator often appears *in media res* having just made, or about to make, some mistake about which he is anxious. In this instance, he is both a man with a job and a "little boy writing in a room," screwing up and being taken to task. The Leo/Cody/father composite personifies Kerouac's uneasy relationship with authority in general, and the traditional masculine role of the responsible "good worker" he felt was expected of him. The narrator's tone is that of a man-child slacker who is chided by

5. "In-stasy" and the Book of Dreams

Dad for writing stories like a child when he should be out working the rails like a man. The sense of discomfort established by this image makes the meanings of the "dad dreams" fairly apparent. But the hierarchy of this dream implies that it's "the Mother Image down the line" that runs the show.

Mom Dreams

As in his waking life, Kerouac's mother was a major and welcome companion. Ever faithful, ever loving, solicitous and caring, she participates in Kerouac's dream life to the max. These entries are thoroughly unapologetic, often tender, and sometimes raw and darkly humorous. She hops trains with him (30), leaves him to go to Chicago for "an abortion" (34), goes driving in a car with him and a bunch of kids (39), she looms over sexually charged scenes with his ex-wives and lovers in dreams (103, 135, 177), she lives with him in a fellahin domesticity where they subside on spectral detritus (42), and, in one instance, Kerouac dreams of the two of them together in a sexual and languorous moment (123). Of the all the iconic figures in the Legend of Duluoz (such as his father, Neal Cassady, his brother Gerard, his boyhood friend Sebastian Sampas — all "ghosts" with whom he communes in this ecstatic technique), it is his mother who abides as the most viable "helping spirit" in his cosmos. A particularly vivid entry telescopes down to the nitty-gritty value of Mother in a dream both beautiful and pathetic.

In this dream, Kerouac goes to New Orleans, where a war has broken out — nationwide calamity, general unrest. He runs into Cody, notes the sad shape of his *über*-hero, and sees in it not only Cody's failure, but also his own. Cody has a broken nose, is unemployed and in a state of complete breakdown (*BOD* 85–86). The noesis thus far in this dream is foreboding. Cody Pomeray, besides being a portrayal of a flesh-and-blood person named Neal Cassady, was also a character that Kerouac, at least in part, dreamed up. When it came to the Beat impulse, as Cassady went, so went Kerouac (at least for a significant amount of time on the page). But Cassady's vitality, as Kerouac's own, followed a characteristically shamanic and entropic arc that evinced a kind of devolution.[13] Whatever vestigial shamanic powers

Kerouac (as modern writer) and Cassady (as modern avatar) possessed had weakened over the course of their lives even as the shamanic ecstasy has decayed over time. In this entry, Kerouac sees this as "a serious reality." What could rescue this nightmare and its waking trauma?

He leaves Cody and dream-jumps on home, to his living room. No war, just safety. No desperate vision of the Beat breakdown. Just his mother, who cares for him and looks over him "with an expression of unfathomable meaning I know is love on earth" (*BOD* 86). (The scene parallels Leo Percepied's vision of maternal salvation in *The Subterraneans*.) Though all else has degraded and fallen short, his mother abides, endures, and never fails to play Madonna to his divine child. It is both a lovely image and a pathetic one.

Kid Dreams and the Nostalgia for Paradise

There's been much conjecture as to the degree that arrested development played in Kerouac's life and writing. Was he a boy who refused to grow old, who regressed "over-fondly" to his youth and dwelt there on the page, psychologically expatriated from the duties of maturity? I think such claims are probably valid. This nostalgia was an essential tool of his trade, and integral to his ecstatic technique. As noted earlier (in close readings of *Visions of Gerard* and *Doctor Sax*), in *Book of Dreams* Lowell remains the root metaphor for a childhood Kerouac lost but never abandoned (as long as he could dream and write). For him, it is the setting that evokes (and functions in the same way as) the Cosmic Mountain that shamans climb in dreams during their initiatory illness and then later visit on their ecstatic journeys. "To summarize very briefly," Eliade writes, "palaces, royal cities, and even simple houses were believed to stand at 'The Center of the World,' on the summit of the Cosmic Mountain" (269). (*Doctor Sax* itself is a narrated dream and tells the full story of Kerouac's boyhood Lowell, as discussed earlier.) The "kid dreams" in *Book of Dreams* elaborate on and presage the paradisal significance of childhood and the "child essence" evident in much of his other work.

The word "paradise," meaning the "abode of the righteous, a place of extreme original beauty and delight," comes to us through the Latin

5. *"In-stasy" and the* Book of Dreams

paradisus, from the Greek *paradeisos*, which means "park or pleasure ground," from the even earlier Iranian *pairi daeza*, which simply means "enclosure" (*Random House Unabridged* 1406). For Kerouac, childhood Lowell, enclosed in time with its locales and milieu, is the center of the world and an ecstatic creative locus. Lowell is his "Hugeroom House of Eternity" (*BOD* 115). In *Book of Dreams*, the child counterpart to the man becomes an inner-other, a muse, and a means of communing with his "child's soul in a grown-up body" in order to fathom a kind of redemption (*BOD* 47).

In twenty entries, Kerouac transports back to the 1930s Lowell as a kind of Adam in the Eden of his existence. He writes, "I'm just a little kid and I just woke up to the fact of the morning of life—and stand in the yard, dew wet" (*BOD* 38). There, sports and play, the serious goofing of youth, make his world go round. The children of Lowell take "railroad buses to pray novenas in church" (*BOD* 80), and they play "fungoes" with balls of rolled-up tape (*BOD* 91). What Kerouac describes as the happiest dream of his life shows a riotous adult presence and awareness transposed onto a reverie of childhood past, and contains all the major motifs, metaphors, tones and themes of *Book of Dreams*.

In the "Night of Miraculous Dreams" (*BOD* 46–50), normal life in America is shut down due to a "national catastrophe," even as the flood undeniably intervened in the Lowell status quo in *Doctor Sax*. With violent riots and bodies in the street, this dream presents Kerouac with a nightmare that he again erases by a flight to Lowell. Here he lands in the midst of a great festival of family and friends during which, in dream elision, he succumbs "to the sexual invitation in public of a girl or woman who wants to prove that men are not priests" (*BOD* 49). (This evolves into a kind of apology for male sexuality that was clearly an afterthought.) The eventual vision of this dreamer as composite man-child is thoroughly modern and unsentimental in its tone, as well as both Vedantic and shamanic in meaning.

"All children are gorgeous," he writes, "because they are the beginnings of our evil, make golden foundations for mountains of crap our later years multiply and ferment our early childhood years are not years at all but a sweet outpouring of eyes" (*BOD* 48). The sacred perception of the child *and* the jaded experience of the adult coexist in this dream. The dreamer recognizes childhood as part of samsara, the Buddhist (and before that Hindu) concept of the series of death and rebirth to which we are all subject. (In *Mexico City Blues* Kerouac calls it "The Wheel of the Quivering Meat Conception" [211].) Also, his reference here to the "outpouring of eyes" that is childhood is a common shamanic trope used to describe the ecstatic experience. "My body is all eyes. / Look at it! Be not afraid!" (Eliade 290).

In *Book of Dreams*, Kerouac seeks to rescue the child from the man, to write from that perspective and abide there for the sake of his vision quest. Childhood is a fundamental condition of his creative writer's soul because children have "that crazy potentiality, potency, of language" that he needs to perform his dreams authentically (*BOD* 170). There is a need to "be in your soul the child the same child again, forget literature and English" (*BOD* 34). What most characterizes this dream as "the happiest of this life" (as well as other dreams that he refers to as "happy" in *Book of Dreams*) is that he is received, recognized, and embraced by others. Conversely, other, more nightmarish entries often include references to being a stranger, unrecognized and ignored. In those instances, he writes (from beyond his childhood, beyond his grave even) that "my throat aches to find my way back to the place where I am mourned and I can't even remember any more where that is" (*BOD* 67). The final lesson of this happiest dream summarizes Kerouac's nostalgia for the paradise of childhood, and expresses the ultimate value of his "in-static" trips there on the pages of his dream catalogue. "We should never left Lowell — but now we're back with everything saved again" (*BOD* 50).

Throughout his Legend, Kerouac pursues a childhood that is doomed by maturity. In *Book of Dreams*, Kerouac amplifies this threat. Talk about kids "at risk." Children are held hostage at gunpoint in church (40), they work the treacherous railroad (43), outrun killers (80), and wander the world in a lost ship out of which, significantly, he emerges "with languidj" (79). Children are frequently cut adrift and left to their own devices.[14] Therefore, in his dreams one will often see Kerouac as the would-be protector of children (*BOD* 160). An entry in the critical (and increasingly nihilistic) final sequence of *Book of Dreams* typifies this role.

Here, Kerouac is a wounded savior (a shaman type) who flees the police and encounters a parade of children chanting his name. He then

5. "In-stasy" and the Book of Dreams

leads them joyously "into Mongolia" and notes, ominously, this was "dreamed the day after the publication of ON THE ROAD)" (*BOD* 173–74). It's a menacing postscript because it implies that the Beat impulse as he initially perceived it (innocent, childlike) was led *by his own device* to a barbarous place where it would be defiled and crushed because, like his modern America, this "Mongolia" is a place where he sees the vision of his "child's soul" broken, spit upon, and cursed at. (And all this recorded in the "happiest" dream of his life.) This entry (as do others that I'll discuss later in this chapter) reflects Kerouac's critique of the reception of the Beat impulse by both his critics and those who came enthusiastically in his wake. In the final analysis of *Book of Dreams*, there is no living in the paradisal past (a noesis that Kerouac performs in a much more formal and comprehensive way in *Vanity of Duluoz*, the final novel in his Legend). His nostalgia for paradise yields the same message here as it does in all of his work: a first-hand comprehension of the both/and nature of death that comes in images at once archaic and modern.

> I walk along home down dark Moody, dark Gershom ... to my dark house on Sarah — everything has that darkness of things buried in the ground decomposing — it's ME! — I see my tree sprouting from my hand now, I see November through the bone, I'm waiting for further Springs and blossoms for my black, I'm the Frankenstein of my own 6 foot grave goodbye little golden children of the glee mad world [*BOD* 41].

In the archaic traditions, the shaman is able to see himself as a skeleton freed from his mortal flesh (Eliade 62). For the narrator of this dream (as for the narrator in *Doctor Sax*), this skeletal vision is both a reminder of death and a sign of imminent transcendence. Similarly, the miraculous presence of a tree growing from his hand evokes the common shamanic symbol of the World Tree, another regenerative image.[15] This is a vision of a shamanic self that is ecstatic in the lost paradise. The narrator's identification with Frankenstein, however, undercuts the promise of this dream, somehow, with a sense of self-blame. In this dream, like Doctor Frankenstein, Kerouac realizes that he has dug his own grave. At this point, I am unsure of exactly how and why this is so. (Does "Frankenstein" trump "The Bone" and "The Tree"?) It is a tone and theme we see echoed in the self-laceration of *The Subterraneans* and the self-loathing of *Big Sur*.

However you cut it, in *Book of Dreams*, this entry is clearly a farewell to the "kid dream."

Now, for the world without a center.

"Shroudy Stranger/Traveler" Dreams

It's not until almost halfway into *Book of Dreams* that Kerouac describes a "shroudy stranger" as a "mortal enemy." Based on a kid named "Fish" who once punched him, this character becomes (characteristically in *Book of Dreams*) a composite type rather than a single presence. It is a significant root metaphor with multiple meanings in these dreams (and one that connects and coalesces with the meaning of other root metaphors in this work). Based on what we've discussed so far in this chapter, the Shroudy Stranger (or Traveler, as he is eventually called) might represent adulthood, the authoritarian status quo (literary or otherwise), and/or death itself. In any case, he is a looming, formidable and frightening adversary, who, Kerouac writes, emanates hostility even in his absence (*BOD* 78). In the first of these dreams, the narrator describes how time and again he has bested this Shroudy Stranger, but it takes all of his skills and cleverness to do so. He has to be at the top of his game. Kerouac describes these victories in terms that echo the shamanic cosmography and imagery (*BOD* 78). Kerouac has his skeletal vision and casts this stranger to the underworld in this dream. Nevertheless, in *Book of Dreams*, Kerouac sees him again and again.

Eventually, Kerouac is pursued by another iteration of the Shroudy Stranger, who is now some grown-up who wants to arrest him in a place that's part California, part Africa. The dreamer tries to escape by "shipping out," but that's a no-go. He then decides to hop a train that night and escape "for good," but that doesn't work either.

In due course, in a warped domestic scene shared with his (dead) father and (living) mother and sister, Kerouac rolls and smokes a joint. When Leo touches his shoulder in reproach, everything goes black. The blinded dreamer is terrified to realize that it's the "Shroudy Traveler" who's got hold of him (*BOD* 131). He continues to see an "out," not through childlike cleverness, not on a ship or train, but through a sense of Buddhist

5. "In-stasy" and the Book of Dreams

detachment, that is, "by not being concerned not believing in either life or death" (*BOD* 131). But that doesn't seem to work for long either.

Before the next visitation of the shroud, the dreamer is attacked by two birds who seek to pick out his brains through his ear. Creepy. In the following entry, the Shroudy Traveler looms in white shirt observing him in a hallway (*BOD* 134). Now Kerouac concludes, "These 2 dreams are madness and death" (*BOD* 134). The encounters with the Shroudy Traveler become more frequent, and seem to be heading somewhere. It's like his soul is being besieged in his sleep.

In his dreams, when Kerouac revisits the set where he last encountered the white-shirted stranger, he's beset with a sentient ecstasy in which all his life flashes before him, and it concludes with the aphoristic question, "O path of sweet Permanency, through what wood, what raindrop?" (*BOD* 149). Embodying the Buddhist idea of the impermanence of all created things, in this instance, Kerouac's yearning for the everlasting also shows a Gnostic bent as in the Gospel of Thomas (77:2–3) where Jesus says, "Split a piece of wood; I am there. Lift up the stone and you will find me there" (Miller, *The Complete Gospels* 317). This is yet another strategy Kerouac employs to keep off the Shroudy Traveler, that is, a connection with the divine "Permanency."

In the climactic dream involving this shady character, the narrator is a little homeless boy who has done something mischievous for which another "shroud" doppelganger is chasing him to punish. Kerouac spies safe haven and makes for "a sand bank beyond (primal, scene of world redsun birth)" (*BOD* 154). But he gets hung up in the interiors and closed spaces of Lowell that, so far in *Book of Dreams*, have always given him sanctuary and marked the center of his world. Houses, yards, rooms, halls, crawlspaces under porches — he hides in them all but is finally, hopelessly, cornered. As in other iterations of this dream crisis with the Shroudy Stranger, here the boy narrator remains confident in his ability to escape the deadly hand of madness and death, but here, simultaneously, for the adult dreamer, the borders have been permanently blown, and Kerouac's composite style of dream transcription reaches a shamanic peak in a breakdown or a breakthrough, depending on your perspective. He writes, "[B]eing a kid I have great potentiality and all the world yet and left to hide in ... (Who the boy? Who chaser?) Who objective? Who subjective? Who real?

What real?" (*BOD* 155). Where has Kerouac written himself in this "instasy"? To a world without a center, or a world that doesn't need one?

In *Book of Dreams*, we never find out how this final confrontation between the dreamer and the Shroudy Stranger, his mortal enemy, ends.

Apocalypse Dreams

As indicated in earlier discussion of *Book of Dreams*, war, cataclysm, violence and dread of the same are all major motifs that are contextual to numerous entries. In the dreams that have the "noetic quality" called "apocalyptic," Kerouac retunes Armageddon to the specific key and imagery of his day. He builds up to this over a series of entries.

In the first, he sees a mechanistic world where hobos and winos are pressed into chain gangs and tortured, and where children fist-fight as adults look on, bored and aloof (*BOD* 17).

In the second, he plays a game of catch with the railroad brakemen and does so with "sensational" skill and innovation, until he drops one. This "screw up" brings on a sunset vision through a huge tree that's like a shamanic axis. He picks up his ball and, in a sense, "goes home" by hurling it "up through the hole." Game over. Equating himself with a cosmic train conductor, Kerouac concludes, "This is the way the world will end, in rays, red, people watching silent, tired" (*BOD* 64).

In the third, he stares the Cold War paranoia in the face. He sees New York City teetering on the brink of nuclear oblivion where everything and everyone, including himself, is waiting "in ecstasy" to be destroyed (*BOD* 77). When the bomb finally explodes in his dream, everything disintegrates except the dreamer's "consciousness."

In the fourth, he dreams about creating "the Giant World Crab" (in writing) that will destroy the world. In it, he sees "families adventuring in the rubble" (*BOD* 108). ("Be nice to the monster crab," Kerouac writes in *Old Angel Midnight*, "it's only another arrangement of that which you are" [18].)

In the fifth he witnesses an apocalyptic comedy that juxtaposes the "old" American paranoia and fear of "Indians" the 1850s with the "new" paranoia and fear of nuclear holocaust in the 1950s. All the Cold War

5. "In-stasy" and the Book of Dreams

dread that has been internalized by the collective American psyche comes to view in this dream. There's a cloud shadowing America's soul and there's "Armageddon in the Dark Air" (*BOD* 104–5).

The sixth apocalyptic dream captures our nuclear neuroses with uncanny insight. Kerouac describes a city that has erected a tower to mark, not where the bomb will be dropped by the enemy, but where it will be *planted*, presumably, by *us*. Armageddon, in this dream, will happen as scheduled, and it will be self-inflicted (*BOD* 145). In this dream, you have a month to evacuate if you want.

In the seventh, Kerouac experiences the Cold War grown "hot," the sum of all America's fears but portrayed now according to "the party line" (as opposed to the previous apocalyptic entry, which implicates America as the cause of its own destruction). Here the citizens are encamped to protect themselves against Russian planes that overfly California threatening to drop the H-bomb. The whole country prepares for what he calls "H-Hour." Some are medicated against radiation sickness; others, like Kerouac and his friend, Julien (whom he cares for like a little brother), are not. The dreamer pens "a great Idealistic poem" for when "H-Hour" happens for real (*BOD* 163).

The final apocalyptic dream, a few entries from the end of *Book of Dreams*, is simple, straightforward, and doomed. The narrator and Garden (Allen Ginsberg) are amazed "that the Apocalypse has finally come and [they're] together in its Moment" (*BOD* 175).

Except for the dream where his consciousness remains intact after the final end, the regenerative notions of apocalypse in these entries are, well, *missing*. In these instances his apocalyptic visions have succumbed, it seems, to the degenerative spiritual awareness of his time. I wager nine out of ten contemporary Americans will tell you "apocalypse" means "the end of the world," without entertaining any notion of the rebirth or renewal that comes along with it. For the most part, this sequence of dreams that are dispersed in *Book of Dreams* embody this impaired understanding and halt at the despair and terror of it all. This is a modern shamanic performance that holds up "a mirror ... for the walking dead" (Kaldera and Schwartzstein, xv).

To reiterate, Kerouac as writer-shaman appears at the low end of a very long shamanic arc. Perhaps it might be more correct to refer to these dreams as "half-apocalyptic." They are indicative of "incomplete apocalypses" that reflect the weakened spiritual condition that enabled us, as a species, to invent the means to destroy ourselves in the first place. (As if death doesn't come soon enough.)

In his preface to a 1959 edition of *The Subterraneans*, Henry Miller comments on Kerouac as a writer in the Cold War era: "Believe me, there's nothing clean, nothing healthy, nothing promising about this age of wonders — except the telling. And the Kerouacs will probably have the last word" (*JKSL 1957–1969* 198). If the apocalyptic message in *Book of Dreams* isn't one of regeneration, then an ecstasy of resignation might suffice. As Kerouac notes in *Some of the Dharma*, "all your life you lose, and then you die / And lose the losing too" (38). The apocalyptic entries of *Book of Dreams* consistently reflect this tone. The drama and theatricality so characteristic of the visions here and elsewhere in his Legend are replaced by a straight deposition of the end times as he and America-at-large are witnessing it awake and asleep.

Dream Notes on the Beat: "Soon everyone realizes the party is a sad failure" (BOD 24)

As noted earlier in this chapter, numerous entries in *Book of Dreams* reveal Kerouac's ambivalent relationship with his Beat legacy, a major theme that he explores in *The Subterraneans*, *Big Sur* and elsewhere in his work. Certain entries of *Book of Dreams* provide moments of (counter)cultural critique where Kerouac's views on the "enthusiasts" who came in his wake are made apparent. I use quotes around that word because while the "subterranean" (or the "hipster") might have claimed to be taking up the Beat ethos (or were ascribed that role by literary and cultural critics of the day), the "beatnik" by any other name was stereotyped, even by Kerouac, for his "cool," not his enthusiasm. Sullen, bored, brooding, and wearing black — that was the Beat image culturally repackaged as "Doby Gillis," and it was an image diametrically opposed to Kerouac's founding notion of the Beat impulse as a modern celebratory and sacred journey to a fading essence. This is the "acceptance," the "popularity" that impaired Kerouac's shamanic influence on mid–twentieth-century America more than the deri-

5. "In-stasy" and the Book of Dreams

sion of his critics ever could. The contempt of the status quo is of vital importance to the shaman. He is most effective only as an outsider who remains a symbol of contrast when he is received back into his tribe. But when he is recast according to the shallow projections of popular culture by marketers or ideologues of any stripe, the modern shaman becomes an endorsement, a talking head, a brand. As Kerouac notes in *Some of the Dharma*, "I don't want to be a drunken hero of the generation suffering everywhere with everyone" (63).

The first and clearest indictment of the compromised state of the Beat comes very early in *Book of Dreams*. This entry tells of a birthday party for Jack held in his boyhood house in Lowell, the center of the world, but now Jack is grown, famous and "honored" by his peers (*BOD* 24). Significantly, his mother is "around," but does not attend the event. (This is Kerouac's "adult life" with his mother at a distance, but always within reach.) Certain Beat "patriarchs" such as Neal Cassady, John Clellon Holmes, and Allen Ginsberg are in attendance. Describing them as "cool," Kerouac senses that they are "almost hostile to my fame" (*BOD* 24). The party begins, although it is quiet and staid. The party proceeds until Kerouac asks them a worrisome question: "Does everybody recall my saying 'Something that was supposed to happen just didn't happen?'" (*BOD* 24). This kills the party outright. The "bad signs" of a decayed Beat impulse in this scene are evident in the apparent embarrassment and disappointment at his bringing up this question. There's no conversation or laughter, and "Cody is stony silent" (*BOD* 24). Noesis? This party (the "Beat Generation") is going downhill.

Factions, cliques, and private side parties further scuttle a sense of Beat camaraderie here. When Cody makes an enigmatic exit (leaving nothing but twelve joints for the bleak dream) the narrator retreats (again), refocuses (in extreme detail) and throws (as always) his spontaneous prose at the center of the world, his "little house of eternity" in childhood Lowell (*BOD* 25). He expresses gratitude for the abiding resource of his past (*BOD* 26). But the adult *Beat* resource has dried up and become a real letdown. The entry gives no good reason for this to be the case, but just lets it stand. Some sad snipper has nipped the Beat in the bud. "Everybody is crushed to realize that people could have made such a disastrous mess of a poor party" (*BOD* 26).

After a humorous sexual elision in this entry, the setting becomes a composite of "work" and "party." The scene continues, dismal and soulless, until a character named "Wallington" begins preaching about the need to "work in love" (*BOD* 27). Kerouac recognizes that it was the crisis of his own "party" that's responsible for (and necessitates) Wallington's oracle of "love." As he sees it, that's what's missing from the evolution of his Beat impulse. It is one of the longest entries in *Book of Dreams* and, on waking, it leaves the dreamer deeply stirred and somehow enlightened by this fact (*BOD* 29).

In another entry, one he calls "THE MOST INCREDIBLE BEAT DREAM in the world," (*BOD* 31), we are shown a comedic critique of Kerouac's shaky idea of himself as a writer, and by extension, of his legacy in general. Set in Lowell (of course), there's a confusing situation that involves Dinah Shore living up the street, and a fan seeking her out, and Kerouac conflating Dinah Shore with Olivia de Havilland. He winds up awkwardly in Dinah's living room with the fan, his mother, and sister. In the midst of this clamor, Kerouac recognizes and announces that he's a failed writer mooching on his family (*BOD* 31). What follows is the open confession of a poseur. He sees himself acting a part of the "writer," and the comedy of all this (as I initially thought) puts a major dent in the foundation of the Beat impulse itself (*BOD* 32). If Kerouac perceives his "hipster" disciples as fakers, then perhaps the Beat apple he's criticizing didn't fall far from the tree. This dream appears to be self-incriminating from this angle.

However, the shamanic perspective complicates this interpretation. Given the decadence of shamanic power that has been well documented, the shaman, for the longest time, has *always* been an actor of original ecstasy. That's the unique and driving premise of the shamanic experience, that is, the technique (the show, the act of ecstasy) equals and is identified with the ecstasy itself. (This reflects the mystical "both/and" quality that I've noted numerous times.) In this light, Kerouac's confession of acting a part (as "writer") is not incriminating in the least, but a simple statement of fact. The problem then lies not in the playing of a shamanic role, but in the reception of that performance because, in a sense, all shamans start out "faking it." They always first build, then buy into, the mythos they've re-created, and only then, if it's received and recognized by the tribe, does

5. *"In-stasy" and the* Book of Dreams

the myth become "revelation." Shamanism is a "con game" in the most denotative sense of the term, but then so is religion, science, economics, politics and any ideology whatsoever. Wherever our "confidence," our belief, individually or collectively, is, *there* is our reality. That the Beat ideology as he saw it received so little confidence, so little good faith, in this dream at least, is laughable.

Along these lines, another entry comments on Kerouac's anxious rapport with Beat fame and his hipster following. In this dream, he shows up naked in a scene that is part hotel, part school, and populated by schoolboys and subterraneans (*BOD* 81). Ginsberg is singing Kerouac's praises and recounting Kerouac's genius prodigious writing feats to the hipsters who are poring over his manuscripts. Kerouac says nothing, just looks on, naked, vulnerable and helpless to their interpretation of him. He realizes that the myth Ginsberg is laying on him is the myth that Kerouac had earlier laid on Ginsberg.

In a subsequent entry, this theme of vulnerability that comes with being in the spotlight of fame (this time through the mass media) remains. We see Kerouac, again naked, and reading his work in a crowded field. Simultaneously, he is on the Jack Paar show, being interviewed and televised worldwide. At this moment he encounters a helping spirit of sorts as his friend (Julien) warns him against such exposure (*BOD* 175). The implication here is that Kerouac's broadcasting of his precious vision will lead to its popularization and commodification (or vice versa). (It's difficult to tell which comes first.) Kerouac concludes an earlier entry with the cranky editorial aside, "TV-itis I think has ruined the culture cold" (*BOD* 61). And, as far as the Beat impulse is concerned, *Dobie Gillis*, at least, proved him right. Hilariously (and pathetically) this dream ends with the narrator throwing a "feeble punch" at Mr. Paar (*BOD* 176). Resistance to the mass marketing of the Beat, at least in this dream, is futile.

Finally, just five entries from the end, we read about a weird catastrophe. At a "BIG BEAT CONVENTION" in Philadelphia, a huge obelisk (similar to the tower that served as a ground-zero marker in an earlier apocalyptic dream) falls and rolls away in a field. Its movement is powered from within by a great number of "rabbits"; dream versions, perhaps, of his Beat devotees and "convention goers" who have multiplied swiftly, out of control. Kerouac didn't envision a Beat conformity. Conventions, after all, are so "conventional." Furthermore, this particular Beat gathering is rife with gangster intrigue. The FBI is looking into it. The whole show, and this *Book of Dreams*, is about to come down.

In these "Dream Notes on the Beat," we see Kerouac saddened, if not alienated altogether, both from his peers and the generation he supposedly founded.

The Final Dream: "Down I go to my doom" (BOD 183)

In the final entry of *Book of Dreams*, Kerouac writes, "We're all prisoners of the Communists" (*BOD* 183). Is all American held captive, or just Kerouac and his Beat cohorts? It's tough to say. However, the dreamer is incarcerated for being a revolutionary and for other offenses having to do with the exercise of his freedom, presumably, of expression (*BOD* 183). After the prisoners pose for a group photograph, in a bizarre scatological scene, he is led to the peculiar netherworld dungeon complex complete "with women cooks & waitresses who need man-love" (*BOD* 184). So, in *Book of Dreams*, Kerouac ends up in a hell that is nevertheless paradisal to some extent; at least, that's the "both/and" impression the dreamer leaves us with. Besides the straight interpretation of Communism and the perceived threat it posed in the Fifties, this prison might be seen as a stand-in for a fascistic status quo on both sides of the Cold War dilemma, a status quo that Kerouac always seemed to resist, but here embodies. So, in this last dream, the revolutionary peril represented by Kerouac and his Beat alternative has been contained. *Book of Dreams* ends in a prison where "the Captor Authorities are forever puzzled" (*BOD* 184).

Conclusion

I have only scratched the surface of the *Book of Dreams* as best I could. The meanings of numerous motifs, metaphors, and allusions demand further attention. In Kerouac's dream transcriptions, we see various aspects of the writer as modern shaman, such as "the ecstatic, the ritualist, the

5. *"In-stasy" and the* Book of Dreams

performer, the quick-change artist/trickster, and the visionary who brings inaccessible layers of reality to light" (Mayer 85). Matt Theado has accurately observed that "Kerouac sought an immediate relation between the object and the writer. The prose that results from this relation is an unmediated representation in language that Kerouac suggests will be recognized by readers via telepathic shock" (33). In his preface, Kerouac presumes a connection between the dreamer and the reader, and argues for the commonality of dreams in the human experience. Reading some of these entries gives one the feeling of a firefly that wanders into the room; while reading others, it's more like a bat's done the same thing. In these dreams, these "in-static" flashes, we run the gamut with Kerouac as he communes with the dead and gone, glimpses the varieties of immortality, previews hell, travels in time, rides the warp of his subconscious experience, and wonders about it all in words.

6

Old Angel Midnight
"Space Prose for the Future"[1]

If *Book of Dreams* shows Kerouac transfixed, staring at his dreams and transcribing what he sees, then *Old Angel Midnight* shows him transfixed, listening and transcribing what he hears. Written in notebooks between 1956 and 1959, *Old Angel Midnight* is a project of chronicling the "inner" by concentrating on the surround (the "sounds of the universe"). The goal of this exercise is to give voice, if not always meaning, to what he hears. In a letter to Lawrence Ferlinghetti dated April 5, 1959, Kerouac describes the project as

> only the beginning of a lifelong work in multilingual sound representing the haddal-da-babra of babbling world tongues coming in thru my window at midnight no matter where I live ... ending finally in the great intuitions of the sounds of tongues throughout the entire universe.... And it is the only book I've ever written in which I allow myself the right to say anything I want ... God in His Infinity wouldn't have had a world otherwise — Amen [*JKSL 1957–1969* 193].

Just as *Book of Dreams* is a spontaneous prose experiment directed at his subconscious experience, *Old Angel Midnight* provides the challenge of setting down his aural experience in the conscious moment as it happens. In his correspondence, Kerouac claims that *Old Angel Midnight* has no intentional narrative, that it is a listening/writing enterprise on which to hone his spontaneous prose technique. Though published, it originated as a private exercise. Michael McClure's essay "Jack's *Old Angel Midnight*" (which prefaces the work) emphasizes his personal "participation mystique" in this work. McClure writes, "I know this is the real thing as I read it" (xvi). However, I think it is difficult for any reader (for anyone besides Kerouac himself, for that matter) to evaluate the mimetic success or failure of this project.

Most readers of *Old Angel Midnight* (like *Book of Dreams*) need to be

6. Old Angel Midnight

predisposed by an interest in Kerouac's life and/or his spontaneous prose to take it on. Readers (myself included) generally enjoy literary convention, and gravitate to the familiar in books. In literature, we look for and derive pleasure from, if not the elements of storytelling (plot, character, setting, conflict, etc.), then at least "sense." These are the traditional elements that let a reader "into" a traditional text. *Old Angel Midnight*, which Kerouac described as a long poem, keeps the reader at a distance, yet, I contend, it has a sense all its own. A shamanic reading of this highly experimental text reveals a narrative, albeit in an extraordinary way. If we take Kerouac at his word, *Old Angel Midnight* represents "the writing of what I hear in heaven" (*JKSL 1957–1969* 45).

McClure perceives a metaphysical and archetypal value in *Old Angel Midnight* akin to the Hindu concept of "seed syllables": a belief that the physical universe originated in sounds that were caught in a veil. (We see this notion echoed in the opening line of the Gospel of John, "In the beginning was the word.") In *Old Angel Midnight*, words are the veil that reveals the underlying universe Kerouac hears. There are passages where Kerouac's re-presentation of his listening moment is clear, and others where a reader can only scratch his head. These sequences, inscrutable as they may be, are nonetheless enjoyable (like scat singing, McClure notes) if the reader's sense of play is commensurate with that of the writer (*OAM* xvi).

Although *Old Angel Midnight* is Kerouac's wildest and most maddening work, it can (and should) be understood in the conceptual continuity of his Duluoz Legend and his spontaneous prose technique. It is literature-gone-ecstatic, the writer-shaman getting down with and breaking through to an ultimate reality. From this perspective, *Old Angel Midnight*, then, is more than a private experiment or preparatory exercise. It becomes what Kerouac calls, in *Some of the Dharma*, "a single act of true mindfulness" (25) that leads, if you look close, to what biographer Dennis McNally calls "a high argument between Jack and God" (216).

The Original "Windows" Operating System: "A story as vast as this" (OAM 1)

As stated, Kerouac's technique in *Old Angel Midnight* is simple enough: sit by the window and write what you hear. The premise is mimetic.

The style is necessarily free-wheeling and ongoing as befits both his prose technique and his subject. Driven by sound, his language is often onomatopoetic, neologistic, and entirely irrational. Kerouac is writing unmediated from the ear in real time. "Because I made the world, I have to listen to it now," he writes in *Some of the Dharma* (21). It is, therefore, a most ambitious undertaking.

The opening lines of *Old Angel Midnight* establish the narrator (the listener) in specific time ("Friday afternoon"), contextual space ("the universe"), and boundless perspective ("in all directions in & out") (*OAM* 1). Immediately Kerouac establishes the limitless scope of this project. His ear is a window (an eye), and through it he hears and sees "Old Angel Midnight," the polyphonic voice of the Creator, who promises to "find a name for this Goddam Golden Eternity & tell a story too" (*OAM* 1). So, despite his categorization elsewhere that *Old Angel Midnight* is a poem (and it does look and "act" like a poem in many places), it also tells a vast narrative, the story of everything everywhere as it sounds right now. All on the first page, he hears-translates-sees (inward and outward with alarming simultaneous perception) house painters, ants, and microbes, all dreaming in the universe he describes as a "vast empty atom." Buddhist and Native American imagery, the drunk neighbor next door and Mrs. McCartiola are all combined in sound, silence, alliteration, and wild wordplay.[2] It is a prodigious opening fugue that proposes the aspiration of Kerouac's scheme to "ward off the inexistency devils" (*OAM* 2). That is precisely the value of this exercise, and the purpose of all his writing. As long as the Old Angel keeps "sounding" through the window, and the narrator (or "you," for that matter) keeps listening and translating, the world will continue to exist. Stop listening and the vast story of the world ceases to be.

The Quantum Buddha: Waves of Being

In this work, Kerouac seems to intuit (and express) key aspects of quantum theory, which is an authentic modern iteration of shamanism (i.e., an alternative way of looking at the universe). In the quantum view, the condition of the world ("the surround") is dependent upon and

6. Old Angel Midnight

influenced by our observation of it. So, in *Old Angel Midnight*, for Kerouac, we see that "ashcans turn to snow and milk" when he looks at them (*OAM* 4). The universe of *Old Angel Midnight* comes into being only when Kerouac turns his ear to the window of his perception. His creative attention gives it definition, and produces a kind of certainty out of the superpositional uncertainty that is the world unobserved, the world that is *in*definite, the world that most resembles a wave, fluid and indeterminate. Section 9 of *Old Angel Midnight* is an essay on this notion.

The "scene" (or soundscape, in this instance) opens with a vision of impermanence as the narrator looks over the sports page. It segues quickly into the elemental shamanic proclamation: "Dying is ecstasy" (*OAM* 11). Since the passing of his brother Gerard (when Kerouac was a toddler), and especially since the death of the "watermelon man" on the Moody Street Bridge imprinted itself on his mind (as recounted in *Doctor Sax*), this realization has always filled Kerouac with equal parts horror and creative awe. It is the shamanic cornerstone to his artistic impulse. This death-insight generates questions and visions.

He asks, "What is the universe but a lot of waves" (*OAM* 11), and "In a universe of waves quell difference betwixt one wave & t'other?" (*OAM* 12). In section 9 of *Old Angel Midnight*, his identification with Jesus and Buddha, and with profane literature and spiritual literature, coalesces into a third order of experience and being: "Ti Jean / a great big sweaty wave" (*OAM* 13). He pronounces, "I am the new Buddha—and I shall call myself ELECTRON" (*OAM* 14). He spies the quantum aspect of the physical universe as a movie screen brimming both particulate and wavelike and declares, "I'm going to the other side" (*OAM* 14).

Allusion, Motif, and Metaphor on the "Other Side"

Old Angel Midnight is peppered with allusions to real-world personalities, such as the classical composers Shostakovich and Elgar, jazz saxophonist Lester Young ("Prez"), pop group Danny & the Juniors, and screen celebrities such as Fatty Arbuckle and Ava Gardner. However, references to literary figures predominate. In this regard, Beat notables include Burroughs,

Ginsberg, Corso, Creeley, Bob Kaufman, Philip Whalen, Gary Snyder, John Clellon Holmes, and Lawrence Ferlinghetti. Other literary dignitaries mentioned are Hart Crane, Gore Vidal, Henry Miller, Jack London, Kenneth Rexroth, Poe, Sterne, Balzac, Baudelaire, Hawthorne, Melville, Joyce, Fitzgerald, Hemingway, Gogol, and Dostoevsky. And though he mentions no names, in section 3 of *Old Angel Midnight*, Kerouac refers to the "poets of France" being burned alive in a kind of Inquisitorial *auto de fé*. What are they all doing there? These figures generally do not speak or participate as they might in a novelistic scene. They are not characters. Rather, they are intoned like "notes" that Kerouac translates from the actual sounds through his window. If nothing else, from the reader's point of view, they are recognizable fragments in the overall weirdness of the piece.

Similarly, the few motifs in *Old Angel Midnight* might help the reader negotiate the strange environment of the "other side" he is describing from his sonic window. The words "sound" and "Friday afternoon" recur and signify pivots that introduce new tangents in this performance. "Gossip(ing)" seems to be set opposite the edict to "shut up and tell it straight." Both are employed frequently in *Old Angel Midnight*. Graphic sexual images recur, as do scatological references that might lend comedy to this "vast story" (depending on the reader's sense of humor). They certainly are evidence, at least, that the censorial filter has been removed, and that Kerouac's expressive freedom in *Old Angel Midnight* is absolute, as he claims in the correspondence quoted earlier. Finally, in three sections of *Old Angel Midnight*, variations of the compound "robeflow" (or "robeflowing") signal the motif of a cultured and bookish renaissance, as in a "deep revival of world robeflowing literature" (*OAM* 6). The narrator seems to call for this revitalization and sees himself taking part in it as he pursues this exercise.

The "window" itself is the most plastic and evocative metaphor in *Old Angel Midnight*. At various times, the window represents (and functions as) an ear, an eye, Old Angel Midnight, heaven, and God itself. In all cases, the window is the shamanic portal between the listening scrivener and the ultimate reality. In section 35 of *Old Angel Midnight*, the window delivers a long message to Kerouac. Unfortunately, he has no idea what it means. (Neither do I.)

6. Old Angel Midnight

Shamanic Showdown: "Angel Midnightmare" versus "Crack Jabberwack" (OAM 33)

For the reader, confusion and disorientation are the prevalent tones in *Old Angel Midnight*. Even though he states in section 26 that "Old Angel Midnight just writes itself" miraculously[3] and proclaims himself "John Kerouac transliterator of perfect knowing, angel from heaven, messenger of the right hand of God," the plot of this vast story he hears through the window, and its universal simultaneity, are often inscrutable to the reader (*OAM* 30). What does come through clearly is surprising. *Old Angel Midnight* does not present the reader with the typical God-prophet (or muse-artist) dynamic. Instead, in Eliade's terms, it communicates "a sort of 'psychophoria' leading to a dramatic encounter between the god and the shaman and to a concrete dialogue (the shaman sometimes going so far as to imitate the god's voice)" (199).

This describes exactly what happens in section 29. Old Angel Midnight-the-character (as equated with both *Old Angel Midnight*-the-written-project and the Old Angel as God) takes over completely and dresses Kerouac down in no uncertain terms. Full of coarse invective and threatening overtures, this dialogue begins with an extended jeremiad that condemns the narrator and basically says, "Stop writing and leave me alone." ("Why don't you mind your own bexness!" and "You're a good enuf old boy but my God you write too much" [*OAM* 31 and 32].) This "cease and desist" decree is long, thorough, and, in places, hilarious. Old Angel Midnight tells him to go drink, play piano, paint pictures, have sex, masturbate — do *anything* but write another word! When Kerouac asks if he's dreaming this diatribe, the answer is "You dream not," coupled with the portentous announcement that "there's a white cross marked X on the road where you will die yr dog's death" (*OAM* 33). What troubles me is that now, almost halfway through the book, Old Angel Midnight is starting to sound like "the inexistency devils" that Kerouac claimed this undertaking would "ward off" in the opening section (*OAM* 2).

A kind of point-counterpoint exchange ensues between the Old Angel and Kerouac (or between Kerouac and this inner-other, that is, between Kerouac and himself).[4] This exchange reaches its crisis when Old Angel Midnight commands Kerouac to "close your window"; in other words, shut down the metaphor, end the report, and let it be. The crux of Old Angel's complaint is that writing somehow taints the immediate purity of the universal essence (which, of course, it does). Old Angel says, "Let the stars fart their message unpolluted by human one, please hee?" (*OAM* 34). The sounds of the universe coming through one's window, it seems, are not a sensible or even practical subject to be pursued in writing. The essence of existence cannot be adequately translated in writing. Stick to love stories and other such popular accidents, Old Angel says, to which Kerouac responds, "[But] I'll go mad as a bush" (*OAM* 34). Unmoved, Old Angel Midnight alludes to Poe's "Tell-Tale Heart" and underscores his dismissal of Kerouac and his aspirations to contain the universal in writing: "And burn, please, the hardwood floors hiding me" (*OAM* 34).

Section 30 (only four lines) describes a dark night of the soul where Kerouac doubts the authenticity of the preceding exchange and of the project as a whole. He asks himself, is the Old Angel/God just a personal projection? Is he "making it all up"? Is the Old Angel/God, therefore, unreal? The answers to these questions in order are "yes," "yes," and "no." In this way, *Old Angel Midnight* strikes at the paradox that rests at the heart of shamanic experience.

Yes, *Old Angel Midnight* is a projection of Kerouac's subjective experience (of his listening at the "window"). It is "made up." As in the creation myth put forth in the Book of Genesis where God creates man in his own image, Kerouac creates Old Angel Midnight (and its many attendant identities) in *his* own image. My claim here describes the opposite directions of a reciprocal dynamic. It is an affiliation of equality that shamanism can let be — the mystical "both/and." In other words, the human experience is a projection of the divine, *and* the divine is a projection of the human. This is no hanging matter from the ecstatic perspective. In this light, the authenticity of Old Angel is beyond question. You can't have "shamanism" without a "sham." The show, the performance, *is* the reality. As Eliade tells us, the technique equals the ecstasy. "This series of facts," he notes, "falls under a 'law' well known to the history of religions: *one becomes what one displays*" (179). Shamanism, even in its modern iterations, is a tradition that privileges imaginative creativity of and participation in an alternative reality over the cold hard facts of the consensus modern reality (or, for that matter, of the moralistic obligation of institutionalized religious faith).

6. Old Angel Midnight

The dialogue between the two continues. Having chastised the writer, in the next section Old Angel allays Kerouac's despair (by continuing to speak) and consoles him (by confirming his eternal love). In section 31, Old Angel recommends that Kerouac be a student of the divine, and not a transcribing secretary, when he says, "Let heaven instruct thee, earth no bug thee" (*OAM* 35). Nevertheless, Kerouac continues to record the sounds of the universe through his window for 36 more entries. Soon, in a jeremiad of his own, Kerouac upbraids priests, philosophers, critics, poets, and publishers for their misguided attention. But most significantly, in section 32, he takes to task the Old Angel divinity (the "Snow Dad") for creating mortality (and the artistic impulse that comes with it) in the first place. This is a complaint Kerouac raises in many of his works. And before the end of this book, *Old Angel Midnight* reveals visions of cats, Beat nirvanas, frozen Siberias, Christian/Buddhist amalgams, grapefruits, American follies, birds at dawn, and ant wars, not to mention the many sections that are completely beyond my, perhaps, facile interpretation. It is a wild ride, but what's it worth?

Goofing: "We'll soothe the forever boys and girls"? (OAM 1)

What's the value in all this spontaneous report? Another of McClure's claims in his preface suggests the shamanic potential in *Old Angel Midnight* "allowed people to be the spirit lives that they were" (*OAM* xvii). Hmmm. So, experiencing the spiritual origin of our physical existence in writing — as in *Old Angel Midnight*, to decipher the voice of God in the sounds coming through his window — that's how the writer-shaman might beget and renew the ecstatic experience on the page in all this apparent gibberish. That has been the founding claim in the whole of my report on all of Kerouac's work. This is the primary disposition a reader must bring to *Old Angel Midnight* or any of Kerouac's writing: there *is* a spiritual world contextual to what we call "reality." The assertion is that our spiritual essence can be interrogated, reflected and perceived through art. In Kerouac's day and age (where the shamanic capacity had been necessarily cheapened for its modernity), and all the more in our postmodern age (where our attention is grabbed by so much more and so much less as I write this in "The Summer of LeBron," Lindsey Lohan's legal mess, and Mel Gibson's latest meltdown), this notion is a tough sell, to say the least. "Art for art's sake," let alone any notion of communing with "the other side," has been a dismissible concept in the incrementing cynicism of our species for a long time. So few of us try, or put any stock in, what Kerouac went for in *Old Angel Midnight*. Who can pay attention? And why would we even try?

Even for attentive readers, the diffused, even disclaimed, narrative in this work describes the withered rapport between ourselves and our spiritual essence. Contact is made, the Old Angel is reverently listened to, skillfully translated, and still it says "don't bother" because you're no longer able to tell it. Well, anything worth doing is worth doing badly, I suppose. That's all that's left for Kerouac, or any modern post-shamanic figure. In a letter to Ginsberg dated April 23, 1959, Kerouac admits

> I feel silly writing Old Angel ... because it is an awful raving madness, could make me go mad, I'm ashamed of it ... I wish other writers wd join me I feel lonely in my silliness writing like this is space prose for the future and people of the present will only laugh at me, o well let em laugh [*JKSL 1957–1969* 198].

Sadly, few writers have joined Kerouac in this "silliness" as far as I can see, at least to the committed degree that he pursued it. And it's too bad. Might have been soothing to the lot of us if more had.

The only thing that's left is all our "Big Surs."

7

Big Sur and the Memoir of Disintegration

> One fast move or I'm gone.
> —*Big Sur* 9

The "Unhappy Exhaustion of Harvest Time"

As he entered his final stage as a writer in the summer of 1960, almost three years after he had become a sensation, Kerouac's alcoholism reached a critical state. He had passed through both the imitative early style of *The Town and the City* and the breathless middle form of *On the Road*. The years between the publication of these novels (1950 to 1957), as noted, proved to be Kerouac's most creative, when he invented and incessantly practiced his "modern prose." Using this high style and spontaneous technique, he wrote thirteen major works in half as many years: *Visions of Cody* (1952), *Doctor Sax* (1952), *Book of Dreams* (1952), *Maggie Cassidy* (1953), *The Subterraneans* (1953), *Tristessa* (1955), *Mexico City Blues* (1955), *Some of the Dharma* (1955), *Visions of Gerard* (1956), *Old Angel Midnight* (1956), *The Scripture of the Golden Eternity* (1956), the first part of *Desolation Angels* (1956), and *The Dharma Bums* (1957). These were not published until *On the Road* created a feeding frenzy around Kerouac's prose and perceived lifestyle. Though he longed (like any working writer) for further publication in these years, he knew that much of what he was writing was too unrestrained for the literary climate of the day. Kerouac notes in his *Book of Dreams* that during this most prolific creative period he often felt like "a sheepish guilty idiot turning out rejectable unpublishable wild prose madhouse enormities" (20). The sheer volume of his work in the Fifties testifies to a need deeper than mere publication. He simply *had* to write whether he was being read or not. In his journal, Kerouac summed up the stages of his career in seasonal terms. "ROAD was learned in my Springtime, & prepared incredible work of summer (CODY, SAX, MAGGIE, SUBS, GERARD, ANGELS etc.) — Then came Autumn to which BIG SUR belongs & all my present unhappy exhaustion of harvest time" (*JKSL 1957–1969* 355).

Eliade observes that a shaman is likely to fall ill if he doesn't shamanize (28). The ecstatic technique of writing, which was Kerouac's practice, enabled him to seek and find what was left of the soul in himself, his heroes, and his culture. Modern prose became a means of confessing and confirming his existence, as best he could, *en toto*. His novels evidence the power he attained in this written performance. The written life became Kerouac's primary reality. In August 1954, he wrote Carolyn Cassady, "I do feel like I'm writing myself to death" (*JKSL 1940–1956* 442–43). Writing, living, and dying were always inseparable in his experience.

When success came with *On the Road*, it pulled Kerouac from the cloister of his notebooks and typewriter and dropped him into the harsh and hungry glare of American celebrity. Burroughs once insightfully noted that Kerouac "was always primarily a writer and not a person. He felt that everything he was doing as a person he was pretending to do" (George-Warren 180). The "pretending" that Kerouac had to do off the page as the "King of the Beats" took a great toll personally and professionally. In the twelve years between publication of *On the Road* and his death in 1969, Kerouac drank more and wrote less, completing only three full-length novels: *Big Sur* (1961), *Satori in Paris* (1965), and *Vanity of Duluoz* (1968).[1] As his backlog of completed manuscripts was published and he was in demand as a "celebrity" of sorts, he simplistically told Ginsberg, "Fame makes you stop writing" (Watson 294). In a 1968 *Paris Review* interview, he blamed his lack of output on "the attentions which are tendered to a writer of 'notoriety' (notice I don't say 'fame') by secretly ambitious writers" who sought his help in furthering their own careers (Plimpton 124).

As a result, the scope and tenderness of Kerouac's earlier works shriveled under the adulatory, confused awe of his proponents and the cruel appraisal of his critics. Nevertheless, these last agonizingly myopic novels display the confessional purity of his best work even though they are writ-

7. Big Sur *and the Memoir of Disintegration*

ten in the spare style of a depressed and disillusioned man who knew for sure that his dreams of literary respect would never come true. Most importantly as regards what I have called "the writer-shaman," the novels of his late style are self-portraits of Kerouac unhinged not only from his Beat legacy, but also from any abiding sense of physical or spiritual humanity whatsoever. If *On the Road* was a wild search for his soul, his final novels give the impression that Kerouac isn't sure he even has one. This is the ultimate nadir and shamanic crisis he sought to remedy in the first place.

All pretenses (literary, romantic, philosophical, religious, mystical) had been stripped away from "the King of the Beats" by the time he fled to Lawrence Ferlinghetti's Bixby Canyon cabin on the Northern California coast, hoping to pull himself together in the summer of 1960. Kerouac's sense of life at the time was highly karmic. He felt he was reaping the whirlwind harvest of his experience and influence at every level. If Kerouac was writing himself to death in the Fifties, he was clearly drinking himself to death in the Sixties for reasons he makes manifest in *Big Sur*, the first novel he had completed in four years. *Big Sur* proves to be the most harrowing and cautionary tale in the entire Duluoz Legend. It is a modern morality play on the demon rum with a first-person vengeance and the "nadir ray" turned up to "11." It was Kerouac's last roar.

In the fall of 1961 (a year after the experience depicted in the novel), taking what he described as huge amounts of benzedrine, he typed the 60,000-word single-spaced manuscript of *Big Sur* in ten days on a 60-foot-long teletype roll (*JKSL 1957–1969* 302). "To celebrate the completion of the novel," biographer Gerald Nicosia reports, Kerouac "bought a case of cognac. Two weeks later, he woke up in a hospital, unable to remember how he got there" (629). Clearly, as Ben Giamo notes, *Big Sur* "marks Kerouac's rite of passage from modernistic mystic to hopeless drunkard" (179). Nevertheless, this memoir of disintegration is nadirally ecstatic in its style and abject confession. No swan song this, but more like the prolonged bellow from an alcoholic deathbed.

Bottoming Out: The End of the Road

> All the kids are fascinated by the upside-down car wreck.
> —*Big Sur* 129

Kerouac in Ecstasy

In terms of narrative content, *Big Sur* proves to be an "anti-road" novel that examines both the desperate alcoholic stasis characteristic of Kerouac's last years, and the demise of "the road" as a viable myth in modern American culture. Seeking to escape his Long Island home that is overrun by thieving groupies and interviewers, Kerouac ("Duluoz") makes secret arrangements to get away to Ferlinghetti's ("Monsanto's") cabin for a spell of solitude and sobriety. But what starts out as a healthy escape from a maddening situation soon devolves into a nadiral circuit that finds the narrator careening back and forth between San Francisco and Bixby ("Raton") Canyon in an incremental state of nervous breakdown and delirium. Despite his plans to the contrary, he can neither keep his visit a secret nor remain alone for too long. Furthermore, he is utterly incapable of sobriety. Leaving his mother and the cat behind, Duluoz makes the trip west "so easy and dreamlike" on a transcontinental train. (After his breakdown in *Big Sur*, the King of the Road will take a plane back to New York.) The irony is not lost on him:

> All over America high school and college kids thinking "Jack Dulouz is 26 years old and on the road all the time hitch hiking" while there I am almost 40 years old, bored and jaded [*BS* 5].

In fact, except where a blissfully drunk Duluoz wills the highway to be the ecstatic thoroughfare it was in his earlier novels, *Big Sur* consistently shows the mystique of the American Road to be a failed experiment that is no longer descriptive of the narrator's (or America's) primary impulses.

In the novel, he no sooner gets off the train in San Francisco than he embarks on a two-day binge. Waking up, already drunk-sick and late, he takes a bus to Monterey, then a cab to Raton Canyon that drops him off on the coast highway in the middle of the night. He has to walk the rest of the way. Kerouac's description of this particular leg of the trip indicates a shamanic flight to the netherworld, and stands as a metaphor for the devolution of "the road myth" in his life. Holding a dim lamp, he negotiates the foreign, rugged Big Sur coast along a narrow trail that descends hundreds of feet to the unseen cabin on the canyon floor where Duluoz will, in effect, sit still at the bottom of his life and try to rise again. Fearful every step of the way and soon rattled to the core by a landscape he can only sense is malevolent to his presence, Duluoz descends into a world that mirrors the darkness and jaggedness of his own experience.

7. Big Sur *and the Memoir of Disintegration*

This pathetic fallacy in *Big Sur* is effectively an inversion of the dynamic in his earlier road novels. Gone are the wide-open vistas of America where God once spoke to him directly through the sun-shot clouds as he flew by in a car. In Raton Canyon, Duluoz stumbles haltingly in the dark, his arm held out in front like a blind man. He studies each and every step in fear and stares into the faint light at his feet. His progress is slow and unsure; his disorientation in the pitch-black night is complete. He hears voices in the wild ambience, fears unseen rattlesnakes, and, humorously, is terrified for a moment by piles of mule dung when he finally reaches the canyon floor. Far from being welcomed by nature in Raton Canyon, Duluoz feels "like a man in the presence of a dangerous idiot he doesn't want to annoy" (*BS* 11).

The morning reveals the precipitous descent he made the night before, and (like his own soul, like his modern America) Raton Canyon impresses him as a place "once inhabited by Gods or giants of some kind but long ago vacated" (*BS* 17). On a short hike Duluoz finds the perfect objective correlative for the "death of the road" in the form of the rusted chassis of a car that had crashed to the canyon floor years before (*BS* 15). To Duluoz, the sight is "like a terrifying poem about America" (*BS* 17). It symbolizes the unexpected and final end to the American road myth proclaimed long ago in Whitman's "Song of the Open Road." In the upside-down car wreck, Kerouac intuits the end of motion as an ecstatic technique, and the return to stasis.

What follows for Duluoz in *Big Sur* is a three-week spate of praying, writing a sound poem at the edge of the surf, and performing humble tasks that, though he finds them boring overall, give him a sense of self-reliance and childlike innocence (*BS* 30–31).

But then visions ensue. He begins to see Raton Canyon with a thousand-year stare that places him on a continuum with its original Indian inhabitants. In expansive imagery, Duluoz understands the impassive efflux of all life into and out of death, and the sky assures him that "all you talkers are in paradise" (*BS* 36). But the paranoia that will clutch at Duluoz as his last stay in California disintegrates is already just below the surface. This brief Thoreau-like respite is undercut completely in a split second when he takes in a deep breath of sea air that (he's convinced) poisons him with "an overdose of iodine, or of evil" (*BS* 41). This strange incident leaves him in a nadiral swoon. He almost faints and perceives himself (and all humanity) as vulnerable, diseased, and doomed. "I'm just a sick clown and so is everybody else" (*BS* 41). This episode sets the tone for all of the narrator's ecstasies in this novel, save one.

Beyond comfort, Duluoz momentarily doubts the existence of God, and in a novel full of aural hallucinations, the sea now screams at him to "GO TO YOUR DESIRE DON'T HANG AROUND HERE" (*BS* 41). Thus he intuits that the very setting of Raton Canyon, as he suspected on the first night's descent, is hostile to his presence, which is impure, intrusive, and "sick."

Ignoring completely the despair that drove him to seek refuge in the cabin in the first place, Duluoz decides to flee the new "mortal hopelessness" he finds in the canyon by numbing it with another binge in the city. He simply cannot abide with the sound techniques of ascetic solitude. His alcoholism has metastasized and trumped all his other "kicks" (i.e., his ecstatic techniques). As John Clellon Holmes notes of Kerouac in September 1962, "Booze alone can seem to produce in him the 'ecstasy' he needs to get thru time" (*JKSL 1957–1969* 348). So the next day, Duluoz scrambles up out of the canyon to hitch a ride to Monterey and then take a bus back to San Francisco. He's on the road again with his thumb out. But there's a problem: no one picks him up.

Kerouac uses this 14-mile stretch of coast highway and the countless station wagons that strand him there as a critique of a modern America that is thoroughly hobbled by fear, apathy, and the self-absorption of a "square" status quo. Duluoz laments the timidity and insularity that have crept into the American lifestyle (and into which he is already descending). He lashes out in preposterously misogynistic terms, and places the blame accordingly. American husbands are put upon by their domineering wives. He reserves his harshest reproach for "wifey, the boss of America," who has "bitched" the American male and sapped him of his virile adventurous appetites (*BS* 44). That's just cranky Jack at his deplorable best straight out of a macho Hemingway phantasm. (In *Some of the Dharma*, Kerouac writes, "Imaginary histories of sentient beings on earth — suddenly they get married etc — It's a confused, vague, dull comedy about marionettes" [166].)

Understood in its broadest light, though, both this sequence in *Big*

7. Big Sur *and the Memoir of Disintegration*

Sur and the novel as a whole show that the sympathy so intrinsic to *On the Road*, and so characteristic of Kerouac's inception of the Beat impulse has not caught on in the least. In the Sixties, the American road is no longer wide open and replete with ecstatic potential like it was in the Forties, but has become a closed corridor between the suburban home, work, and the yearly family vacation (*BS* 46).

In any case, Duluoz is stuck on it, so he resolves to hike up the coast on foot. Here, as we have seen elsewhere in Kerouac's work, the narrator assumes the posture of a suffering Christ. After walking nine miles, his feet are blistered and bloody, and he can go no further. Though his predicament is obvious to passers-by in vehicles, no one offers a ride because, as Duluoz sees it, the media has imprinted upon them suspicion and paranoia (the darling fears of the Cold War era). Christ-like, the narrator lets them off the hook: "I don't blame them" (*BS* 47). Fifteen years earlier, Kerouac had tried the road, found it good, and offered it to America in the true sense of "religion," a means of reconnecting with an estranged divinity. Now, in 1960, he sees that this creed has been rejected, that his dear Thomas Wolfe was right: "You can't go home again." Eventually in the novel, a bearded folkie picks up Duluoz and drives him to the bus station in Monterey, bringing an end to this significant episode. The narrator's bleak experience that day clearly indicates that the theory of a Beat salvation on the open American road has been disproven. Duluoz notes that it was the last time he ever hitched (*BS* 48).

Upon his arrival in the city, Monsanto gives Duluoz a letter from his mother saying that his cat had died some weeks before.[2] In his already fragile state, this is yet another premonition of mortality closing in, and causes Duluoz to embark upon a three-week bender that will lead to the climax of the novel. For this half-healed shaman, it'll be the aberrant technique of alcohol and its nadiral ecstasy from here to the end of *Big Sur*.

By the Sixties, Kerouac had fallen away from the original cast of characters celebrated in his road novels. In *Big Sur*, he is occasionally running with the second-wave Beats, a younger crew that essentially idolizes him. Duluoz describes many of them as "wanna-bes and posers" (*BS* 56). Though he mostly despises these "beatniks," and is increasingly suspicious of them, he does manage to forge what seems like a genuine relationship here and there. Chief among these is his friendship with a poet named

"Dave Wain" (Lew Welch) who can talk and drive as well as the greatest road hero of all, Cody Pomeray (Neal Cassady). Still, this "new driver" is only an echo of the old. In order to fully investigate the demise of the Beat impulse and write the epitaph to the ecstasy of the American road in *Big Sur*, Kerouac brings Neal Cassady on the stage one final time. So, in an attempt to integrate some of the pieces of his crumbling identity and to keep off the encroaching madness before "losing it" completely, Duluoz arranges a meeting with Cody. He's on the road again, this time fifty miles down the highway to Los Gatos. In this antithesis of *On the Road*, the short trips reveal everything. They're all that remains before the final stasis.

Cody and Jack: Smith and Shaman

Everything Duluoz sees and hears now confirms either the corrosion or the cancerous multiplicity of American life (and his perception of it). He describes the broken seat he occupies in Wain's jeep in static terms as "a rocking chair on a porch" (*BS* 62). Urban sprawl has eaten up California's farm tracts and destroyed its spacious beauty (*BS* 63). Wain's rambling apocalyptic monologue triggers an overwhelming sense of futility that calls into question the viability or worth of Duluoz or any writer (*BS* 63). Wain's monologue corroborates what the narrator earlier realized in the canyon after taking "the iodine breath," namely, the incapacity of "poor protective devices" (such as writing) to keep off our existential woes.

As far as Duluoz can see from the moving jeep, the world and everything in it is crowding him out, pushing him off an edge. In fact, a hanger-on, named Stanley Popovich, one of his beatnik imitators, sits in the back seat poised, as he sees it, to "take over" (*BS* 64). On the way to Los Gatos, as on the floor of Raton Canyon, Duluoz translates all his confusion and fear into endless gulps from a bottle. Finally, as if he has internalized all the closeted paranoia of the "too big" modern world, Duluoz sees a flying saucer hovering in the sky over Los Gatos.

The meeting with Cody is further evidence that the carefree days on the road to heaven are long gone. Images of the fallen Cody myth abound. Having just served a two-year sentence in San Quentin for possession of

7. Big Sur *and the Memoir of Disintegration*

marijuana, Cody (though he has a mistress who soon becomes involved in Duluoz's *Big Sur* breakdown) is ostensibly living a happy domestic life in the suburbs with his wife and children. Because of his criminal record, Cody has lost his archetypal job on the railroad and now makes a living (still in the "road business") as a tire fitter. Even Cody's car, a broken-down Nash Rambler, has to be push-started before the motor kicks in. Duluoz wants to perceive Cody in the same way he sees himself, as a persecuted Beat dissident, hobbled by a moralistic and joyless society, and justifiably indignant. But Cody is not bitter from his experiences. He invites his old friend and the others to watch him recap tires on the night shift. A pivotal scene of mythical allusion and shamanic implication follows when the "King of the Beats" and his acolytes (Wain and Popovich) attend the compline of Cody Pomeray. In the Duluoz Legend, this scene proves to be one of the very few remaining glimpses of Cody as a Beat deity.

Cody at work reminds Duluoz of "Vulcan at his forge" (*BS* 69). Cody lays into the task with the same strength and loquacious energy that made the myth of Dean Moriarty so charismatic. This allusion to Vulcan bears a closer look. Even as Vulcan, the god of fire, is cast from heaven to earth by his father (Zeus) and mother (Hera) as a boy, Cody is abandoned to the road by his father (the legendary hobo tinsmith) and a mother he didn't live with until he was six, and then only for a short time. Like Cody in 1960, whose mobility is impeded by his circumstances, Vulcan is the lame "workman of the immortals" (Hamilton 35). Vulcan spends all his time laboring under a volcano, and Cody, like him (in his Beat prime and long after), is a powerful underground center of heat and commotion. Finally, while Vulcan's wife is Aphrodite (goddess of love and beauty), Cody's wife, Evelyn, is often the object of the Jack's amorous attention in fact and fiction. A shamanic point of view reveals other significant symmetries here, as Eliade explains.

> The craft of the smith ranks immediately after the shaman's vocation in importance.... Shamans cannot "swallow" the souls of smiths because smiths keep their souls in the fire; on the other hand, a smith can catch a shaman's soul and burn it [470].

The relationship between Neal Cassady and Jack Kerouac (as rendered under various pseudonyms in his Legend) is complex, to say the least. Kerouac variously portrays them as brothers, metaphysical lovers, rivals, alter egos, co-paramours of women, and even fellow Catholics! Undoubtedly, Cassady was Kerouac's primary muse and soul-mate. Cassady, like a smith, had the big medicine of a soul in the fire. Kerouac, like a shaman, had the craft to show that magic to the world in his writing. As is commonly understood by his biographers (and as I discuss from the ecstatic perspective in Chapter 2 of this book), the primary reason Kerouac developed his spontaneous prose technique with its whole mystical bent and breathless urgency was to imitate Cassady's wild, shameless soul, and thus immortalize it on the page.[3] To a degree determinable only by those who personally knew Cassady, Kerouac succeeded in this, although it's well documented that Cassady was never pleased with his portrayal in *On the Road*, and that the friendship between the two suffered greatly after its publication.

Cassady's spirit (true to the smith-shaman trope) was kept too hot in the forge of existence for Kerouac as writer-shaman to capture (and re-create) it unadulterated. Instead, it was Cassady who "captured and burnt" Kerouac's soul (as seen in *Visions of Cody*). Cody's ongoing vitality, as contrasted with Duluoz's helpless alcoholic march to the grave in *Big Sur*, attests to this. Whether he is being punished by the status quo for his hot instinctive "Yes!" or simply acquiescing to a more moderate lifestyle, Cody's energy is now spent "keeping up the constant noise" of working for a living in America. For the last time in any of his novels, in *Big Sur* Kerouac describes Cassady's raw energy and indefatigable spirit, and portrays the soul he spent much of his lifetime trying to actualize in writing. No longer running wild off to new adventures, to Jack, Cody has become a martyr (*BS* 70). Though the road has ended in so many ways for both of them, Cody endures, though bent, as always, to the necessity of his circumstances.

After this visit with Cody, Duluoz is driven back to the city, where he passes out. When he wakes up groaning, he feels "trapped." By this point, the reader knows that what's ambushing the narrator wherever he goes cannot be evaded because he's caught in his own alcoholic skin. Though Duluoz has a way to go in this novel before he shares that realization, there's no place for him to retreat or advance to in this widening, deepening nadir. Mortally stuck, there's no road that will deliver him from himself.

Duluoz spends the remainder of his stay in the city in a state of delir-

7. Big Sur *and the Memoir of Disintegration*

ium and continuous drinking (*BS* 74). Though he is eager to get back to the Big Sur cabin, he is helpless before his own appetite for oblivion. He drifts in and out of near-hallucinatory encounters with sundry Bay Area beatniks. He trades his tattered sneakers for those of a callow admirer named Joey Rosenberg, whom he sees as "some sort of beat Jesus" (*BS* 72). Duluoz becomes convinced, in fact, that Joey really *is* Jesus after having a drunken dream of the youth leading a pilgrimage to the East and walking on the water, with the whole excursion being terrorized by "I.B.M. machines trying to destroy this 'Second Coming'" (*BS* 73). It is an odd, modern theophany that doesn't encourage our narrator.

More dispiriting still is a hospital visit he pays to a poet friend named George Baso. Even as George is wasting away with tuberculosis, Duluoz is mortifying his own body with drink. Though he finds George detached from a fear of death, and the visit is filled with playful goofing, Dulouz is locked in a downward spiral (*BS* 78). To complete the nightmarish stay in the city, Duluoz is taken on a high-speed joyride through the pre-dawn streets of San Francisco by a complete stranger.

Things are well out of hand when a call comes from Cody, who's lost his job (and his car) and needs a hundred dollars from Duluoz to make ends meet. What starts out as a second jaunt to Los Gatos to deliver the money morphs into a return trip to Raton Canyon, this time with a whole slew of new and old Beats (including Monsanto) and their women. Cody comes along (*BS* 88). So, it's back to Big Sur.

Though all are awed by the coastal landscape and Cody boyishly revels in it, Duluoz cannot extricate himself from the nadir. Again, he spies only an impassive, sinister place that stokes his fear (*BS* 90). Furthermore, he is filled with guilt and shame to see the cabin, the creek, the trees (all of it), as they remind him of a commitment to recovery, to getting clean, that he has abandoned. Worst of all, perhaps, is the great distance that has opened up between Duluoz and the "Cody dynamism" that inspired and sustained him in his earlier novels. As the entourage breaks into a flurry of activity—Monsanto axes at a log for no particular reason, Arthur Ma draws a picture, Wain unpacks and sets up the cabin, Fagan meditates by the creek, Ron Blake sees to the food—Duluoz's initial happiness is (as always) underpinned by his sadness (*BS* 93). His spirit crashes further. Jack opens the wine bottles expertly and his stasis at the "end of the road" is perfected for another day. When night falls, everyone starts drinking in earnest, and Duluoz spies through sick, scornful eyes yet another symptom of the general deterioration of his Beat vision.

"Yakking": Symptom of the Beat Terminus

> Not being able to talk or communicate ... the whole generation afflicted.
> —*Book of Dreams* 26

In New York City, during the mid–1940s, when the Beat Generation was essentially Burroughs, Ginsberg, Kerouac and their avatars Herbert Huncke and Neal Cassady, before "being Beat" was taken up and tried on like the uniform it never was, their primary (and nonexistent) Beat manifesto might have read in part, "See the way we talk *with* each other." James Fisher notes:

> Burroughs and the others introduced Kerouac to the mysterious world of Times Square and environs, and he responded to that world as though he had rediscovered a lost universe of immense human variety and color [219].

For the original Beats, sympathetic communication of the variety of human experience was truly a rush in which they could share worlds and confirm their existence in an open-ended exchange of ideas, philosophies, intuitions, and inquiries. They were receptive to each other's unfolding notions and, in a give-and-take manner, each greatly informed the others' literary techniques. Burroughs said to read Spengler, so they all read Spengler and turned on to the fellahin alternative. Kerouac proclaimed that Cassady's "Joan Anderson Letter" with its first-person confessional and acutely detailed narrative style was the fulfillment of "Goethe's prophecy that the future literature of the West would be confessional in nature," and all of them, each in his own manner, went on to dedicate their careers to the often-shocking confessions of their distinct subjective experiences (Plimpton 101). As an extension of this, Ginsberg became committed to Whitman's idea that literature is only valuable to the degree that it is personal and honest. In a 1966 interview, he explains,

> You have many writers who have preconceived ideas about what literature is supposed to be, and their ideas seem to exclude that which makes them most

7. Big Sur *and the Memoir of Disintegration*

charming in private conversation ... there should be no distinction between what we write down, and what we really know to begin with. As we know it every day, with each other. It's also like in Whitman, "I find no fat sweeter than that which sticks to my own bones," that is to say the self-confidence of someone who knows that he's really alive, and that his existence is just as good as any other subject matter [Plimpton 40].

It is clear that honesty became a harsh priority for each of these "source Beats." They called their nascent theory "the New Vision."

This discourse of discovery was as anthropological as it was literary. They immersed themselves in the countercultural fringes of American society and ran with the pariahs they found there. The criminal, the hustler, the drifter, the drug user, the homosexual, and the lunatic (Huncke and Cassady were all of these to one degree or another) were looked upon as having some secret knowledge that might free their disciples from the moralistic shackles of the status quo. The now-famous New York City "commune" of Joan Vollmer (Burroughs's future, ill-fated wife) where Burroughs, Kerouac, and Ginsberg spent much time became a Beat Lyceum that was "an Uptown outpost for an elite group of prostitutes, addicts and thieves" (Watson 60). For Kerouac, for all of them, it was an eager era full of potential escape and experimentation on all fronts. Their literary identities had not yet formed and they shared a feeling that heroes and mystics brushed shoulders on the American streets everyday and all you had to do to access their wisdom was seek them out, talk to them, and listen. Ginsberg confirms this "Beat Eden" of New York City in the late Forties as a communicator's paradise: "I spend my whole lifetime rushing out meeting people, connecting with facts & dramas; I do not know the facts and I am not a good actor" (Watson 64). Kerouac seconds the notion.

> By 1948 it began to take shape. That was a wild vibrating year when a group of us would walk down the street and yell hello and even stop and talk to anybody who gave us a friendly look [*GBO* 60–61].

It was all a fervent, guileless matter of seeking and sharing visions. The *exchange* of information was vital.

Flash-forward to August 1960, where we find Kerouac playing a poisonous end-game in *Big Sur*. At this time, in "real life," Neal Cassady, as we have seen, is making a go of it comparatively "in the middle of the road." Allen Ginsberg is off in Peru eating the telepathic vine called *yage* and in a few months he will take LSD under the tutelage of Timothy Leary. William Burroughs is experimenting with his "cut-up method" in order to inoculate his fiction against what he considers to be the viral manipulation of language. They have all evolved. Kerouac, now notorious as a personality more than famous (or even consistently working) as a writer, understands none of this. He has fallen out of contact with the co-founders of the New Vision.

Kerouac explores two major symptoms of this implosion in *Big Sur*. The first is obvious by now. "Drinking," Kerouac writes in *Some of the Dharma*, "you abandon people and they abandon you—and you abandon yourself—it's a form of partial self-murder" (112), or a mortification of the body (as I will discuss in the next section of this chapter).

The second is a malady that has become endemic to his circle. He calls it "yakking." Here, as Kerouac sees it, the original Beat richness of excited, genuine and revelatory conversation has devolved into a poverty of soulless blather. This secondary Beat*nik* manifesto might read, "See the way we talk *at* each other."

In *Big Sur*, Duluoz perceives that conversation is no longer an enlightening or sharing event, and that pretentious grand-standing and guile have replaced any authentic verbal exchange. The narrator's drunken paranoia doesn't really negate his critique of the transformation of "soul talk" to "yakking." Even before *On the Road* catalyzed the disaffected of the American status quo, "Beatness" had been codified, synopsized, and packaged such that anybody could "be one." When "being Beat" became a sort of fashion trend, for Kerouac, what was once a window looking out onto the panoply of human experience became a wall in a tiny room where everyone dressed a part, read their script, and no one listened—a clichéd product where ideas were cheaply emulated and rarely generated. Once the status quo assimilated the Beat impulse (as it has always done to any subcultural phenomenon it can turn into profit), many notions antithetical to Kerouac's vision were absorbed into its ersatz knock-off. Kerouac could neither protect nor distance himself from what he saw in the sneering replication of his vision called "the beatnik." As biographer Dennis McNally notes,

> His greatest gift had come to betray him. His innocent eye could never develop a saving shield of cynicism. And when his creation—the term "Beat Generation"—was defiled in the service of violence and corrupt profit, he could only

7. Big Sur *and the Memoir of Disintegration*

cry, or curse or get drunk enough so that the images blurred or softened; there was no forgetting what was happening to him [274].

In *Big Sur*, the night he and the boys watch Cody at work in the tire shop, Duluoz pines for the genuine communication and connection so characteristic of their Beat heyday, "but there's no chance with everybody yakking" (*BS* 68).

And later on in the novel, the first night the big gang is all closed into Monsanto's cabin on the canyon floor, Kerouac paints a hellish picture of dissonant beatnik entropy. The ten of them are packed in the dimly lit space with the wooden shutters closed against the chill and fog. The fire and lamp fill the place with smoke. All are drunk; many ramble. Duluoz wants to read the sound poem he wrote during his first stay, but McLear (poet Michael McClure) is already reading a poem about having sex with his wife. Although the simultaneous dialogue is absurd and cacophonous, much of the "yakking" betrays an "end of the road" subtext. Cody and Dave Wain (the "old" driver and the "new"), for instance, slam about their views on the parking habits of old men in Safeway parking lots before Cody goes on to explain how he, as a child, had to devise a way of riding a broken bicycle (*BS* 96). Monsanto talks about his bookshop, Fagan laughs, Ron Blake sings like Chet Baker, and Arthur Ma, forever drawing, yells, "Hold still you buncha bastards, I got a hole in my eye" (*BS* 96). Hold still, indeed. Duluoz is in the crosshairs of his own disintegrating vision.

All the simultaneous babble, all the uncircuited energy in this frantic claustrophobic "pit" at the bottom of the world, fire at the narrator as the scene devolves into trauma. A terrifying midnight hike to the sea drives Duluoz into an escapist fantasy where he is "the leader of a guerilla warfare unit ... marching ahead the lieutenant giving orders" (*BS* 97). Providing only a vague sense of self-esteem, such imagined conceits are rapidly becoming the only hedges against insanity for Duluoz. After all have gone to sleep that night, Duluoz and Arthur Ma drink beyond sense and throw non sequiturs at each other until they pass out at dawn. The narrator wakes up weak with a distinct realization of shamanic breakdown. Referring to the Buddhist mystic and renunciant, Duluoz confesses, "I'm no Milarepa who could also sit naked in the snow and was seen flying on one occasion" (*BS* 122). It's all broken down now, the original Beat spirit, slipping to the nadir though a din of "yakking."

"Yak on, crack on, wail & howl on, poor babies of the world," Kerouac writes in *Some of the Dharma*. "There's an end coming" (147).

Cassady's Exit

In one thin chapter of *Big Sur*, Kerouac briefly exalts (for the last time) and debunks (forever) the most compelling character and myth of his career as writer-shaman. The last time we see Cassady and Kerouac interact alone in any of his novels leaves no doubt that, for the narrator, the Beat impulse has faded to black and is gone for good. Here we see the extreme capacity of Kerouac's perception to destroy what he once created. And in it, we can trace the decadent arc of his vision in the opening throes of his final nadir.

So intense is the narrator's yearning for the paradise of his "good old days" that the stretch run of *Big Sur* is, at times, spelled by passing spasms of nostalgia and momentary relief. A prelude to his last reunion with Cody occurs in the cabin one crowded morning when Duluoz manages a "serious" discussion about literature with McLear. In the dark room, in this fragile bubble of "no-yak" calm, Duluoz briefly experiences the essential human connection that he has all but drunk away, namely, "that lonely shiver in my chest which always warns me: you actually love people" (*BS* 122). But too soon the conversation pivots when McLear asks his help in getting published and suddenly the benign moment shatters completely. Duluoz darkens and grows suspicious. Yet again, whether the narrator feels legitimately "betrayed" by a sycophant or is only locked into his own paranoid psychodrama, it's all the same.

"Suddenly, boom," as in *On the Road*, Cody throws the door open, bursts in on the scene, and floods the room with sunlight. Duluoz compares him to St. Michael the Archangel, the one who drove Satan from heaven. It seems that Cody intervenes in this nadiral scene to drive the demons away from the narrator, who is now "ecstatically amazed as tho [he's] seen a vision" (*BS* 124). To Duluoz's great relief, Cody still "carries that strange apocalyptic burst of gold" (*BS* 125). Cody's presence in the canyon (with Evelyn and their three children) pours some light in a corner of Duluoz's madness, and he walks toward it instinctively. After all, as

7. Big Sur *and the Memoir of Disintegration*

often noted, Cody-as-muse once embodied that Whitmanic "wild yea-saying overburst of American joy." "He's an angel," Kerouac writes in *Visions of Cody*, "I'm his brother, that's all" (298). Now in *Big Sur*, Cody's got a new job and a new Jeepster parked down the road. So he and Duluoz go off to "talk and walk just like old times" to see Cody's "splissly little old beautiful new jeep!" (*BS* 126). Just what the doctor ordered, it would seem.

But again, in the blink of an eye, the serene promise of communion, even with Cody, twists Duluoz into a paranoid and hopeless isolation. Away from the crowd, Cody proffers a joint. They smoke it and immediately fall into an uncomfortable silence with nothing to say. Their null-node stupor illustrates a breakdown of the ecstatic technique that yields only bad trips to "the nethers." Marijuana, alcohol, and so forth, once the "Beat sacraments," no longer uplift. In *Book of Dreams*, Kerouac presages this scene, noting, "I've laid off tea, it alienates my soul from me as it has done Cody's from himself" (25). Now, for Kerouac, alcohol remains and is more a rite of suffering and penitence. In *Big Sur*, this pot session hopelessly and finally separates him from Cassady, once his greatest inspiration. Yakking soon fills the gap between the two.

Fleeing the silent, stoned moment, Cody starts up a heartless soliloquy about his new vehicle. But the car is no longer the mystical chariot it used to be since Sal Paradise was forced off the road, or ran out of gas. These two "heroes" take a short ride (their last roadtrip, under a mile) back to the cabin in a brand-new station wagon, and afterward, "what started as a big holy reunion and surprise party in Heaven deteriorates to a lot of show-off talk" (*BS* 129). It's not the first time Cody deserts Duluoz to his madness, but it is the last in any of Kerouac's fiction.

Back amid the bustle in and around Monsanto's cabin, *Big Sur*, in elegy, takes one last fond look back at Cody as Duluoz reminisces with Evelyn about the psycho-sexual *ménage* they once shared. Duluoz concludes that "you can at least write that on his grave someday 'He Lived, He Sweated'—No halfway house is Cody's house" (*BS* 128). For her part, Evelyn promises, "I'll get you Jack, in another lifetime.... And you'll be very happy" (*BS* 130). But it's all yakking in the void now for Jack. In *this* life, in *Big Sur*, all the symbols of the Beat myth are worn out and its shamans can no longer fly.

Besides, his crew has run out of liquor again. They pile into cars to go get more. It's the only ritual left.

Buddha, Jesus, Jack and the Critics

Kerouac's autodidactic foray into Eastern thought provided an invaluable resource during his intense output in the Fifties. However, *Big Sur* shows that by the Sixties he had returned to a predominantly Western view of spirituality. The Buddhist journey toward nirvana, an obliteration of self, offers a mysticism of emptiness. But the Catholic focus on the Passion and death of Jesus Christ, via the mortification of the body, embodies a mysticism of sacrifice. The Buddhist endures lifetimes in the pursuit of escaping suffering, while the Catholic penitent tries to perfect suffering in this life and hotshot it to the hereafter by paying the price of, not a thousand lives, but a single fantastic death.[4] In a way, Buddhism (a philosophy "of silence that renounces all ways of naming the absolute") was antithetical to Kerouac's literary ambition (*TEOR* vol. 1, 250). Catholicism, however, a "religion of the word," suited his creative drive as much as the figure of a brutalized and misunderstood savior reflected his self-image. Kerouac's obsession with Christ crucified is well noted by his biographers. The Duluoz Legend consistently shows that, in his last years, the desperately Catholic Kerouac saw the trajectory of his life as analogous to that of Jesus. There's something to that.

Both of their public lives as seekers of souls (hence as shamans) begin in prayer and are accompanied by a vision of divine commendation. And both end in a prayer of self-abandonment. After his baptism in the desert,

> while Jesus was praying, heaven was opened, and the Holy Spirit came down upon him in bodily form like a dove. And a voice came from heaven, "You are my own dear Son. I am pleased with you" [Luke 3:21–22].

And, at the end of his road, just before dying on the cross, "Jesus cried out in a loud voice, 'Father! Into your hands I place my spirit!'" (Luke 23:46).

As portrayed in *Visions of Cody*, Kerouac received his divine call while traveling west to see Neal Cassady in the late Forties. In *Big Sur*, many years after this calling, Kerouac thoroughly identifies his "crucifixion" (that is, the accelerated disintegration of his life since publication of *On the*

7. Big Sur *and the Memoir of Disintegration*

Road) with that of Jesus by describing a night-long vision of the cross that provides him an ecstatic moment on the brink of his own death.

> Suddenly as clear as anything I ever saw in my life, I see the Cross.... I see the Cross, it's silent, it stays a long time, my heart goes out to it, my whole body fades away to it, I hold out my arms to be taken away to it, by God I am being taken away my body starts dying and swooning out to the Cross standing in the luminous area of the darkness. I start to scream because I know I'm dying but I don't want to scare ... anybody with my death scream and just let myself go into death and the Cross....—"I am with you, Jesus, for always, thank you" [*BS* 204–5].

It is easy, though callous and simplistic, to dismiss this scene as a "deathbed conversion." Few readers and even fewer critics of his time were fully attuned to the consistent and ardently spiritual import of Kerouac's Legend. So it is not surprising that *Big Sur* "was later advertised as the 'crack-up of the King of the Beats,' not as the experience of a deeply religious mystic" (Charters 336). Criticism of the novel largely followed suit. Typical was the review in *Time* that scorned the author as a "confirmed one-vein literary miner" and cynically panned the effort as "ridiculous" and "pathetic" (*JKSL 1957–1969* 346).

From *Visions of Gerard* on, Kerouac could never cotton to the notion that there is anything "ridiculous" or "pathetic" about dying, nor would he censor himself from writing about the pain of existence in a style that was true, not to literary convention, but to the texture of his subjective disasters. To comply with the views and expectations of his critics would be to cut himself off from what Anne Charters calls "the force of his genius," namely, "to create novels out of the tragedy of his life" (355). "The best writing," Kerouac claims, "is always the most painful personal wrung-out tossed from the cradle warm protective mind" (*GBO* 70). As he writes in *Big Sur*, "If I don't write what actually I see happening in this unhappy globe which is rounded by the contours of my death skull I think I'll have been sent on earth by poor God for nothing" (167).

In a fiery response to *Time*'s "snide, sneering, condescending, semi-literate, semi-dishonest, spiteful attack" on *Big Sur*, Lawrence Ferlinghetti rushed to Kerouac's defense by pointing out the critics' blindness to *the abiding and fundamental spiritual motif in Kerouac's fiction*. He writes, "Perhaps this is just what you had in mind. For you are all great experts in the killing of the spirit, and here you have killed another great one" (*JKSL 1957–1969* 346).

In correspondence and conversation Kerouac often predicted that it would be years before the spiritual depth of his fiction would be fully appreciated. This problem has been rectified by Beat scholars like John Lardas and Ben Giamo, whose works explore "Beat religiosity."[5] Of the two, Giamo more fully delineates the alcoholism of Kerouac's last years as a mortification of the body, an active technique of self-waste with an eye on mystical union.

Via Purgativa, *Mortification of the Body, and Happy Hour in Eternity*

> I'm trying to drive my madness away by self-torturing ordeals.
> —*Big Sur* 201

> Not to what most pleases, but to what disgusts; not to matter of consolation, but to matter for desolation.
> —William James, *The Varieties of Religious Experience* 305

The closeted Puritanism that brings about our moral judgment on the use of narcotics and alcohol today (as it did in Kerouac's time) still proscribes assent to Giamo's view of Kerouac's dissipation. Though advertising and the popular media capitalize heavily on the dissipate culture, we are still loath in America to discuss with any seriousness the use of consciousness-altering substances. We reflexively understand the terms "alcoholism" and "religious technique" to be antithetical. As Aldous Huxley points out, "Drinking cannot be sacramentalized except in religions which set no store on decorum" (68). But, as noted earlier, according to one common translation of the Latin root of the term (*re-ligare*), the function of religion is to "reconnect," even as ligament connects muscle to bone, strength to strength. So if you give Kerouac any credence at all as a seeker of mystical experience, as a shaman performing on the page, then you have to start with his primary means of reconnecting with the divine essence and proceed from there. Ted Spivey, in *The Writer as Shaman*, notes, "The shaman, as Eliade, Jung, and others have shown, plunges into the midst of his own physical dissolution and discovers the transcendent power in

7. Big Sur *and the Memoir of Disintegration*

the form of a center of creativity" (9). "The drunken consciousness," as William James aptly indicates, "is one bit of the mystic consciousness, and our total opinion of it must find its place in our opinion of that larger whole" (387).

Ginsberg felt that Kerouac drank because he was bored (*WHTK?*). Giamo expounds on this observation. "Kerouac knew deep in the marrow of his bones that boredom was the minimal counterpart to that enormous burden of time ticking off our mortality; and his quest sought to evade or surmount the solemn awareness of such final human matters" (197). Carl Solomon (another Beat avatar, specifically for Ginsberg) simply thought that Kerouac drank to enjoy himself (Foreman, *The Beat Generation*). In a letter dated March 31, 1962, Kerouac agrees with Solomon, with a significant qualification that highlights a shamanic recognition of the role of drink in his experience. He writes, "I am a hopeless paralyzed drunken mess and I don't know how long I'm going to live, if I keep on like this. ... Yet I have such a good time when I'm drunk, I feel such ecstasy, for people, for books, for animals, for everything. It's a shame there's a string tied to everything, huh?" (*JKSL 1957–1969* 333).

Many of his biographers hasten to suggest that Kerouac drank to numb out the anguish brought on by his celebrity. But it wasn't in Kerouac's artistic interest to anesthetize anything; besides, he drank to excess long before he was "famous." Although he orchestrates the rationale behind his drinking in a variety of tones, the Duluoz Legend is a song of mortal pain and suffering, and to numb it out would be to deny his creative sensitivity and vision. As Michael McClure notes, "Each novel of Jack's is an act of desperation and of vision.... He is really an outlaw of the sensorium" (*WHTK?*). John Lardas further comments on the dynamic between Kerouac's pain and his perception, and nods as well to the idea of psychic, if not physical, mortification as a conscious, informed act on the writer's part. "Kerouac was 'attacked' and overwhelmed by sacred messages. He had bared himself to the mercy of the universe. By steadfastly absorbing everything, he became absorbed, and pain became a form of mystical pleasure" (151). In this light, Kerouac's alcoholism can be seen as a masochistic vocation.

Kerouac's long-time parish priest and friend, "Spike" Morrissette, asserts that he knew the writer primarily as a mystic whose devotion to the crucifixion matched his ardor for the bottle (*WHTK?*). There is no discerning where devotion ends and pathology begins for the alcoholic Kerouac or where, as Giamo notes, he "lost sight of that very fine line between ecstasy and destruction" (199). What is clear from the Duluoz Legend is that his alcoholism was not a diversion but a deadly earnest technique of realizing vision in the pain and suffering of a mortified life. Kerouac knew the final cost of this aberrant ecstatic technique, and in fact yearned for it. "I'm a Catholic," he told his friend Fran Landesman, "and I can't commit suicide and I wouldn't do that to my family, but I plan to drink myself to death" (*WHTK?*).

Jack Kerouac, on his way down in life, drank to hasten and perfect his exit from this world. But why the hurry? My study here, like much Kerouac criticism, has considered a variety of responses to this question. It could have been the fallout of Kerouac's mystical obsession with the death of Gerard, or the conflicted sexuality and consequent shame and guilt that so disturbed his adulthood. Maybe the consistently withering criticism of his work or seeing his Beat vision co-opted in ways he never imagined got to him.[6] Perhaps his personal and professional development was stuck on some romantic back road when most of America traveled the new superhighways designed as evacuation routes in case of nuclear attack. Any of these rationales would explain (and all, it seems, contributed to) Kerouac's immolation. His self-destruction became an agonizing ritual that he took very seriously in fact and fiction. Why put it on the literary record in such a raw manner in a novel like *Big Sur*? Certainly not for reasons of conversion, for Kerouac raced, unreformed and without apology, to the grave. What's the message? Here again, I think Kerouac's own words on the matter are the most indicative. In his *Scripture of the Golden Eternity*, he writes,

> I was awakened to show the way, chosen to / die in the degradation of life, because I am / Mortal Golden Eternity [24].

In *Visions of Gerard*, situated at the beginning of his arc as writer-shaman, Kerouac shows the holiness (and hopefulness) of death (with a brief nod to a profane context). *Big Sur*, however, located at the end of that career, shows the profanity of Kerouac's death drive in a hopeless tone that is relieved by a scant few moments of sacred understanding. In both

7. Big Sur *and the Memoir of Disintegration*

cases, the final wager and purpose of his existence, and the driving subtext throughout his Legend, is death itself. To paraphrase his words in *Visions of Cody*, he wrote all his books because "we're gonna die."

But, if character is fate, then perhaps the lonesomeness, isolation and disillusion so prevalent in *Big Sur* prove that Kerouac/Duluoz is reaping the whirlwind of a vow he took as a young man. In a notebook entry dated September 5, 1945, he writes,

> I dedicate myself to myself, to my art, my sleep, my dreams, my labours, my sufferances, my loneliness, my unique madness, my endless absorption and hunger — because I cannot dedicate myself to any fellow being. And if it were in my power to dedicate myself to any fellow beings, I would not have myself.... This is the ideal I take with me to my grave [*Kerouac ROMnibus*].

No wonder, then, that the Beat impulse as he conceived it, a great sympathetic promise, struck Kerouac as such a miraculous possibility that didn't pan out. It was his folly to think, live, and write for a time that it might. His "endless absorption and hunger" made happy hour in eternity a grim shift.

That is why, in *Big Sur,* Duluoz falls into the vision of the cross, an external and established symbol. His inner journey offered him no agency of salvation. And no mere mortal, not any of his old heroes, new cronies, ex-wives, his mother, not even Cody or the woman they presently share in *Big Sur* (Billie), can save him from a life spent pursuing a sense of community that was basically counterintuitive to his own impulses. His gesture toward a modern Beat life of the soul was either condemned by the vulgar complacency of his time or, somehow, repackaged and sold to the consumer. This bastardization of his vision, it seems, came as a cruel surprise to Kerouac in his day, but it shouldn't to us. The cynicism Kerouac suffered and lamented has become a hallmark of our modern America, as I will discuss in my conclusion.

Big Sur, then, as experience and literature, becomes an act of atonement and, perhaps, a warning to the modern visionary of the toll exacted on those who wander from established religious and literary tenets in search of the soul. We have seen in *Big Sur* that Kerouac puts to an agonizing death the Beat myth he risked so much to build, and renounces, as well, the validity and legacy of that vision. Hoping to be saved now by the cross of Christ (which had so frightened him as a child), Kerouac flays himself with alcohol (which had so pleased him as a younger man), and records his last journey in mind and body to the netherworld. Six years after the publication of *Big Sur*, Kerouac's bodily mortification would be complete.

The End of the Story

> "Does anything in modern life make you sick?" the interviewer asked. "I'm sick of myself," Jack said.
> —Amburn 350

> Death hovers over my pencil.
> —Kerouac, in Watson, *Birth of the Beat Generation* 98

Though the night visions of the cross in Raton Canyon cause Duluoz to momentarily fancy that "we'll all be saved," his torment is far from over (*BS* 206). First a pesky bat, then the hum of a flying saucer, and the bizarre leg-stomping of a sleeping child in the cabin (Billie's son, who, he's sure, is a warlock) all conspire to keep him from sleep. He is not saved, just yet, from the paranoia of his delirium tremens. In time, though, he sinks into exhausted sleep, and falls into a recurrent though transfigured dream wherein he revisits "Mien Mo," the vacated mountain home of the gods that is populated by a terrifying army of flying horses only he can see.[7] But now, Mien Mo is transformed into a Raton Canyon cut through by a river, in the middle of which "on many rocks are huge brooding ... fornicating vulture couples on the town dump" (*BS* 208).

> These are humanly formed vultures with human shaped arms, legs, heads, torsos, but they have rainbow colored feathers, and the men are all quietly sitting behind Vulture women slowly somehow fornicating at them in all the same slow obscene movement — Both man and woman sit facing the same direction and somehow there's contact because you can see all their feathery rainbow behinds slowly dully monotonously fornicating on the dumpslopes.... They're so human! [*BS* 208].[8]

The significance of "dream work" in Kerouac's fiction, as in shamanism, I hope is clear by now. "It is only when dreams lose their importance," he writes in *Book of Dreams*, "that the dirty business of evil begins" (49). In the same book, he further claims, "It is in dreams that the pure sacred life is entered" (103).

7. Big Sur *and the Memoir of Disintegration*

The hellish eroticism of the Vulture Dream in *Big Sur* reflects his (typically) disastrous relationship with a woman (in this case, Billie). However, it also asserts that the world, at root, is really profane, and that the human experience has devolved into the routine joyless pursuit of pleasure in a filthy hell on earth. Giamo aptly notes that this dream is not an escape or release from the agony of Duluoz's waking life, but a further penance. This dream, he contends, is "not only ... a desolate caricature of libertine excesses [Duluoz has] committed in the past, but also (considering the torturous episode in the novel) a way of offering atonement for them" (Giamo 198). The cross, however, has not provided the narrator with any abiding sense of peace. The cross is not revealed to Duluoz as a free ride, but rather as a model he must embrace until he gives up the ghost. Furthermore, his misery doesn't diminish with the dream of the vultures. Instead, it multiplies as the chastened narrator awakes to realize his damaged faculties are beyond repair: "All my self sayings suddenly blurting babbles so the meaning can't even stay a minute I mean a moment to satisfy my rational endeavors to hold control, every thought I have is smashed to a million pieces by millionpieced mental explosions" (*BS* 211). His madness and anguish are perfected in this nadiral dream and the penance of his ecstatic nadir is perpetuated. Awake or asleep, only a burial will bring an end to Duluoz's nightmare in *Big Sur*.

Only now does the novel resolve, and quickly, on an absolutely panic-stricken morning where even Duluoz's thoughts yak at him beyond sense. Again he renounces any romantic impulses he's harbored as a writer.

> The words I studied all my life have suddenly gotten to me in all their serious and definite deathliness, never more I be a "happy poet" "Singing" "about death" and allied Romantic matters.... "Sleep is death, everything is death!" [*BS* 213].

Death is now personal, very, very close, and finally, real. Duluoz has made a shambles of this visit to Big Sur. He manages to explain to Dave Wain that he must leave this place at once. The others set about cleaning up the cabin before leaving. The mother of the "warlock child," Billie, digs a garbage pit that, to Duluoz, looks like "a neat tiny coffin-shaped grave" (*BS* 213). In a final flight of hysteria and vision Duluoz rushes to shovel the debris of the visit (and, figuratively, the tragic offal of his consciousness) into the pit for good. The child, in a fit of crying, tries to stop him. Duluoz prevails and completes the burial. Suddenly but, perhaps, not inexplicably, he experiences a strange, rapturous deliverance, and rest. "There's the golden swarming peace of Heaven in my eyelids—It comes with a sure hand a soft blessing as big as it is beneficent, i.e., endless—I've fallen asleep" (*BS* 214–15).

He awakes only a minute later, but, this time, the sense of wellness abides. The chaotic yakking has ceased. There is peace and silence in a canyon that is no longer hostile to his presence. He feels "perfectly normal again.... All the dark torture is a memory" (*BS* 215–16). Duluoz can't understand it in the least. Neither can I.

Today, though, with the benefit of the intervening years, the reader knows that this condition did not last. This "golden swarming peace" comes not with the desperate vision of the cross, nor with Duluoz's "hell harrowing" in the Vulture Dream (though both are key elements in this hybrid Catholic/shamanic journey). Rather, his deliverance, however suspect, is the result of an actively engaged mortification of the narrator's body and spirit. Death is the only breakthrough point, life's only release. In *Big Sur*, Duluoz pursues death and tastes its ecstasy only as the novel "dies."

The remaining 49 lines of the novel convey Duluoz's blithe hopes for abiding peace in a saccharine, lobotomized tone to make you cringe from all that has come before and all that, we know now, will follow. The suffering human condition, the anguish of existence has both a purpose and an end. Only death completes the circuit of a life (mortified or not) and returns you to God, if that's where you want to go.

Thus ends this nadiral and ecstatic threnody to Kerouac's "adult disaster of the soul through excessive drinking" that is *Big Sur* (*BS* 216).

8

Conclusion
"Be Lamps Unto Thyselves"[1]

> He claimed, in his drink, that he was Christ, Satan, an Indian chieftain, various holy men of half a dozen cultures, the universal genius, and who knows who else, who can remember. The search for the role. The mile-deep puzzle of identity that goes on in someone who can imagine all alternatives, all roles.
> — John Clellon Holmes

My primary claim in this book has been that Jack Kerouac's role in post-war America was that of writer-shaman; that he was a modern, post-shamanic figure who realized his own soul as well as internalized the soul of his culture, and performed both in his writing. Clellon Holmes's description of Kerouac (quoted above) as "someone who can imagine all alternatives, all roles" in part corroborates this claim. However, while the résumé of the archaic shaman (classically defined) included the role of healer, in the end, Kerouac could not cure his own soul sickness or that of his culture. He was poised to perform in literature a religious function for a tribe that had long been "demystifying" and was rapidly secularizing in its modernity. His reception by critics and worshippers, as well as his alcoholism (i.e., his aberrant ecstatic technique), doomed any curative aspect that Kerouac's vocation might have offered. At the beginning of that career, Kerouac wrote to Cassady of his "ambition to be a tremendous life-changing prophetic artist."[2] Although Kerouac's America had notions of ecstasy that differed from his own, the prophetic aspect of his art as writer-shaman has proven to be, for the most part, accurate.

Kerouac's prodigious output in the Fifties indicates that he lived to re-create his own experience in writing as authentically and immediately as he could, for whatever it was worth. His was a confessional style that said "this is me" in unapologetic wonderment. His prose technique was shamanic in that its practice revealed the ecstatic context of his subjective experience. His spontaneous prose, like much of the Duluoz Legend, flouts literary tradition and decorum, demonstrating a paradoxical content and highly innovative style that blend into an apotheosis of the individual voice. From the shamanic perspective, each of Kerouac's books is a séance that translates the ecstatic highs and lows of his own visions.

Like most innovations (or innovators) that suggest an alternative to the status quo, Kerouac's writing (and he personally) attracted much scorn in his day. The vehement tone of this rejection is indicative of the threat that the Beat vision posed to the post-war ideologies that his critics sought to perpetuate and protect. The conventional notions of the American Dream such as God, family, and consumerism were all challenged by the content of his work, but even more by his prose style, which was drastically committed to the ecstasy of the individual voice. As writer-shaman, Kerouac liberated language for the purpose of ecstatic expression. This stylistic freshness made him a literary outlaw, the enemy. Language is the front line in this conflict. Aldous Huxley comments upon why this is so.

> Verbalists are suspicious of the non-verbal; rationalists fear the given, non-rational fact.... This being so, the subject is, for academic and ecclesiastical purposes, non-existent and may be safely ignored altogether or left, with a patronizing smile, to those whom the Pharisees of verbal orthodoxy call cranks, quacks, charlatans and unqualified amateurs [77].

Kerouac was condemned as all of these by the keepers of literary convention. The shaman, even in the modern era, is always a provocateur, as is any authentic artist who challenges the perceptive and cognitive limits of his audience. A shamanic reading of Kerouac affords one a prism of critique comparable to the content, style, and process of his writing. Shamanism is a critical *entrée* to his work that doesn't snag on essentialist ideology. Jack Kerouac, at least in his fiction, was never a strident "ideology man," and, as such, his writing cannot be fairly evaluated or understood by any fixed criteria, be it "ecclesiastical" or "academic," as Huxley notes above.

Kerouac's trip as writer-shaman was more intuitive and less codified than that. An actual search in real time, his writing reveals something of the human footfall toward the "the given, non-rational fact" of the soul. As his life could not be separated from his art, his work became a project

8. Conclusion: "Be Lamps Unto Thyselves"

of keeping "body and soul together" (*JKSL 1940–1956* 270). The Duluoz Legend is the report of what Kerouac saw, felt, and dreamt on the journey to his own essence in modern America. Clearly, his self-portraiture in this regard can be bewildering. The motivations and actions of his narrators often conflict, and quite often Kerouac's Legend exhibits the mugshot of a multiple offender that is self-incriminating. My study has not focused exclusively on *what* Kerouac said in his writing, but rather *how* he said it, and, even more, *why* he said it at all. Reviewing his life and death for the sake of his art in shamanic terms — that is, as an ecstatic project — seemed to be the most objective way to understand the decadent arc of his career.

The shaman's initiation and gathering of power necessarily involves the experience of death. Kerouac establishes his familiarity with death early on in his Legend in *Visions of Gerard* and *Doctor Sax*. "All you do is head straight for the grave," as Kerouac writes. "A face just covers a skull awhile. Stretch that skull cover and smile" (*VOC* 12). Early in his career, Kerouac's preoccupation with death is somehow bright and full of creative potential. Ginsberg's eulogy illuminates the dynamic between creativity and mortality as Kerouac saw it:

> He'd already scribed a million dreams, one thousand pages of dharma, a million words that sounded like a million ears. His heart was tender. He'd already died and become recording angel [*WHTK?*].

Late in his career, as we have seen in *Big Sur*, Kerouac's perspective on death dimmed to the point of blackout. Like his vision of the golden cross in that novel, his strident Catholic orthodoxy and conservative politics in the Sixties indicate a tired, reflexive diminution of an authentic shamanic vision that had evolved far beyond the tenets of each.

Even in his most nadiral prose, though, Kerouac refuses to deny the existence of the soul. Though he suffers its apparent absence, he remains stubborn in his assurance that the soul's divine credential cannot be revoked as long as he yearns for it. James Fisher asserts that, for Kerouac, "doctrinal formalities paled before his desire to have 'God show me his face'" (218). This freedom from religious convention is characteristic of the post-shamanic figure. Gerhard Mayer explains, "The figure of the shaman in its popularized and modern interpretation is not bound to religion but represents a cipher of an individualistic and experience-oriented access to transcendence, with its manifold ways of manifestation in different realms of modern society" (99).

Once this hunger for theophany grabbed hold of him in the spiritual wasteland of post-war America, he fed it on the fact and fiction of his earthly avatars ranging from Thomas Wolfe to Dizzy Gillespie, from Jesus and the Buddha to The Shadow, Neal Cassady, and Gary Snyder. Kerouac then rushed to the essence of his soul by performing and satisfying this hunger in a writing style of his own design that often seemed chaotic but was always disciplined, and expressive of, not the consensus reality, but an eternal one.[3] This is the ultimate alternative any shamanic figure can offer.

Kerouac wagered everything to share the Dulouz Legend with the world in his writing, in some instances, like a shy boy venturing to introduce himself, and in others, like a prophet entering the city; always like a shaman returning to the tribe with visions written down. He established death as "the only decent" subject in *Visions of Gerard*. He ritualized the passage into the life of the writer in the "Faust Part Three" he called *Doctor Sax*. He portended the rise and fall of the Beat impulse in *Visions of Cody*. He lacerated his tortured ego to full confession in *The Subterraneans*. In *Book of Dreams* and *Old Angel Midnight*, he journeyed inward to delineate the psychic landscape of his Legend. And in *Big Sur* he recorded the final mortification of the body that anticipates the theophany of the eternal soul-cross. The gamble of his life-fiction, as biography and criticism have shown, had dire personal and professional consequences for Kerouac, and an undeniable, though now long-dispersed and still contentious effect on those who came in his wake. As Lucy Lippard notes, "[The] best artists, like traditional shamans, consciously and unconsciously take risks for the common good outside the circumscribed boundaries of professionalism" (Tucker 73).

Matt Theado contends, "Spontaneous Prose is Kerouac's foremost literary characteristic and may yet be his chief claim to literary longevity" (6). I agree and further contend that as an ecstatic technique (i.e., full confession in an authentic voice distilled of craft and censor on the run in time), Kerouac's spontaneous prose is a shamanic practice as well as a literary one. His work reveals a dogged love of life (if only for his art's sake) even when he was tired of life. There is an unconditional sense of the dignified soul in the individual experience, and a solid recognition of ecstasy-

8. Conclusion: "Be Lamps Unto Thyselves"

as-reality in his Legend — all of which evince the shamanic aspect of his mission as a writer. With the publication of *On the Road* imminent, in a 1957 letter to editor Sterling Lord Kerouac discusses the purity and scope of his artistic vision and warns against the consequences of its rejection:

> I'd rather die than betray my faith in my work which is inseparable from my life, without this faith any kind of money is mockery —... My whole believing heart is involved here — I can see it clearly, there will be no American Literary Renaissance unless the sanctity of personal speech is honored, that indefinable personal quavering sound of each and every writer [*JKSL 1957–1969* 11].

It has been my aim to discuss Kerouac's participation in the shamanic tradition that is deeply embedded in the human consciousness. It is a practice that has been much hybridized by time, and in Kerouac's case, involves the written performance of the private experience, the alchemy of life into art that originates in the shamanic urge. Whereas Mircea Eliade documented shamanic traditions, and Carlos Castaneda wrote about shamans, Jack Kerouac *shamanized* in his novels. By filtering the soul of his time through his own on the page, he realized an ecstatic technique that was an end unto itself. His early writing enacted a shamanic healing through a sacred realization and mystical journey in his modern art of words. The confidence he exudes in a letter to Cassady three days after Christmas in 1950 could well be addressed to any of his readers: "My report to you in the pit of the night and to God in the pit of the night, will carry me through" (*JKSL 1940–1956* 248). And this description of the boy Cassady in *Visions of Cody* could well characterize any of us at our child-like ecstatic roots:

> There were no images springing up in the brain of Cody Pomeray that were repugnant to him at their outset. They were all beautiful. There was a clarity and pureness in his mind. It was just a matter of believing in his own soul; just a matter of loving your own life, loving the story of your own life, loving the dreams in your sleep as parts of your life, as little children do and Cody did, loving the soul of man [306].

"Loving the soul of man" certainly describes a "common good" for which, as Lippard notes above, the shaman-artist might take risks. Though malicious criticism often dogged his writing style, the cynicism leveled toward Kerouac's message of love for the direct and positive soul is most telling of our modern age. Then, as now (more easily than ever, perhaps), we tend to, if not sneer at, then simply dismiss such a high-minded notion because the historical tally sheet shows that, in numbers, "love" has always been more of an ideal than a reality. Ginsberg hypothesized that "America by [Kerouac's] day was sick. Hard heartedness had taken over. So I would say America broke his heart" (*WHTK?*). Yet, even in the final throes of his dissipation and career-long sadness with the reception of his vision, Kerouac hung on, writing in *Big Sur*, "It always makes me proud to love the world somehow — hate's so easy compared" (141).

Kerouac's writing, in every facet of its ecstatic content, ranging from rapturous highs to nadiral lows, exudes a desperate hope that his audience might follow him on an affirmative road to the soul. In a speech delivered to a forum entitled "Is There a Beat Generation?" at Brandeis University in the fall of 1958 (one year after publication of *On the Road*), Kerouac pleads for an ecumenical Beat positivity.

> I want to speak *for* things, for the crucifix I speak out, for the star of Israel I speak out, for the divinest man who ever lived who was a German (Bach) I speak out, for the sweet Mohammed I speak out, for Buddha I speak out, for Lao-tse and Chuang-tse I speak out, for D.T. Suzuki I speak out ... why should I attack what I love out of life. This is Beat. Live your lives out? Naw, love your lives out. [So] when they come and stone you at least you won't have a glass house, just your glassy flesh [*GBO* 56–57].

Such is the essence of his shamanic vision: a message to love. On the one hand, this passage encourages you to stay positive and "in love with" life by maintaining and celebrating the common soul connection with others. If you can remain "naked" in that way (which takes much skill, dedication, and guts), then you're unbreakable, because there's no such thing as "glassy flesh." It's when you're defined by negativity (i.e., "I'm against this" or "I oppose that") that you are most fragile, and most doomed when "they" come to get you. Because, as he has learned in the year since the publication of *On the Road*, Kerouac has no doubt about it — they will come to get you, no matter how much you deal in the soul. They (the critics, the admirers, the sycophants, the guardians of the status quo) will come for you, no matter what. The only thing you can cling to is the sense of your own abiding soul when they find you. For all this, it is a hopeful vision.

For reasons well documented in his Legend, and all the criticism and biography directed at it, Kerouac's tone had changed considerably by the

8. Conclusion: "Be Lamps Unto Thyselves"

Sixties, though his vision remained resolute. In a 1965 letter to Sterling Lord, he prophesied in modern culture:

> a trend towards the Ian Fleming type of sadistic facetiousness and "sickjoke" grisliness about human affairs, a grotesque hatred for the humble and suffering heart, an admiration for the mechanistic smoothy *killer of sincerity*.... I just felt that nobody is going to care anymore about my vow to write the truth only as I see it, and with sympathetic intention, "thru the keyhole of my eye," (i.e., autobiographically, in transcriptive detail directly from my own mind, arriving at the universal point of view ... rather than from the objective point of view, literally "non-fiction" because you know what I think of fiction and its definition in the dictionary and its tall-told IF), I just felt nobody cared anymore whether I or anybody like me lived or died anyway let alone write. But I remember my father's tearful blue eyes and honest Breton face, and I am mindful of what my mother just said: that my way and my philosophy will come back, some great catastrophe is going to make people wake up again, my works and my fellow human beings who work in the same spirit, will outlast the sneerers, the uncooperative and unmannerly divisionists, the bloody Godless forever [*JKSL 1957–1969* 408].

Nearly fifty years later, it's difficult to scoff at his prophecy. The "sickjoke grisliness" of terrorism, counter-terrorism and reality TV, the smooth neglect of the "humble and suffering heart" in a culture where rich and poor alike are blinded by wealth and celebrity, the mechanistic insincerity of mass media that pour out a numbing flood of slick images about anything real or imagined for the millions plugged into the machine — all have come to pass in soul-deadening, authentic voice-stifling time. What the precipitating "catastrophe" will be that will wake people up to the "way and philosophy" of love as iterated this time around by Jack Kerouac might be closing in and is anybody's guess. Listen to the news, hear the static of calamity.

In the doomed, half-healed nature of Kerouac's visions of America as writer-shaman, personal tragedy and social critique become a single expression. If, as Joseph Campbell says, "dream is the personalized myth, myth is the depersonalized dream," then Kerouac's Legend, "so quirked by the peculiar troubles of the dreamer," also relates a message in the public sphere even now (19).

Eliade cites a Yukagir belief that "the dead return to earth and begin a new life. But sometimes, when the living forget their duties toward them, the dead refuse to send their souls" (246). So I write this study not so much to further the recognition of Kerouac as "a tremendous life-changing prophetic artist" but as an inquiry into a viable perspective on his writing as a modern ecstatic technique that is an expression of the decadent shamanic impulse. This decay has to do with individual shamanic power and influence, and does not imply that shamans are an endangered species, just the opposite.

Gerhard Mayer observes that "the pop star has become shaman, and the traditional shaman has become pop star. Both of them ... provide projection surfaces for individual wishes and ideals. The mythic charging of that alien figure into one of our own making it an idol, a modern myth" (96). It's the decay of our wishes and ideals, and our diminishing notions of myth, that ensure the atrophy of the shamanic impulse over time. This was a problem for Kerouac as a modern shaman. He was received by the tribe, but in a diminished manner where his Beat visions were reversed and projected onto him in ways he never intended (including mine, perhaps). It is possible that writing a book about Kerouac is the most "un-Beat" thing one could do. "Be lamps unto thyselves," said the Buddha. "Leave the paper on the desk unwritten," said Whitman. Yet I cannot. There is something about the fading imprint of the archaic shamanic light on our experience that compels me to seek it out, chasing the shadows of Kerouac's visions. As Gloria Flaherty has noted,

> Much still needs to be studied about the line of descent from the primordial shaman to the Roman mime, and then to the medieval minstrel, the eighteenth-century performer, the nineteenth-century star, and the celebrity superstar of today [214].

Somewhere along that descent you'll find Jack Kerouac forsaking the notion of storytelling for the human resonance of *story-being* and putting up his ecstatic "moan for man" (*VOC* 295).

"I'll write long sad tales about people in the legend of my life," Kerouac tells us in the last line of *Tristessa*. "This is my part in the movie, let's hear yours" (96).

Chapter Notes

Introduction

1. Because of the wide range and application of his powers, the term "shaman" can be used interchangeably with "magician," "medicine man," "psychopomp," "priest," "mystic," and "ecstatic" (Eliade, 39).

2. Flaherty notes, "Some scholars have attributed the rise of the late Hellenistic novel to the trances of shamans, while others have seen in those trances the origins of theater and fairy tales. Still others have believed shamans responsible for the very creation of Greek mythology" (3).

3. "My work comprises one vast book like Proust's except that my remembrances are written on the run instead of afterwards in a sickbed.... [My novels] are just chapters in the whole work which I call The Dulouz Legend.... The whole thing forms one enormous comedy seen through the eyes of poor Ti Jean (me) ... the world of raging action and folly and also of gentle sweetness seen through the keyhole of his eye" (Kerouac, preface to *Big Sur*).

4. "Woe to the man who is different, who tries to break down all the barriers. Woe to the man who tries to stretch the imagination of man, he shall be mocked, he shall be scourged by the blinkered guardians of morality" (Marquis deSade).

5. "Look into the mirror. You have just captured the essence of what Jack Kerouac spent his entire literary career doing" (*www.charm.net/~brooklyn/Lists/KerouacWorks.htmlc*).

6. "[Kerouac's] literary awakening came at the age of twelve, when he began recounting his personal history. These writings were long, secret, semi-ecstatic outpourings that often culminated in masturbation — a habit that would continue through his life. From the beginning, writing was not only aimed at an end product but was also a self-stimulating process" (Watson 21).

7. "At the center of ... all [Kerouac's novels] is an unreconcilable, unresolvable duality of grief and ecstasy" (Hunt 207).

8. "[Kerouac's] collective of characters ... exemplifies a pivotal paradigm in twentieth-century American literature: finding the highest spirituality among the marginal and dispossessed, establishing the link between art and pathology, and seeking truth in visions, dreams, and other non-rational states" (Watson 6).

Chapter 1

1. "It was by virtue of his pain-on-earth, that [Gerard's] black was turned to white" (*VOG* 24).

2. There are two interpretations of the term "religion" based on its Latin root. One is to "re-read" (*re-legere*). The other is to "re-connect" (*re-ligare*). Either interpretation serves to define the primary purpose of both "religion," as it is commonly understood (i.e., Judaism, Chris-

tianity, Islam, etc.), and shamanism, which predates any of these traditions. "Religion" is an impulse to "know again" and/or "get back to" our divine essence.

3. The same dynamic is present in *Visions of Cody*.

4. Gerard chastises the cat on this account, warning, "We'll never go to heaven if we go on eating each other and destroying each other like that all the time!" (*VOG* 11).

5. This presents a singular and sort of troubling aspect of the Catholic child in relation to the Sacrament of Penance. At about the age of eight, the baptized Catholic is educated about his sinful nature and, as a result, required to go to confession on a regular basis. In Kerouac's day this meant entering a dark booth and speaking your shortcomings through a curtained screen to a priest who sits in an adjoining dark booth. (These days confession can take place in a face-to-face manner, but the function remains the same.) The priest then absolves you from the sins you've confessed contingent upon your completing an assigned penance (usually the recitation of a prescribed number of prayers), then you're "good to go," so to speak (i.e., returned to a state of grace). Speaking from experience, the biggest problem of this sacrament for a kid in the third grade is "coming up with" sins to confess. This dilemma is, of course, much alleviated for the adult Catholic.

6. Significantly, here and elsewhere in the novel, Kerouac's Buddhist awareness that the root of our suffering is attachment does not figure in explaining away any of our existential pain.

7. The second point of the prevailing criticism, and I think a more valid one, has to do with the inconsistent and occasionally forced characterization in the novel that shows Gerard and even Kerouac's father having thoughts and making observations that obviously reflect the author's Buddhist and Beat views. These are instances where Kerouac works his characters like ventriloquist dummies rather than letting them speak for themselves.

Chapter 2

1. *Jack Kerouac: Seleted Letters, 1940–1956* 371.

2. "Sax's name may derive from Saxon, suggesting that he is charged with helping Jackie make the linguistic transition from his French-speaking neighborhood ... to a polyglot Pawtucketville, and that this transition paved the way for his literary career" (Jones 43).

3. This hybrid form, the "book-movie," shows Kerouac's insistence on his own freedom to blur distinctions in his "wild form." It also explains what he considers the visual import of his writing.

4. The painful awareness of mortality and the preoccupied tone of the novel evoke the shamanic initiation that always involves a fearful death experience and a consequent rise from death's grip. (Also note the characteristic ineffability of the mystical experience: "there's no telling what it is I really see in that dream.")

5. This is similar to the Gnostic view, as in the Gospel of Thomas (29:1–3) where "Jesus said, 'If the flesh came into being because of spirit, that is a marvel, but if spirit came into being because of the body, that is a marvel of marvels. Yet I marvel at how this great wealth has come to dwell in this poverty'" (Miller, *The Complete Gospels* 310).

6. Kerouac describes Sax's lair as a place where the Wizard of Oz might live (*DS* 49). Like the Great Oz, Sax's powers

(it will be shown as the apocalyptic vision plays out) are only apparent and, in the end, unnecessary. That Sax is an inept savior who fails to deliver the goods of salvation doesn't matter in the least.

7. "[Kerouac] was never fully aware of the degree to which Van Doren guarded a vision of literary orthodoxy. A bohemian lifestyle was one thing, but once Kerouac began his experiments in verbal sketching and 'spontaneous prose' around 1949, he virtually cut himself adrift from the arbiters of taste" (Fisher 221).

8. James Joyce had made a similar proclamation about *Ulysses* when he met with the rejection that greets any innovator. It's safe to say that Kerouac's "wild form" is Joyce's "stream-of-consciousness" with a post-war American beat. The echo of Leopold Bloom is clearly heard in the narrator's father, Emil Duluoz, with his "circuit ads sticking out of pocket." Kerouac even refers to *Doctor Sax* as "[his] *Ulysses*" (*JKSL 1940–1956* 205).

9. "The shaman personifies the seemingly paradoxical combination of will power and control with abandonment and letting go" (Mayer 89).

10. In his interpretation of *Doctor Sax*, Richard Howe argues that the narrator and, by extension, Kerouac achieve a kind of temporal and spatial bi-location. "Cohabitating Massachusetts in the 1930's and Mexico City in 1952, Duluoz has a kind of double presence" (*Moody Street Irregulars*, vol. 6–7, p. 17).

11. "Hence the guardian and helping spirits without which no shamanic séance is possible can be regarded as the authenticating signs of the shaman's ecstatic journeys in the beyond" (Eliade 95).

12. Furthermore, by novel's end, as the boy's journey reaches an integral threshold, Jackie will come to know Sax as a kind of Jungian "shadow self."

13. "Kerouac could recall a time when Catholicism was an integral part of community life; by the late 1940's he was estranged from the church in large part because the Lowell of his boyhood now existed only as a powerful goad to his imagination" (Fisher 216).

14. *Murder by the Clock* is a 1931 horror/mystery about an old woman who installs a loud horn in her crypt in case she's buried alive (which eventually happens). The plot also features a nefarious beauty in tight satin dresses and a drug that can raise the dead. Kerouac was nine years old when this movie was released.

15. In an apocalyptic rapture of the final book of the novel, Sax does take Jackie flying above the town and accompanies him to a netherworld below Lowell. I will examine this ecstatic sequence in some depth later in this chapter.

16. The continuous crashing of the Merrimac River through town (and throughout the novel) provides what Jackie intuits to be the only truly living and dynamic thing on the Lowell landscape (*DS* 125). The river cutting through Lowell endures as a terrible and unfathomable sign of regeneration. If the "wrinkly tar corner" is the image-object of the bookmovie that is *Doctor Sax*, then "the roar of the river" is its soundtrack.

17. The "snake" references in this chapter are mostly adjectival in form. They affect a tone of secrecy and imminence of something concealed that will soon be revealed.

18. Sax's portrayal of the Transcendenta crowd of the Twenties presages Kerouac's depiction of the hipster subculture of the Fifties in *The Subterraneans*, written a year later (i.e., effete, pretentious, self-absorbed, bored, and boring). Both groups profess tolerance of diversity, but reflexively close ranks when they encounter it.

19. Throughout Kerouac's *oeuvre*, it is the month of October (when the days grow chill and dark) that he hails as his season of joy and fulfillment, not March (though it is poised just before the regeneration of spring). This reflects a shaman-like appreciation of death as a door that doesn't close but opens. Kerouac was born in March and died in October.

20. Here again, Kerouac echoes one of the biblical tropes of his Catholic upbringing. In the Book of Genesis, Noah is similarly greeted by a dove as he tries to get a handle on his own flood troubles. (See Genesis 9:10–11.)

21. *Jack Kerouac: Seleted Letters, 1940–1956* 251.

22. The power and meaning of the circle in shamanism is profound. Typical of this motif is the Malayan tradition where the séance, or shamanic rite, "takes place inside a round hut or a magic circle, and the object ... is cure ... or knowledge of the future" (Eliade 345).

23. "[A] number of myths refer to a primordial time when *all human beings* could ascend to heaven, by climbing a mountain, a tree, or a ladder, or flying by their own power.... The *degeneration of humanity* henceforth forbids the mass of mankind to fly to heaven; only death restores men (and not all of them!) to this primordial condition; only then can they ascend to heaven, fly like birds and so forth" (Eliade 480).

24. Again this echoes a Gnostic notion, as in the Gospel of Thomas (70:1) where "Jesus said, 'If you bring forth what is within you, what you have will save you'" (Miller, *The Complete Gospels* 316).

25. "Lingering traces of the shaman's trance as a model for mystical experiences can be seen in the phenomena of later stages of religion: yoga, the Buddha's enlightenment, and the transfiguration of Jesus" (Ellwood 58).

Chapter 3

1. America has always been fascinated with those at the criminal margins of its status quo. From Billy the Kid to Al Capone to Charles Manson on through to the present day where convicts, gang-bangers, and drug addicts effectively have their own TV shows on the Discovery and History channels, our voyeuristic attraction to the criminal element has long been apparent.

2. Part 2 of *Visions of Cody* is a transcription of taped conversations between Cody, Jack, and others. This is a very conscious, conceptual, and high-minded (for the time, technology, etc.) exercise in the ecstatic technique of this book; a representation of a spontaneous event that leaves me unmoved, as I'll discuss later on.

3. Besides use of the first person plural, Kerouac frequently employs direct address as a more aggressive strategy of ensuring the reader's participation in his visions. It is a primary point of his style by which the writer begs the image in the sense of "you too have seen this Cody and already know what I'm talking about." Essentially, it is the rhetorical stance of the "illuminator."

4. Descriptions of the sky in *Visions of Cody*, as in other chapters of the Duluoz Legend, are a motif of the heavenly context of Kerouac's point of view.

5. At the time of writing *Visions of Cody*, Kerouac was preoccupied by his second wife's demands for child support (Nicosia 370). This could only have heightened his suspicious view of women during the composition of *Visions of Cody*, though it is never much in doubt elsewhere in his oeuvre.

6. In the Catholic tradition, the novena is a prayer for a particular intention that is said over nine consecutive

days. Inasmuch as the novena is a ritual supplication to the spirit world to affect the real world, it might be seen as a vestigial shamanic element that endures in Catholicism.

7. Notably, the penultimate entry of this section is a vision of "A GREAT AMERICAN INTERSECTION"—a still life of America, static, poised, lovely—that symbolizes the road that leads anywhere, anytime—all you have to do is get a move on (*VOC* 37). The road is, of course, a primary metaphor for Kerouac. The road is also the essence of Cody. This entry portends a pivot in these visions, and forecasts movement.

8. A shaman can also be selected by the tribe. However, this dynamic doesn't apply as much to Cody's rise at this point as it does when, more than twenty years later (having arrived at his own legend), he was "proclaimed" in this way by the post–Beat hippies in his career as driver of the "FURTHER" bus with Ken Kesey, the Merry Pranksters, et al. Cody's vortices won him few popularity contests when he was center ring with the Beats.

9. I.M. Lewis notes that shamans "as a whole [are] extremely excitable, almost hysterical, and not a few were half-crazy. Their cunning in the use of deceit in their art closely resembles the cunning of the lunatic" (161). Elsewhere he notes that the shaman's behavior often features "gross non-reality ideation, abnormal perceptual experiences, profound emotional upheavals, and bizarre mannerisms" (163). I find both these characterizations to be supported in Kerouac's descriptive visions of Cody.

10. Lewis explains that the shaman's initiatory experience involves a surrender "into the chaos which the ordered and controlled life of society strives so hard to deny, or at least keep at bay.... The shaman is not the slave, but the master of anomaly and chaos" (169).

11. Biographers tell us that Kerouac wrote much of *Visions of Cody* after smoking marijuana in his Ozone Park bedroom once his mother went to sleep. (He finished it in Cassady's attic in San Francisco.) John Clellon Holmes claims that "the reason those sentences are so long and exfoliating and so incredible is because of pot" (Gifford and Lee 77). I agree to a point. As noted, use of marijuana and other substances has its legitimate function in the shamanic practice in which Kerouac (as artist) participates. However, the primary reason for the "exfoliating" style and form of *Visions of Cody* is the fact that Kerouac was a skilled practitioner of the ecstatic technique of spontaneous prose. On the other hand, the "writing while high" technique, in and of itself, is not a guarantee of fantastically innovative sentences, or much else.

12. *Visions of Cody* contains several passages where Kerouac seems to be in contested dialogue with the spontaneous impulse as to who is telling the story and who is calling the shots (as on *VOC* 251). This dispute reaches its apex in *Old Angel Midnight*, as I discuss in Chapter 6.

13. Even the most attentive reader, one who is well-acquainted with Kerouac's biography, who *might* grasp the meaning of many of these wild passages, can only guess at the rest. In this section especially, I am generally at an interpretive loss except for the more concrete moments I have cited because the themes expressed there are significant and present in his other work. "Frisco: The Tape" and "Imitation of the Tape" are literature gone punk in a language, form, and intention of their own. According to Ginsberg, *Visions of Cody* is flawed by "a lot of meaningless bullshit ... that doesn't make sense to anybody except someone

who has blown Jack" (McNally 161). In any case, one could use a decoder ring reading many of these entries.

14. Most Kerouac scholars have amply and duly noted the stylistic affinity between Kerouac's spontaneous prose and jazz improvisation (as has Kerouac himself). "Imitation of the Tape" has the same effect on me as late-phase Coltrane and Ornette Coleman, both of whom I value beyond understanding or even enjoyment. The pure voice, the actual moan, always upsetting, could be frightening.

15. *Visions of Cody* 279.

16. Because Kerouac witnesses the filming of *Sudden Fear* out of context with the rest of the movie, he perceives the Joan Crawford character as a victim in this scene. In the full context of the film, actually, at this moment, she is actually quite in control for the moment, envisioning how she will orchestrate the perfect crime and exact her revenge on the murderous lovers.

17. *Visions of Cody* 296.

18. Titled "Visions of Neal, Parts I and II," you can hear Kerouac read this section of *Visions of Cody* (300–306) on tracks 7 and 8 of the CD, *Jack Kerouac—The Beat Generation*. Besides catching the rhythm and flow of Kerouac's voice, it is interesting to follow along and note what he deletes and revises in this reading in order to skirt objectionable material.

19. As noted elsewhere, the words "ligament" (that which holds the body together) and "religion" share a common Latin root, *ligare* (to connect, tie, or bind).

20 Cody's confession of his love for Jack precipitates Kerouac's struggles with the notion of Cody as "average." It also brings on a sudden realization in Jack that women would love him, too— something he had forgotten in his obsessive discipleship under Cody. However, it seems that Jack still appraises the love of a woman as "the clay endeavors beneath the Golden Spear of God," that is, as an inferior substitute for the complete love of and with Cody (*VOC* 328).

Chapter 4

1. By contrast, as we have seen in *Doctor Sax*, Kerouac made a Faustian bargain wherein he became inextricably *bound* to a cosmic subjectivity, the value of which he and his readers could never agree upon. By the time he writes *Big Sur*, we will see that, though the nature of his Faustian dealings is reversed at the outset, the same effects of diffidence and isolation that we see here in *The Subterraneans* remain.

2. "Kerouac's attentiveness to ethnicity—however pointed or perhaps unsavory at times—was an aspect of his resistance to the growing conformity of American culture after the Second World War" (Fisher 210).

3. This veneration doesn't really benefit their relationship, of course. Eliade tells us, "The love of such a semidivine woman becomes an obstacle rather than a help for the hero" (79).

4. Kerouac explains this "old dream" in *On the Road*. He wishes he were "a Negro," "a Denver Mexican, or even a poor overworked Jap" because "the best the white world had offered was not enough ecstasy for me, not enough life, joy, kicks, darkness, music, not enough night" (*OTR* 179–80).

5. Paradoxically, I don't think this was Kerouac's intention to "out himself" here. Rather it seems like this content just "came up" in the spontaneous prose ecstasy that he was so dedicated to. He could have edited this sequence out.

Again, like so much of *The Subterraneans*, the content of this unapologetic sequence is enigmatic, to say the least.

6. Kerouac revisited this mystical realization in a mescaline vision that he explained to Ginsberg in this way: "This is the whole visit ... / And how can it be a visit when you are God Yourself? / Like, I realized that Christ has a cunt ... and Jesus Christ and the black cunt are reconciled at last. Easy enuf." (*JKSL 1957–1969* 221–22).

Chapter 5

1. "The Plotinian union with the One has been called ec-static, but the term in-static might be more appropriate for describing a movement of inwardization" (*TEOR* 252).

2. "Eidetic"—pertaining to visual imagery vividly experienced. This realness of dreams is often lost "in terms of Ahsen's I-S-M model [when] verbal description often causes the visual image (I) to lose its vital sensory/sensual qualities (S) in favor of its semantic meaning (M) alone" (Jennings 256). Causes for this degradation? Self-censorship due to shame of the dream's content and/or verbal paralysis due to the rules and limitation of language. Kerouac prescribes for these crises in his "Belief and Technique for Modern Prose," where he writes, "Something you feel will find its own form.... No time for poetry but exactly what is.... Remove literary, grammatical and syntactical inhibition.... Don't think of words when you stop but to see picture better.... No fear or shame in the dignity of yr experience, language & knowledge" (*GBO* 72–73). Using this technique in *Book of Dreams*, he does an admirable job of preserving the eidetic quality of his dreams. The bizarre visuals and the feelings of the dreamer (for the most part) are clear to the reader because Kerouac was a practiced and skilled spontaneous writer. For years, he attuned his creative psyche and ecstatic technique to this dream record. The goal is to be fully immersed in the eidetic dream life re-created. As a result, the writer and reader alike might become privy to scenes from "the other side."

3. See, for example, the entry where we see the dreaming Kerouac, like a vision questing neophyte, awaiting "a sign from the shroud of Arab eternity" (*BOD* 66).

4. Reference Kerouac's identification with Christ crucified in a dream (*BOD* 90), or witnesses an apocalyptic showdown where a "chalice, having a Cross, makes the devil hiss and shiver back" (*BOD* 57). Overall, however, Catholic symbolism doesn't predominate in *Book of Dreams*.

5. "Later I'm back in the West Street cottage with Ma wondering if the organ is still in the shed" and "I have a seven foot salami on my shoulder" (*BOD* 65 and 72).

6. In his dreams, Kerouac observes that "the whole world swims by, archetypal as plots" (*BOD* 75).

7. Though Kerouac frequently uses neologism in all his novels, *Old Angel Midnight*, another odd duck in the Duluoz Legend, exhibits this characteristic most frequently and effectively. It is his most experimental and ambitious work of spontaneous prose, as I will discuss in the next chapter.

8. Of the experience of rereading *Book of Dreams*, Kerouac writes, "What shame I'd feel sometimes to see such naked revelations so insouciantly stated" (*BOD* preface). Taboo dreams of incest, pedophilia, homosexuality, and corporal ephagia pepper this volume. They don't predominate or signify in any primary sense I'm interested in. I let them be.

9. As a point of style, this "goofing around" with identities shows a vestigial shamanic influence since the shaman "is a master of the game of identities — a requirement the individual has to fulfill more and more in postmodern culture" (Mayer 90).

10. "'Face value' is the direct, self-evident meaning of dream images ... it is the perfect embodiment of a complex of feelings, perceptions, and personality features. The key is that [a dream's] 'face value,' when encountered in its full impact, is not trite, but profound and enriching" (Jennings 273).

11. For a Catholic, Kerouac, like so many, was non-practicing and dissolute. And for a Buddhist, he surely wrote about himself a lot, and couldn't do without the self (let alone obliterate it). Still, *Book of Dreams* often embodies the Catholic notion of mortification, and, especially down the stretch in the final entries, a grim Buddhist hope for the Void. The shamanic view encompasses both these views. "The phenomenon of shamanism itself displays ... specifically Buddhist (Lamaist) elements" (Eliade 496).

12. "Sad" is Kerouac's first-string mantra that somehow I never sicken of, because he's so often accurate in his appraisal throughout his work. "Sadness" is Kerouac's métier and creative fuel.

13. Eliade cites "a general conception of the decadence of shamans ... according to this view, the 'first shamans' *really* flew through the clouds on their horses and performed miracles that their present day descendents are incapable of repeating" (67).

14. In one terrifying nightmare, Kerouac sees himself as both father and son trying to hop a too-fast freight train and escape hobo brigands. There is no resolution to this dream, only Kerouac confused and wishing he was Buddha (*BOD* 137).

15. In *Some of the Dharma* Kerouac asks, "Remember when you were a tree? / I do — arms, heaviness, blear peace" (82). See Chapter 2 of this study for a detailed discussion of the shamanic significance of skeletal visions and trees as played out in *Doctor Sax*. (And see pages 7, 140, and 175 in *BOD* for other entries that involve skeletons/skeletal vision.)

16. A partial list of important aspects of *Book of Dreams* that I haven't discussed includes the "white horse dreams," allusions to Tolstoy and Dostoevski (specifically his character, "Stavrogin"), the role and portrayal of Native and African Americans, the motifs of cats, birds, and other animals, and the recurrent dreams of "the land of the great guitar."

Chapter 6

1. *Jack Kerouac: Seleted Letters, 1957–1969* 198.

2. This first section of *Old Angel Midnight* might be best appreciated by hearing Kerouac read it himself on track 3 of the CD, *Jack Kerouac — The Beat Generation*. (Kerouac also reads section 6 of *OAM* on track 4 of this disc.)

3. Kerouac compares *Old Angel Midnight* to Jesus' miracles in Capernaum: casting out the evil spirit, healing the paralytic, and walking on water (*OAM* 28).

4. Reading this puzzle of a book gets rather frantic and bewildering even here in one of the more likely sections, meaning-wise. The fact that Kerouac (afoot with spontaneous vision) makes up words at will and doesn't use quotation marks to designate who's saying what makes this reader feel like he's eavesdropping on a conversation being held in another language in another room. There is no other work in his Legend (as I see it) that demands such a high level of par-

ticipation mystique from his reader as does *Old Angel Midnight*.

Chapter 7

1. Steven Watson notes in *The Birth of the Beat Generation*, "Kerouac's writing during the last ten years of his life appeared mostly in such sex-oriented magazines as *Nugget*, *Escapade*, and *Playboy*," which indicates his exclusion from "the literary Establishment [that] considered him puerile and anti-intellectual" (293).

2. Of this episode, Ferlinghetti recalls that Kerouac "started belching and throwing up.... He was shivering like he was cold so I rapped [sic] him up in a blanket then he started to throw up all over me. And that was the last of him" (McNally 284).

3. In a 1968 interview, Kerouac said of Cassady, "In my opinion he's the most intelligent man I've ever met in my life. He's a Jesuit by the way.... He was a choirboy in the Catholic churches of Denver. And he taught me everything that I now do believe about anything that there may be to be believed about divinity.... He was perfect" (Plimpton 111).

4. "The Christian notion of mortification ... derives from this originally Pauline ideal [that] was exemplified by the early martyrs, and when the persecutions [of the early Christians] eventually came to an end mortification began to function as a sort of self-imposed martyrdom" (*TEOR* vol. 10, 113).

5. *The Bop Apocalypse* by Lardas (2001) and Giamo's *Kerouac, The Word and the Way* (2000) both offer invaluable insights into the religious import of Kerouac's fiction.

6. "I feel horrified and fear my Blake humilities which I can stand will become unbearable if worth thousands to writers like [John Clellon Holmes] ... as if and just like, Christ and his thorns pounded into a golden Chalice, the bible a Bestseller,—the Agony in the Garden a smash hit!" (*BOD* 90).

7. Kerouac first recorded the nightmare of "The Flying Horses of Mien Mo" in his *Book of Dreams* (180).

8. In his study of Kerouac as "spiritual quester," Ben Giamo notes that the "singular image of the Cross ... comes only after [Duluoz] purges himself of the sordid vision [of] the bestial vulture people fornicating on the dump" (198). Actually, the sequence is significantly reversed in the novel.

Chapter 8

1. These were Buddha's last words, quoted by Kerouac in a 1964 letter to Italian translator, Fernanda Pivano (*JKSL 1957–1969* 378).

2. *Jack Kerouac: Seleted Letters,* 1940–1956 274.

3. Lack of discipline was one of the most common, and unfounded, criticisms leveled at Kerouac's work. He addressed this in his correspondence. "Altho I had to learn to handle the reins I still needed the horses — I mean by that, critics have failed to realize that spontaneous writing of narrative prose is infinitely more difficult than careful slow painstaking writing with opportunities to revise — because spontaneous writing is an ordeal requiring immediate discipline.... They don't know how horrible it is to learn immediate and swift discipline and draw your breath in pain as you do so —... Alas, lachrymae rerum, yet how good it is that everything will vanish eventually —(some people, it makes 'em mad) (but it makes me feel god) (how just is God) ... how clever" (*JKSL 1957–1969* 325).

Bibliography

Amburn, Ellis. *Subterranean Kerouac.* New York: St. Martin's, 1998.

Bangs, Lester. *Psychotic Reactions and Carburetor Dung.* New York: Vintage, 1988.

Brustein, Robert. "The Cult of Unthink." *Horizon,* vol. I, no. 1 (1958): 18.

Bukowski, Charles. *Love Is a Dog from Hell.* Santa Rosa: Black Sparrow, 1977.

Bulkeley, Kelly. *The Wilderness of Dreams: Exploring the Religious Meanings of Dreams in Modern Western Culture.* Albany: State University of New York Press, 1994.

Campbell, Joseph. *The Hero with a Thousand Faces.* New York: Pantheon, 1949.

Charters, Ann. *The Portable Beat Reader.* New York: Penguin, 1992.

———. *The Portable Sixties Reader.* New York: Penguin, 2003.

Confraternity of Christian Doctrine. *The New American Bible.* Nashville: Thomas Nelson, 1971.

Eliade, Mircea. *Shamanism: Archaic Techniques of Ecstasy.* Princeton, NJ: Princeton University Press, 1964.

———. ed., *The Encyclopedia of Religion.* New York: Macmillan, 1987.

Ellwood, Robert S. *Mysticism and Religion.* Chapaqua, NY: Seven Bridges Press, 1999.

Fisher, James Terence. *The Catholic Counterculture in America, 1933–1962.* Chapel Hill: University of North Carolina Press, 1989.

Flaherty, Gloria. *Shamanism and the 18th Century.* Princeton, NJ: Princeton University Press, 1992.

French, Warren. *Jack Kerouac.* Boston: Twayne, 1986.

George-Warren, Holly, ed. *The* Rolling Stone *Book of the Beats.* New York: Hyperion, 1999.

Giamo, Ben. *Kerouac, The Word and the Way.* Carbondale: Southern Illinois University Press, 2000.

Gifford, Barry, and Lawrence Lee. *Jack's Book: An Oral Biography of Jack Kerouac.* New York: Penguin, 1979.

Hamilton, Edith. *Mythology.* New York: Penguin, 1940.

Holmes, John Clellon. *Visitor: Jack Kerouac in Old Saybrook (The Unspeakable Vision of the Individual).* California, PA: Arthur and Kit Knight, 1981.

Howe, Richard. "Interpretation of Dr. Sax." *Moody Street Irregulars: A Jack Kerouac Newsletter,* vol. 6–7 (1980): 16–18.

Hunt, Tim. *Kerouac's Crooked Road: The Development of a Fiction.* Berkeley: University of California Press, 1996.

Huxley, Aldous. *The Doors of Perception.* New York: Harper & Row, 1970.

Hyde, Lewis. *Trickster Makes This World: Mischief, Myth and Art.* New York: Farrar, Straus and Giroux, 1998.

James, William. *The Varieties of Religious Experience.* New York: Penguin, 1982.

Kaldera, Raven, and Tannin Schwartzstein.

Bibliography

Urban Primitive: Paganism in the Concrete Jungle. St. Paul: Llewellyn, 2002.

Kerouac, Jack. *Big Sur.* New York: Penguin, 1962.

———. *Book Of Dreams.* San Francisco: City Lights, 1961.

———. *Desolation Angels.* New York: Perigee, 1980.

———. *Doctor Sax.* New York: Grove Press, 1959.

———. *Good Blonde And Others.* San Francisco: Grey Fox Press, 1993.

———. *Kerouac ROMnibus.* New York: Penguin, 1995

———. *Mexico City Blues.* New York: Grove Press, 1959.

———. *Old Angel Midnight.* San Francisco: Grey Fox Press, 1995.

———. *On the Road.* London: Penguin, 1957.

———. *Satori in Paris and Pic.* New York: Grove Press, 1985.

———. *Selected Letters, 1940–1956.* Edited by Ann Charters. New York: Penguin, 1995.

———. *Selected Letters, 1957–1969.* Ann Charters, New York: Viking, 1999.

———. *Some of the Dharma.* New York: Penguin, 1997.

———. *The Scripture of the Golden Eternity.* San Fransisco: City Lights, 1994.

———. *The Subterraneans.* New York: Ballantine, 1958.

———. *Vanity of Duluoz.* New York: Penguin, 1968.

———. *Visions of Cody.* New York: McGraw-Hill, 1972.

Lardas, John. *The Bop Apocalypse.* Chicago: University of Illinois Press, 2001.

Lerner, Richard, and Lewis MacAdams, dir. *What Happened to Kerouac?* Richard Lerner Productions, 1986.

Levy-Bruhl, Lucien. *How Natives Think.* Salem, NH: Ayer, 1984.

Lewis, I.M. *Ecstatic Religion.* New York: Routledge Press, 1971.

Lippard, Lucy. *Get the Message: A Decade of Art for Social Change.* New York: E.P. Dutton, 1984.

Lommel, Andreas. *Shamanism: The Beginnings of Art.* New York: McGraw-Hill, 1967.

Mailer, Norman. *The Deer Park.* New York: Putnam, 1955.

Marozza, Maria Ilena. "When does a dream begin to 'have meaning'?" *Journal of Analytical Psychology*, 50, (2005): 693–705.

Mayer, Gerhard. "The Figure of the Shaman as a Modern Myth: Some Reflections on the Attractiveness of Shamanism in Modern Societies." *The Pomegranate.* vol. 10, no. 1 (2008): 70–103.

McNally, Dennis. *Desolate Angel.* New York: McGraw-Hill, 1979.

Miller, David, dir. *Sudden Fear.* Joseph Kaufman Productions, 1952.

Miller, Robert J., ed. *The Complete Gospels.* San Francisco: HarperCollins, 1994.

Morrisette, Alanis. "I'm Not The Doctor." *Jagged Little Pill.* Maverick Records, 1995.

Nicosia, Gerald. *Memory Babe.* Berkeley: University of California Press, 1994.

Norris, Frank. *McTeague.* New York: Norton, 1977.

Plimpton, George, ed. *Beat Writers at Work.* New York: Modern Library, 1999.

Podhoretz, Norman. "The Know-Nothing Bohemians." *Partisan Review* (Spring 1958).

Spivey, Ted. *The Writer as Shaman.* Macon, GA: Mercer University Press, 1986.

Staub de Laszlo, Violet, ed. *The Basic Writings of C.G. Jung.* New York: Random House, 1959.

Swartz, Omar. *The View from On the Road: The Rhetorical Vision of Jack Kerouac.* Carbondale: Southern Illinois University Press, 1999.

Bibliography

Theado, Matt. *Understanding Jack Kerouac.* Columbia: University of South Carolina Press, 2000.

Thornhill, Chris. "Karl Jaspers." Stanford Encyclopedia of Philosophy, *http://plato.stanford.edu/entries/jaspers/* (accessed June 28, 2008).

Tucker, Michael. *Dreaming with Open Eyes.* San Francisco: Aquarian/Harper, 1992.

Tytell, John. *Naked Angels.* New York: Grove Press, 1976.

Watson, Steven. *The Birth of the Beat Generation.* New York: Pantheon, 1995.

Whitman, Walt. *Leaves of Grass.* New York: Modern Library, 1921.

Wilson, Edmund. *The Wound and the Bow.* Athens: Ohio University Press, 1997.

Workman, Chuck, dir. *The Source.* Fox Lorber, 2000.

Index

Allen, Steve 25
"The American Dream" 9, 180
Aphrodite 161
Arbuckle, Fatty 147
Arcaro, Eddie 87
Auden, W.H. 48

Balzac, Honoré de 13, 148
Bangs, Lester 97
Baro, Gene 13
Baudelaire, Charles 148
Berle, Milton 87
Big Sur 22, 26, 101, 133, 138, 153–178, 181, 184
Blake, William 47
Bogart, Humphrey 48
Book of Dreams 22, 25, 74, 122–143, 144, 153, 169, 176, 182
Brave Bulls 119
Buckley, William 22
Burroughs, William 19, 42, 45, 100, 113, 147, 154, 164, 165, 166

Capote, Truman 13
Cassady, Carolyn 154
Cassady, Neal 13, 19, 23, 73–98, 128–130, 139, 160–164, 165, 168–170, 182
Castaneda, Carlos 183
Cixous, Hélène 102
The Cold War 136, 137, 142
Cooper, Gary 48, 87
Corso, Gregory 111, 148
Cowley, Malcolm 48, 122
Crane, Hart 148
Crawford, Joan 88–89
Creeley, Robert 24, 148
Cronkite, Walter 9

Danny & the Juniors 147
Davis, Miles 85

The Day of the Locust 88
The Deer Park 104
de Havilland, Olivia 140
DeMott, Benjamin 13
Dempsey, David 48
Desolation Angels 20, 22, 26, 153
deus otiosus 6, 7, 12
Dharma Bums 21, 153
Dobie Gillis 141
Doctor Sax 26, 35, 41, 42–72, 74, 85, 99, 115, 130, 131, 133, 147, 153, 181, 182
Dostoevsky, Fyodor 148
Duncan, Isadora 48

l'écriture féminine 102
Elgar, Sir Edward William 147
Emerson, Ralph Waldo 13
Endymion 123

Ferlinghetti, Lawrence 144, 148, 155, 156, 171
Fields, W.C. 48, 75, 76
Finnegans Wake 46
Fitzgerald, F. Scott 148
Freud, Sigmund 125
The Function of the Orgasm 109

Gardner, Ava 147
Gibson, Hoot 48
Gillespie, Dizzy 182
Ginsberg, Allen 6, 10, 16, 17, 23, 48, 73, 100, 113, 137, 139, 141, 148, 164, 165, 173, 181, 184
Gnosticism 33, 135
Gogol, Nikolai 148
Google, Barney 85
Graham, Gloria 88

Hatto, A.T. 8
Hawthorne, Nathaniel 148

Index

Hemingway, Ernest 86, 87, 148, 158
Holmes, John Clellon 13, 18, 139, 148, 158, 179
Huncke, Herbert 164, 165
Huxley, Aldous 172, 180
Hyde, Lewis 119

Irigary, Luce 102

Jaspers, Karl 123
Joyce, James 39, 125, 148
Jung, Carl 6, 172

Kaufman, Bob 148
Kaye, Danny 87
Kerouac, Jack: adolescence 42–72; alcoholism 15–16, 153–178; Buddhism 33, 70, 122, 125, 132, 134, 135, 147, 170; Catholicism 12, 16, 26, 30, 32, 33, 51, 52, 54, 64, 70, 75, 76, 106, 170, 173–174, 181; childhood 11, 29–41, 130–134; commentary on the Beat Generation 138–142, 164–168; confessional prose 100–102; devolution of American Road myth 155–160; dreams 122–143; as hagiographer 30–31; as "half-healed shaman" 15–17, 23; homosexuality 112–116; on movies 75, 76, 85, 88–89; on Neal Cassady 73–98; as post-shamanic figure 4, 5, 9, 17–19; preoccupation with death 29–41, 52–56, 58, 59, 64, 90; on race 99–121; spontaneous prose 24–27, 43–50; on women 75, 76, 99–121
Kesey, Ken 19
The Keystone Cops 48

Ladd, Alan 48
Leary, Timothy 166
The Lives of the Saints 79
London, Jack 148
Look Homeward, Angel 13
Lord, Sterling 183, 185
Lowell (Massachusetts) 11, 23, 76, 127, 130–134, 135, 139, 140

MacAdams, Lewis 16, 17
Maggie Cassidy 153
Mailer, Norman 104
The Marx Brothers 48
Mason, James 85
McClure, Michael 47, 144, 145, 151, 167, 173

McCoy, Tim 48
Melville, Herman 148
Mexico City Blues 132, 153
Miller, Henry 138, 148
Mix, Tom 48
Morrisette, "Spike" 173
mortification of the body 15, 172
Murder by the Clock 51
mysticism 4, 83

"nadiral ecstasy" 21–24, 99–121
Nebuchadnezzar's Dream 117
"nostalgia for paradise" 6, 130–134

Old Angel Midnight 22, 25, 47, 74, 136, 144–152, 153, 182
On the Road 18, 19, 20, 22, 42, 74, 77, 92, 97, 106, 133, 153, 154, 155, 159, 160, 162, 166, 168, 171, 183, 184
Orphic myth 120–121

Paar, Jack 141
Palance, Jack 88
Paris Review 154
Piaf, Edith 48
Poe, Edgar Allan 148, 150
Popeye 48
Post-War America 9–11
Powell, Bud 85
Proust, Marcel 13, 47

quantum theory 146–147

Reich, Wilhelm 68, 109
Rexroth, Kenneth 148
Rimbaud, Arthur 115
Roosevelt, Franklin Delano 92
Rousseau, Jean-Jacques 13

St. Francis 30
Sampas, Sebastian 23, 129
Satori in Paris 22, 35, 154
Schopenhauer, Arthur 79
The Scripture of the Golden Eternity 153, 174
The Shadow 51
shamanism 3–4; cosmology 19–21, 130; cultural reception of 7–8; decadence 15–16; "half-healed shaman" 15–17; initiation 6–7; mask-wearing 65; as "sham" 71, 140, 141, 150; tree motif 65, 66, 133; use of drugs/alcohol 15–16, 36

202

Index

Shore, Dinah 140
Shostakovich, Dimitri 147
"the sick soul" 6
Snyder, Gary 75, 148, 182
Solomon, Carl 48, 87
Some of the Dharma 139, 146, 153, 158, 166, 168
"Song of Myself" 16, 21
"Song of the Open Road" 21, 91, 157
The Source 10
Spengler, Oswald 100, 164
Sterne, Laurence 148
The Subterraneans 20, 21, 22, 26, 35, 44, 74, 99–121, 133, 138, 153, 182
Sudden Fear 88–89
Susskind, David 13

"Tell-Tale Heart" 150
Thoreau, Henry David 13
The Three Stooges 93–96
The Town and the City 13, 14, 42, 153
Trader Horn 59, 69
Tristessa 20, 22, 153, 186

Ulysses 39, 66

Van Doren, Mark 48
Vanity of Duluoz 22, 24, 133, 154
The Varieties of Religious Experience 6
Verlaine, Paul 15
Vidal, Gore 114, 148
Visions of Cody 25, 26, 35, 44, 73–98, 88, 103, 153, 162, 169, 170, 175, 182, 183
Visions of Gerard 21, 26, 29–41, 99, 105, 130, 153, 171, 174, 181, 182
Vollmer, Joan 165
Vulcan 161

Welch, Lew 160
West, Nathanael 88
Whalen, Philip 148
Whitman, Walt 11, 16, 21, 37, 47, 90, 91, 101, 157, 164, 186
The Wilderness of Dreams 124
Williams, Ted 87
Wolfe, Thomas 13, 159, 182

Yeats, William Butler 87
Young, Lester 147

Zeus 1161

www.ingramcontent.com/pod-product-compliance
Lightning Source LLC
Chambersburg PA
CBHW032059300426
44116CB00007B/808